Infinite Love is the Only Truth
Everything Else is Illusion

Exposing the dreamworld we believe to be 'real'

David Icke

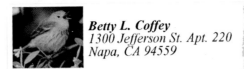

Betty L. Coffey
1300 Jefferson St. Apt. 220
Napa, CA 94559

Infinite Love is the Only Truth
Everything Else is Illusion

First published in April 2005 by

Bridge of Love Publications USA
1825 Shiloh Valley Drive
Wildwood
MO 63005
USA
Tel: 636-273-5951
Fax: 636-458-7823
email: bridgeloveUSA@aol.com

Cover and original illustrations by Neil Hague

Printed and bound by:
Patterson Printing
1550 Territorial Road • Benton Harbour • MI 49022

British Library Cataloguing-in
Publication Data
A catalogue record for this book is
available from the British Library

ISBN 0-9538810-6-7

Original illustrations in this book are by
Neil Hague

Neil is an English visionary artist, writer and lecturer who originally trained in graphics and publishing. He has had numerous exhibitions of his highly imaginative work in London and his paintings have appeared on book covers all over the world.

He has also written two books of his own, *Through Ancient Eyes* and *Journeys in the Dreamtime*, in which he illustrates a personal, and fascinating, approach to art, life and the nature of changing reality. Apart from giving public talks, Neil is currently working on a new illustrated book, *Visions from Beyond the Matrix*.

> "Neil Hague's work is unique – the language of an open and highly creative mind. You look with your eyes, but he speaks to your heart."
> **David Icke**

> "Through Ancient Eyes should inspire even the most dimensionally resistant soul to open up to more benign and sumptuous realities currently convening/integrating on our imperilled planet."
> **Jaye Beldo**

For more information about Neil's work and how to purchase his pictures visit
www.neilhague.com

Other books and videos by David Icke

It Doesn't Have To Be Like This	*Green Print*
Truth Vibrations	*Gateway*
Heal the World	*Gateway*
The Robots' Rebellion	*Gateway*
Alice in Wonderland and the World Trade Centre Disaster	*Bridge of Love*
... And The Truth Shall Set You Free	*Bridge of Love*
I Am Me, I Am Free	*Bridge of Love*
The Biggest Secret	*Bridge of Love*
Children of the Matrix	*Bridge of Love*
Tales from the Time Loop	*Bridge of Love*
Turning of the Tide a two-hour video	*Bridge of Love*
The Reptilian Agenda, parts one and two video/DVD featuring David Icke with Zulu Shaman, Credo Mutwa	*Bridge of Love*
Revelations of a Mother Goddess – two-hour video/DVD with David Icke and Arizona Wilder	Bridge of Love
Speaking Out – two-hour video with David Icke	Truthseeker
The Freedom Road – three-video package lasting more than five hours	*Bridge of Love*
From Prison to Paradise – three two-hour videos/DVDs with David Icke	*Bridge of Love*
***NEW* – Secrets of the Matrix** – a three video/DVD package	*Bridge of Love*

Details of availability at the back of this book

Dedication

*To Royal Adams for all his magnificent work
to keep my books in circulation*

*To Vera Diamond, a great friend and tireless
campaigner on behalf of the ritually abused
and mind controlled. Vera died while this
book was in production and will be sorely
missed by all those who loved her for who she
was and what she did for the victims of
unimaginable horror. Bye wonderful lady.
We'll meet again in a happier 'place'.*

Contents

Eternal Truths . . .

Every man takes the limits of his own field of vision for the limits of the world.
Arthur Schopenhauer

Violent means will give violent freedom.
Gandhi

The dissenter is every human being at those moments of his life when he resigns momentarily from the herd and thinks for himself.
Archibald Macleish

I think we all have a little voice inside us that will guide us … if we shut out all the noise and clutter from our lives and listen to that voice, it will tell us the right thing to do.
Christopher Reeve

It is not worth an intelligent man's time to be in the majority. By definition, there are already enough people to do that.
G. H. Hardy

Any fool can make things bigger, more complex, and more violent. It takes a touch of genius – and a lot of courage – to move in the opposite direction.
Albert Einstein

A coward is incapable of exhibiting love; it is the prerogative of the brave.
Gandhi

Cherish forever what makes you unique, 'cuz you're really a yawn if it goes.
Bette Midler

Always Look on the Bright Side of Life ...

Some things in life are bad
They can really make you mad
Other things just make you swear and curse.
When you're chewing on life's gristle
Don't grumble, give a whistle
And this'll help things turn out for the best ...

If life seems jolly rotten
There's something you've forgotten
And that's to laugh and smile and dance and sing.
When you're feeling in the dumps
don't be silly chumps
Just purse your lips and whistle – that's the thing ...

Life's a piece of shit
When you look at it
Life's a laugh and death's a joke, it's true.
You'll see it's all a show
Keep 'em laughing as you go
Just remember that the last laugh is on you.

And always look on the bright side of life ...
Always look on the light side of life ...
Always look on the bright side of life.

Words by Eric Idle, Monty Python's *Life of Brian*

Illustration by Neil Hague

Who looks outside, dreams; who looks inside, awakes.
Carl Gustav Jung

Great spirits have always found violent opposition from mediocrities. The latter cannot
understand it when a man does not thoughtlessly submit to hereditary prejudices but
honestly and courageously uses his intelligence.
Albert Einstein

All truths are easy to understand once they are discovered;
the point is to discover them.
Galileo

CHAPTER ONE

No Snowflake in an Avalanche
Ever Felt Responsible

Most people are other people. Their thoughts are someone else's opinions, their lives a mimicry, their passions a quotation
Oscar Wilde

In 1990, I consciously began an incredible journey of self-discovery. I had no idea where it would lead, but I was going anyway. I'd had enough. This 'world' had never made sense to me: the injustice, the stupidity, the way the system turns people into little more than machines working through a spin cycle of repeating experience and behaviour they hysterically call 'life'. We don't live life – life lives us.

There are exceptions and many will be reading this book, but most people are told what to think, where to go, what to do and how to do it. Not so? Well, where do you get your 'information' that leads you to reach conclusions about yourself and the world? Who decides what time you get up every workday? Who decides where you go and what you do when you get there? Who decides how you do it? If you are like the overwhelming majority of people currently resident in this dreamworld, those decisions are not made by you at all; they are imposed by the 'system', the spider's web of control that dictates its will upon your 'life'.

You get your 'information' from the mainstream media that sells you the daily falsehoods on which you decide what to think and believe. You have to get up at a certain time because you have to report for work and you can't be late. You go where your bosses tell you to go and you do what they say. If you rebel you get fired and if you don't get paid you can't afford a home or enough to eat. And it's not only you. What about your family and others dependent upon you? If you don't serve the system what are the consequences for *them*? To meet all these perceived needs and responsibilities, you have to spend every day keeping other people happy. In turn, the bosses are also slavishly following the impositions of those who control *them* and *they* dare not step out of line either. Bosses have bosses, too.

Take a farmer supplying food to a supermarket; he dictates to his farmworkers and if they don't do as he tells them they're sacked. But he also has to do whatever the supermarket tells him or he loses the contract and can go out of business. At the next level, those running the supermarket have to answer to shareholders, who will themselves include people who serve *their* bosses, and bosses who serve their own bosses. Round and round it goes, this circle of dependency and imposition of will. One man's slave is another man's master; one man's sheep is another man's shepherd. This is the way the world is purposely structured. The system wants everyone controlling everyone else and this is done in a billion different ways. What we call 'free societies' are Gulags by any other name. The system doesn't serve us – we serve it. We are slaves who delude ourselves that we are free because we don't want to face the reality of our plight.

I was on an American radio show one night when a caller made a great point. He likened humanity to the husband who knows his wife is being unfaithful, but is desperately trying to persuade himself it's not true. When she comes home he confronts her about where she's been and who she's been with. The husband knows the truth, but he is desperately hoping that his wife's explanation sounds credible enough for him to go on kidding himself that everything is fine. He'd rather hear a good lie than accept an unpleasant truth. In the same way, most people don't want to face the conspiracy and corruption of governments or ask why the countries go to war against defenceless civilians, including their own. When governments deliver the lies and excuses for their grotesque actions most people are ready to accept them because they *want* to believe the lies are true. The alternative is to face the fact that the government is not a benign servant of the people – it's the other way round. It is to face the reality that the forces which control the United States are capable of orchestrating the horrors of 9/11 and blaming someone else; and that they can brazenly attend funeral services for the victims while knowing they helped to kill them. How many people are strong enough to face that and what it means for their lives? This is one major reason why the official lies prevail as accepted truth. The alternative is too unthinkable, too unbearable, to contemplate; so most people don't. Pass me a bucket, heavy on the sand.

The same is true of the collective denial we have about our lives: 'I've got a big house and a big car; ain't life great?' Well, the house and the car may be great, but *life*? How many people are doing what they really want to do? How many are truly happy, fulfilled and at peace with themselves? Hardly any, in truth. Isn't that in itself a profound condemnation of the insanity we call 'life'? Most people do what they think they *have* to do and that means serving the system on the system's terms. Why do we confuse 'life' with the world as it is currently experienced? What has life got to do with blowing up children in front of their parents and parents in front of their children and calling it 'liberation'? Where is the life in getting up at the same time every morning to sit in the same jam, or queue for the same train, on the way to the same job that leaves you bored, frustrated and unfulfilled, before returning through the same jam, or same queue, to watch the same nightly TV that treats you like a moron? Where is the life in sending our children to schools and universities designed to spit them out as the programmed cogs of the next generation? But, again, we'd rather convince ourselves that we have a 'good job', 'good career', 'good life', and give our children a 'good education', than face the horror of horrors that life is actually shit. Or shit compared with what it could be and we would like it to be. Indeed, it's not 'life' at all. It is a veil of tears disguised with heavy mascara and massive dabs of self-delusion.

We judge our 'happiness' by our state of unhappiness, and our achievements by the symbols and trinkets that the system has decreed are the essentials of 'success'. On the day I was writing this I saw the results of a study about the mental and emotional health of teenagers in Britain, although the same will apply across the industrialised, computerised, world and beyond. The study: 'Time Trends in Adolescent Mental Health', published in the *Journal of Child Psychology and Psychiatry*, revealed that the number of 15-year-olds suffering from anxiety and depression had increased by 70 per cent in less than 20 years. Hey, we are talking *15-year-olds*! The study concluded that a key cause of this dramatic increase in teenage emotional trauma was the pressure to 'succeed'. It should have added, more accurately, to succeed *on the system's terms*. The study said the 'pressures of succeeding academically and the prospect of debt are contributing to widespread unhappiness'.

In Britain, thanks to the Blair government, students face a mountain of debt when they leave university because of the loans they have had to take out to pay for their education (or what passes for it). Debt means control by the system and that's the real reason for student loans. The study also pointed out the imbalance in time spent at school compared with leisure activities, something I have been highlighting for years. They keep the kids at school for hours on end five days a week and when the prison door opens they send them off with homework! When do children and young people have time to do what *they* want to do? Answer: in between the deluge of academic bullshit designed to turn out the mind-fodder that keeps the system rolling on like some runaway snowball, gathering more and more of our freedoms and uniqueness in its daily wake.

Another study: *The Growing Pains Survey*, reported by the UK Press Association in October 2004, confirmed these trends with three quarters of parents interviewed saying their children were under far more pressure than *they* had been at the same age. A similar percentage said that peer pressure and stresses at school (such as bullying and exams) had the greatest impact on their child's emotional health and well-being. And exams for what, pray? To reveal the extent to which the system controls their minds and perception. According to the survey, seven out of ten parents said the government should be investing more in the provision of mental health services for children and young people. Oh my God, get me out of here! Never mind 'treating' the problem, how about *removing the cause*? How about changing the way your children feel by telling them to relax and have fun because education and passing the system's exams is a pile of crap? 'Education' is there to program, indoctrinate and implant a collective belief in a reality that suits the power structure. It is about subordination, limitation, and the 'I can't', 'you can't', mentality because that's what the system wants everyone to express in their journey to the grave or the hot box. What we call Education doesn't open minds, it screws down the lid. As Albert Einstein put it: 'The only thing that interferes with my learning is my education'. He also said that education is 'what remains after one has forgotten everything he learned in school'.

Why does it make parents proud to see their children getting certificates of 'achievement' for telling the system what it demands to hear? I'm not saying people shouldn't pursue knowledge but, if we are talking freedom here, that has to be done on *our* terms, not the system's. It is also sobering to note that politicians, government officials, journalists, scientists, doctors, lawyers, judges, business leaders and others who administer or serve the system, are invariably those who have been through the same university (indoctrination) mind-machine. Sadly, intelligence and passing exams are so often believed to be the same thing. I was in a disco one night where the dance floor was empty because the DJ was playing music the people didn't want to hear. This ego from hell refused to change it and I asked if that was very intelligent in the circumstances. He was outraged at such a suggestion. He had *proof* that he was intelligent – he had a *degree*! Hilarious. Basic intelligence is to see that people aren't dancing because the music is shite and to change it for something they like; a degree is to tell the system what it has told you to tell it. What is intelligent about that?

Most people kid themselves that they are free by never testing the theory for real. They are like flies caught in a web and so long as they don't try to move they can convince themselves that they could if they wanted to. It's just that they don't want to right now, you see (*Figure 1*). If they tried they would have to face the fact that their arse is superglued to someone else's control system with dinner about to be served – them. They keep doing what the government dictatorships tell them to do, without question or challenge, and perpetuate the illusion that they have free choice by never making one. 'Having my wings stuck to this web suits me fine because I am choosing not to fly.' I have met so many people over the years who thought they were free until they did something that was outside the 'norm'. A big reality check followed because, to quote that great American comedian, Bill Hicks: 'You are free to do as we tell you'. As the Orwellian global state emerges rapidly from the shadows, this self-deception about a 'free world' is becoming far more difficult to sustain. But instead of staring their plight in the face, most just try harder to look the other way. Most people are quick to complain about what is happening in their lives and the wider world, yet they are cast in stone when it comes to doing anything about it. Far better, it seems, to avoid your own responsibility by blaming someone else. The world is like it is because we have allowed the few to make it that way and just pointing the finger at those few is not enough. We are all involved in this. Voltaire captured this theme brilliantly when he said: 'No snowflake in an avalanche ever felt responsible'.

From the time I was seven or eight this 'world' seemed crazy to me and when I began to see what lay behind the illusion we call 'reality', I was an open door. There was no need to push; I was already swinging. There had to be a reason why the world was so ludicrous and why so few appeared able to see it or, at least, admit it to themselves. My incredible experiences since 1990 have shown me that there is indeed a reason, a method in the madness. Society is like it is because those in

Figure 1:

'Fancy going out today, Bill?'
'No thanks, mate, I'm happy sitting here'.
'But we could go out if we wanted to, couldn't we?'
'Sure we could'.
'That's okay, then – ain't it great to be free?'

Illustration by Neil Hague

control want it to be this way. It suits their agenda for global dictatorship. The extraordinary story behind the façade of daily life has been unfolded to me step by step and this book represents the next one – a gigantic leap into a realm and reality where few are prepared to go.

I explain how my journey began in *Tales from the Time Loop* but, in summary, I was told through a psychic that I would be given the 'spiritual riches' to, in effect, lift the veil of illusion that held humanity in servitude. Knowledge would be put into my mind and at other times I would be led to knowledge, the psychic told me. 'One man cannot change the world, but one man can communicate the message that will change the world', she said. Many other psychics repeated the same themes. There were secrets to be revealed – enormous secrets – and I would be led to this knowledge and communicate it on a global scale. One said: 'Arduous seeking is not necessary. The path is already mapped out. You only have to follow the clues'. It sounded fantastic at the time, but how true it proved to be. From that point on, my life became an explosion of synchronicity and 'coincidence'. I have been led to knowledge through people, books and personal experience in more than 40 countries and the clues have been laid out, not only in abundance, but in the

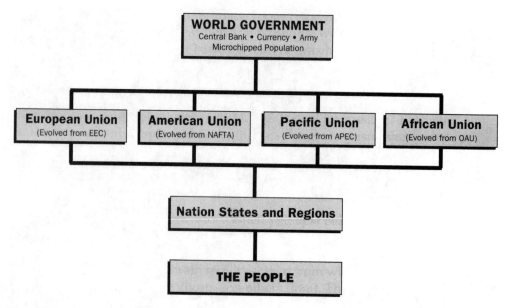

Figure 2: *The Illuminati global fascist state. The plan is for a world government dictatorship that includes a second tier of superstates like the European Union. What we now call 'countries' would be merely administrative subsidiaries controlled by the world government, central bank and army. This structure would allow a few to impose their will on the global population*

right order to most swiftly assimilate. I have been guided along a path that began with an understanding of the manipulation in this 'world', the reality we think is 'physical', and then took me into other realms that interpenetrate this one – what scientists call parallel universes. In the first two chapters I am going to summarise this information before moving to the next amazing stage in the unfolding revelation of who we are, where we are, and what we are doing here.

Through the 1990s, thanks to unseen guidance and synchronised 'coincidence', I began to understand and communicate the 'five-sense' level of a global conspiracy for human control orchestrated through a network of secret societies and interbreeding families known as the Illuminati. These are the families that control governments, the banking system, transnational corporations, oil and pharmaceutical cartels, world media, intelligence agencies, police forces and even what is taught in the schools and universities. All these aspects of society, and so many more, are ultimately controlled by the same Illuminati families pursuing the same agenda of global tyranny. Their aim is a centralised fascist state headed by a world government, central bank, currency, and army that will enslave a microchipped population connected to, and controlled by, a global computer network (*Figure 2*). People laughed when I first suggested that this was the plan, but only the uninformed and concrete-minded are smirking now. The Orwellian 'Big Brother' nightmare unfurls by the day, especially since 9/11. This is not surprising when you realise that those attacks were engineered by the same force that now uses them as an excuse to impose its fascist agenda to 'save us' from terrorism (see

Alice in Wonderland and the World Trade Center Disaster). We can clearly see the rapidly advancing centralisation of power and ownership in all areas of our lives and it has become known as *globalisation*. This is not just about big, greedy corporations, as so many of the 'Left' would have us believe. The major corporations are not the end, but a means to the end. They are part of a coordinated and long-planned agenda for global control which targets every expression of human existence.

In politics we have superstates like the European Union, and its emerging mirrors: the African Union, Asia Pacific Economic Cooperation (APEC), and the planned 'Free Trade' Area of the Americas (FTAA). These are structured to align with a basic fact of life for would-be dictatorships – the more you centralise decision-making the more power the few have over the many. Diversity is the worst nightmare of the dictator because he can't control all the points of decision-making. Uniformity and centralisation are essential to Fascism or Communism or whatever name you give to your dictatorship of choice. Thus, we see the centralisation of everything introduced with an ever-gathering pace.

The world government is designed to be the capstone on this pyramid of political tyranny and the world army's role is to impose its decisions on countries that want to govern themselves. It is for this reason that national armies are more and more subordinate to, and merely a part of, groupings like NATO and the United Nations peacekeeping operations. It is an example of what I call the 'Totalitarian Tiptoe' in which you go step by step to a long-decided goal instead of making colossal changes all at once. If the steps are too big many people would see what was going on and that's not the idea. Our ignorance is their bliss. In Europe, the EEC, or Common Market 'free trade' area, became the centralised fascist state known as the European Union thanks to the drip, drip, drip of change imposed through the Totalitarian Tiptoe, and the same is happening elsewhere.

The Illuminati manipulate their placemen and women into the key positions in politics, and most of the rest who make up the political numbers are ignorant fodder. Intelligence never was an essential attribute of a politician and often it is a bad career move. Tim Collins, a Conservative Member of Parliament in the UK, was sent details by a constituent about flaws in the official story of the 'plane' that was supposed to have hit the Pentagon on 9/11. Mr Collins was offered the chance to see a DVD presentation detailing this evidence, but he refused to even look at it. His 'executive assistant' wrote that Mr Collins '… does not believe in conspiracy theories, and regards it as particularly reprehensible that the creators of the DVD to which you refer should be seeking to play games with such a terrible tragedy'. This was without even bothering to see it, and the fact that people like Tim Collins become politicians might also be considered a terrible tragedy for those they are supposed to represent. When you have Members of Parliament or Congress with this mentality – and Collins is a norm, not a rarity – manipulating the political system is child's play. Politics always reminds me of Albert Einstein's adage that you can't solve problems with the same level of intelligence that created them.

The Pyramid of Manipulation

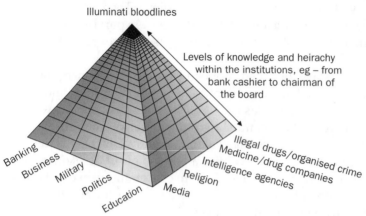

Illuminati bloodlines

Levels of knowledge and heirachy within the institutions, eg – from bank cashier to chairman of the board

Banking
Business
Military
Politics
Education
Media
Religion
Intelligence agencies
Medicine/drug companies
Illegal drugs/organised crime

All the major institutions and groups that affect our daily lives connect with the Illuminati, which decides the coordinated policy throughout the pyramid.

People in the lower compartments will have no idea what they are part of.

Figure 3: *The Russian doll dictatorship. Global society is structured as pyramids within bigger pyramids with one encompassing them all. At the top are the Illuminati families manipulating their agenda for global control through apparently unconnected organisations and institutions. 'Free societies' are a myth because the Hidden Hand is imposing its agenda behind this veil of deceit*

The control of banking and business is already in a few hands and the trend continues. The European currency – the euro – is part of the Illuminati agenda to replace all currencies with a single world currency controlled by the planned World Central Bank. As Mayer Amschel Rothschild, founder of the (Illuminati) banking dynasty, is reported to have said: 'Give me control of a nation's currency and I care not who makes the laws'. Take that a stage further and you have the plan for a world dictatorship in which they control the world currency *and* make the laws. The Illuminati families use their secret society network and interlocking, proxy, gofer directors to control all the major banks and transnational corporations. There may appear to be different names on the major boards of directors, but they are answerable to the masters who put them there and dictate the policy they pursue. As detailed in my other books, the world is controlled on the five-sense level by a structure of pyramids within pyramids, like Russian dolls, one inside the other. At the top of these pyramids, especially the biggest one that encompasses all the rest, are the Illuminati families (*Figure 3*). From there they manipulate and impose their agenda for centralisation of global power right across society. Those involved with pressure groups, which challenge the system on many and various issues, need to understand that they are all dealing with the same Illuminati families at the top of the pyramid.

Through their transnational corporations, the Illuminati control, among much else, the world's oil, gas, electricity and water supplies, drug production and 'medicine', and food production and distribution. Their banking system controls governments, commerce and people by lending money that doesn't exist and

Figure 4: *Money is merely debt; and even 'cash' is only an IOU promising to pay at some time in the 'future'. It is there for all to see on British banknotes*

charging interest on it. What we call money is only *debt* being passed around as cheques, wire transfers, credit and even 'cash'. What we call cash is not money; it is debt. Money is created by issuing credit – a debt – and no matter what form this credit may subsequently take (cash, cheques, whatever) it is always recycling debt. The word *credit* is Latin for 'he trusts' or 'he believes', and that's exactly what 'money' really is: a belief that it is real. It is not. Even the debt bit is an illusion because how can you be in debt if nothing has been given to you in the first place?

When a bank makes a 'loan' it is loaning *nothing*. They simply type into your account the figure they have agreed to 'loan' you against your house, business or land. They don't create money, they create *debt* by tapping the keys of a computer program and from that moment you have to pay them back the non-existent 'money' they have 'loaned' you, plus interest! If you don't do that they can take your property – *for loaning you nothing*. Governments borrow 'money' in the same way and taxpayers become responsible for 'paying back' the banks the non-existent money that has been 'borrowed' on their behalf by governments controlled by the same forces that own the banks. If you wrote this as fiction they would say it was too far-fetched to be credible, but this is the reality of the banking fraud. British banknotes 'promise to pay the bearer on demand the sum of' whatever the note is said to be worth (*Figure 4*). How can this be? If I owe you ten pounds and I give you ten pounds I have given you what I owe, right? Yes, if the ten pound note is money as we understand it to be. But it's not. It is nothing more than an IOU, a promise to pay – a *debt*. When you lend me ten pounds you lend me a debt and when I give you back the ten pounds I give you back the debt. How can we pay money to anyone when there isn't any?

My wife, Pam, had a letter from the police in Hampshire, England, claiming she had been caught on a speed camera doing six miles an hour over the limit on an empty road at midnight. They wanted £60 for this crime against humanity. I wrote to a guy at Hampshire Police, a debt collector for the government who went by the title of 'Manager, Central Ticket Office'. I asked him how the 'money' could be paid when there *was* no money. Wasn't it illegal to pay a debt with a debt and how, therefore, was it possible to pay them without committing fraud? He refused to answer the question no matter how many times I asked him because he had no answer. The police document even suggested that the 'money' be paid by credit card! I also asked the Chief Constable of Hampshire and the 'Justices' Chief Executive' how it was possible to pay when there was no money, only debt. They also gave me the silent treatment because they have nowhere to go except ignore the question. Yet billions go hungry, lose their homes, live in poverty and even die through lack of money when it is only illusory figures on computer screens. A Rothschild family communiqué to associates in New York in 1863 summed up the situation perfectly:

'The few who understand the system will either be so interested in its profits, or so dependent on its favours, that there will be no opposition from that class; while on the other hand, the great body of people, mentally incapable of comprehending the tremendous advantages ... will bear its burden without complaint, and perhaps without suspecting that the system is inimical to their best interests.'

The whole banking system is based on a fraud of stunning proportions to control and suppress the people. There is nothing wrong with having a unit of exchange and calling it money. That is not my point. It is that once you have private banks owned by the same people creating the exchange out of nothing, and charging interest to do so, you have all you need for global tyranny. This is what we have and it has been installed because the same families that control the banks also control the politicians that pass the banking laws. Staggering as it may be to anyone new to this, banks are allowed to lend ten times what they have on deposit. It is called *fractional reserve lending*. Every time you put a pound or dollar into a bank you are giving it the right to lend ten pounds or dollars it does not have. Many people think that banks are lending depositors' money when they are actually lending fresh air, figures on a screen. When you follow 'money' from bank to bank in cheques and transfers etc., you find they are creating more and more 'money' from your original deposit or loan because each time this is spent and ends up in a different bank, more credit is loaned against it. The amount of interest that banks accrue through this fraud is astonishing. The manipulation of the money/banking system is one of the most effective means of dictatorship by the Illuminati families and an example of the depth to which we are scammed.

People work in jobs they hate to 'pay the mortgage'. But what is this mortgage? It is a debt paid by the bank to you in exchange for you paying them back an even bigger debt. But you can't – in law – pay a debt with a debt! And they say *I'm* mad! See my other books for the detailed and extraordinary background to the global banking fraud. This Illuminati network of interconnecting banks and companies is using its influence (control) in government to destroy smaller non-Illuminati businesses and make everyone dependent on the elite families to survive. Why is it that governments continually pass laws that make life easier and more profitable for big corporations, but more difficult and costly for small businesses? Here you have the answer and it is a simple equation: dependency = control; diversity = freedom.

In the media, the power over what we see and hear is now in ridiculously few hands. There may appear to be ever-increasing media 'diversity' with more and more television channels, but the number of those who control them and their output continues to contract. When I became a television reporter/presenter in the 1970s it was unthinkable that the regional Independent Television (ITV) stations around the United Kingdom would not be owned independently of each other. This was thought essential for the free flow of unbiased information. But today one company, Carlton–Granada, controls the whole of ITV throughout England, Scotland, Wales and Northern Ireland. 'Independent' radio is going the same way rapidly. Even that is not the end because the Illuminati agenda demands total control, and all over the world the regulation of media ownership is being reduced or binned.

The British government under Illuminati puppet, Tony Blair, has done this to an outrageous extent and seeks to allow more foreign ownership of the media so that global corporations like Disney, and others, can move in. The United States Federal Communications Commission (FCC), headed by Colin Powell's son, Michael, is continually pressing for limits on ownership to be relaxed still further. This is allowing a few Illuminati corporations to own enormous swathes of the national and global media and destroy what is left of diversity of output and view. The idea is to control information to such an extent that people will only see and hear what suits the Illuminati dictatorship. This is exactly what George Orwell envisioned in his book, *1984*. A media group called Clear Channel, which has close connections to the Bush family, is one example. It has purchased a vast number of US radio stations and dictates the 'news' output. In Detroit alone it owns seven of the city's most popular stations. Before and during the 2003 invasion of Iraq, Clear Channel was funding rallies aimed at gathering support for the war while suppressing alternative views on its airwaves.

Major corporations like General Electric control the US television networks from which most Americans get their 'news'. General Electric owns the NBC network, CNBC, MSNBC, Bravo, Mun2TV, Sci-Fi channel, Trio, WNBC – New York, KNBC Los Angeles, WMAQ Chicago, WCAU Philadelphia, KNTV San Jose/San Francisco, KXAS – Dallas/Fort Worth, WRC Washington, WTVJ Miami, KNSD San Diego, WVIT Hartford, WNCN Raleigh, WCMH Columbus, WVTM Birmingham, WJAR Providence, KVEA/KWHY Los Angeles, WNJU New York, WSCV Miami, KTMD Houston, WSNS Chicago, KXTX Dallas/Fort Worth, KVDA San Antonio, KSTS San Jose/San Francisco, KDRX Phoenix, KNSO Fresno, KMAS Denver, WNEU Boston/Merrimack, KHRR Tucson and WKAQ Puerto Rico.[1] They also own Universal Studios, NBC Universal Television Studio and NBC Universal Television Distribution. Imagine the power that gives them to implant a false reality.

Media tycoons like Rupert Murdoch head companies that control streams of television and radio stations and newspapers worldwide, together with the movie studio Twentieth Century Fox, book publishers like Harper Collins, and the Delphi Internet system. One Murdoch 'asset', Fox News, or *Fix* News to be more accurate, is the most biased television propaganda channel I have yet seen. Through conglomerates like General Electric, Murdoch's News Corporation, Disney and AOL–Time Warner, the Illuminati also control Hollywood and the music industry. You may see 'different' music labels and movie studios, but essentially the same force dominates them and decides what will and won't be seen and heard. You will appreciate when we get to the focus of this book just how vital this media domination is to the Illuminati agenda. It goes much further and far deeper than just telling lies and hiding truths about world events. Without this imposition of what people largely see and hear the rest of the control structure would collapse.

Two small examples of media manipulation and false reporting reveal the bigger story. A former BBC journalist told me how she was asked to take a camera into the streets and record what people thought about the Queen Mother when she died in 2002 at the age of 101. The reporter found that '99 per cent' of those she interviewed said they didn't like the Queen Mother and didn't care that she had died. As a journalist of integrity, she reported the truth of what had happened, but found herself severely reprimanded by her bosses. The official BBC line was that the 'Queen Mum' (a really nasty piece of work) was loved and admired by the nation. The journalist asked her sycophant 'superiors' if they were saying she should have lied. 'In the circumstances you should have bent the truth', they said. She was horrified and resigned. Sadly, there are few like her and the truth is not only bent every day, it is massacred.

While I was writing this book, I had my latest experience (one of many hundreds) that highlighted the media's extraordinary inability to report the facts – and the public's naive belief in what they read and hear. I was approached by a television programme called *Celebrity Big Brother*, in which 'well-known' people live in a 'house' for up to two weeks while being filmed 24 hours a day. The viewers vote to eject the 'celebrities' until there is one left – the 'winner'. I met with representatives of the programme to see if, appalling as the 'show' was, it might be an opportunity to get across information that the public wouldn't normally hear. I quickly decided that it wasn't, and I never heard any further from them, nor them from me. But in the two months and more that followed, newspapers began to report that I *was* going to be on the programme. Right up to the day this was being repeated and one paper even sent a reporter to knock on my brother's door looking for quotes about my appearance. A Sunday paper said that I had been replaced at the last minute by someone else when I had *never* been scheduled to appear. In the ten weeks that the stories were running not *once* did any of these papers ever ask … *me*! Yet, nonsense as the reports were, the public believed them. I was constantly stopped in the street to be asked about my appearance on the show and most people believed that it must be happening because they had read it in a newspaper. Radio programmes repeated the story and it became the accepted truth even though it was 100 per cent *wrong*.

What I have just described is how, minute by minute, people are sold a false reality by the media. The *Big Brother* experience, and the Queen mother story, may

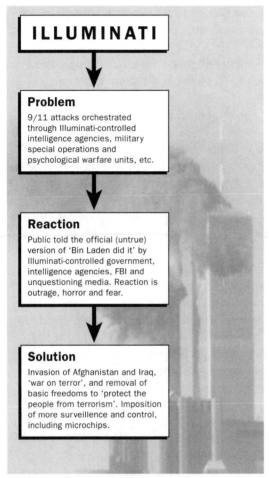

ILLUMINATI

Problem
9/11 attacks orchestrated
through Illuminati-controlled
intelligence agencies, military
special operations and
psychological warfare units, etc.

Reaction
Public told the official (untrue)
version of 'Bin Laden did it' by
Illuminati-controlled government,
intelligence agencies, FBI and
unquestioning media. Reaction is
outrage, horror and fear.

Solution
Invasion of Afghanistan and Iraq,
'war on terror', and removal of
basic freedoms to 'protect the
people from terrorism'. Imposition
of more surveillence and control,
including microchips.

Figure 5: *The September 11th attacks were a classic example of the Problem-Reaction-Solution technique and the 'solutions' were all planned long before the twin towers were hit. (See* Alice in Wonderland and the World Trade Center Disaster *and* Tales from the Time Loop *for the detailed background)*

be minor examples, but the same principles apply to the reporting of wars, politics, business, finance, science and all the rest – as detailed in my other books like *Tales from the Time Loop*. People are constantly misled by a combination of incompetence, ignorance and calculated deceit. It may not matter if people wrongly believe that I am going to appear on some trash television show; but it does when they accept the official story of 9/11 and the manufactured 'war on terror'.

Then there are the microchips and surveillance cameras. You would need an honours degree in self-delusion not to see the monumental expansion of surveillance technology everywhere you go. This has been justified in response to terrorist outrages orchestrated by the very forces behind the introduction of the microchips and surveillance! This is the technique I have dubbed Problem-Reaction-Solution in which you secretly create a problem (like 9/11), tell the people a false story about the perpetrators and reasons behind it and, when the people say 'something must be done', you offer the solution to the problem you have created (*Figure 5*). As we have seen since 9/11, these 'solutions' advance the Orwellian agenda. The technique is to put the people in fear so they will look to their leaders to protect them with new laws that suit the plan for human enslavement. Dr William Sargant, a psychiatrist with the Illuminati Tavistock Institute in Britain, wrote in his 1957 book, *Battle for the Mind*:

'Various types of belief can be implanted in people after brain function has been deliberately disturbed by accidentally or deliberately induced fear, anger or excitement. Of the results caused by such disturbances the most common one is temporarily impaired judgement and heightened suggestibility. Its various group manifestations are sometimes classed under the heading of 'herd instinct', and appear most spectacularly in wartime, during severe epidemics, and all similar periods of common danger, which increase anxiety and so individual and mass suggestibility.

'… We would be advised not to underestimate the effect on the collective psyche in terms of fear and a desire for the authorities to "protect people" from that fear.'

Levels of surveillance have soared to 'protect' (control) the people since the attacks of 9/11. When you walk through towns or cities you are watched by one camera after another. Go into a store and it is invariably the same, as it is with airports, train stations and even, as I experienced recently, in some taxicabs. Sitting in that cab, with a camera recording my every move, was such a symbol of where we are, never mind where we are going. If you have a mobile phone you can be tracked to within a few feet and microchips in cars can do the same. Your credit card records your every purchase and everywhere you go to use it; and the interconnecting databases mean that any government agency, and many others outside of government, can tell you your life story in intimate detail.

We now have iris–recognition cameras being introduced, voice–recognition technology and, oh yes, the microchipped human. How they laughed when I first began to say that this is where we were heading, a system in which every child is chipped within moments of birth. 'You're a nutter', I was told. Do I still hear the sound of laughter? I think not, because human microchipping is well under way. They have used the Totalitarian Tiptoe to make people familiar with chipping. They started with domestic and farm animals, went on to clothing and other products, and finally came the main target – *us*. As always, they emphasise all the alleged benefits of being microchipped cattle while ignoring the true agenda. They say you would be able to track your child, have your medical records available if you are hit by a truck, and get rid of those awful credit cards. 'See how much we care?' Everything could be put on the chip under your skin and you could even fast-track through an airport or pay for your groceries without ever having to reach for your pocket. Now doesn't that justify being a tagged animal? You know it makes sense.

A United Press International (UPI) report I read in April 2004 said the US Department of Health and Human Services had announced a trial to 'more closely monitor and assist the nation's homeless population'. Note the Orwellian use of the word 'assist' when they really mean *control*. Under the pilot programme, the report said that homeless people in participating cities would be implanted with *mandatory* Radio Frequency Identification (RFID) chips so that social workers and the police could track their movements in real-time. 'Supporters of subdermal RFID tracking say the technology will discourage implanted homeless men and women from committing crimes, while making it easier for government workers to provide social services such as delivering food and medicine', the report concluded. When these people say they are launching 'trials', this is forked-tongue speak for: 'We are getting our foot in the door by targeting people that most of the public don't give a shit about, and when chipping is an established method of identification we are coming for the rest of you'.

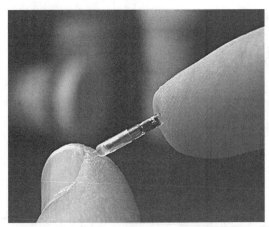

Figure 6: *The rice-sized microchip designed to turn people into robots*

One of the main companies behind all this is Applied Digital Solutions in Florida who produce the rice-sized 'VeriChip' (*Figures 6 and 7 overleaf*). I have seen media reports claiming that the idea of embedding chips in the human body remained 'largely theoretical' until 9/11 when a technology executive at Applied Digital Solutions saw firefighters writing their badge numbers on their arms as identification in case they were disfigured or trapped. This led to the idea of chipping people, it was claimed. What utter trash. I highlighted this company before the attacks in a book called *Children of the Matrix* and its launch of a chip called Digital Angel. Dr Peter Zhou, the chief scientist behind the technology, said *before* 9/11:

> 'Digital Angel will be a connection from yourself to the electronic world. It will be your guardian, protector. It will bring good things for you. We will be a hybrid of electronic intelligence and our own soul.'

Electronic intelligence and our own *brain and central nervous system* more like. The idea of microchipped people was not well received by those concerned about privacy and civil liberties, and promotion of the chip was cooled for a time. But after 9/11, Applied Digital Solutions took the opportunity to strike with a sales pitch of Human Chip = Human Security. It now claims to have chipped thousands of people, but the aim is for everybody to be tagged. One of VeriChip's early clients included Mexico's attorney general to 'protect him from kidnap'; and a company called Solusat, the Mexican distributor of VeriChip, has launched a 'service' to chip children as an 'anti-kidnapping device'. It doesn't mention that these 'VeriKids', as it calls them, are kidnapped electronically the moment the chip goes in. Applied Digital Solutions is planning to introduce the 'VeriKid' scheme in other countries, including the United States.

ORBCOMM, a global satellite telecommunications company, announced on its website in late 2004 that agreement had been reached with the VeriChip Corporation, a subsidiary of Applied Digital, to provide 'satellite and telecommunication services for applications to be developed for use with the world's first implantable radio frequency identification (RFID) microchip …'. Jerry Eisenberg, CEO of ORBCOMM, said the relationship with VeriChip provided yet another new and important industry that will use their satellite system and its ground infrastructure network to transmit messages globally. Yes, to control the people. If you have read my book, *And The Truth Shall Set You Free*, you will know that all this was predicted a long time ago. I wrote in

Illustration by Neil Hague

Figure 7: Digital concentration camps – the microchipped world symbolised by Neil Hague. It is vital for human freedom for people to refuse to be chipped

1994 that the human microchip would be sold to the people as a means of protecting children, having medical records available for doctors, and as a more convenient and thief-proof way of replacing the credit card. Applied Digital Solutions is already using all three ruses in its marketing statements. In October 2004, the Illuminati-controlled Food and Drug Administration gave permission for the company to market the VeriChip (a decision never in doubt) and the US Department of Health and Human Services announced $139 million in grants to advance 'President Bush's' plan for electronic health records (microchipped people) within a decade. The people work to pay the taxes and the taxes are used to further imprison the people. I have even seen an article about a Barcelona nightclub offering people a faster entrance if they would agree to be chipped. Apparently, Tuesday night is now 'implant night' when guests can be chipped between drinking and dancing. How many chipping schemes are being introduced that never make the newswires?

We will see the chip being used and promoted ever more widely in countless ways because the Illuminati global state demands it for the ultimate control of the people. The British government, for example, has announced plans to introduce compulsory ID cards, but this is only a stepping stone, a Totalitarian Tiptoe, to microchipping the population. The same is happening in the United States. A CIA scientist told me in 1997 that the chip is far more than a means of electronic tagging. The messages going from the chip to the computer are one thing, but more important are the messages going the other way. He said they could communicate with the embedded chips, either isolating an individual or doing it en masse, and send frequencies that could cause severe pain or illness, manipulate people mentally and emotionally, and even kill. The chip could make people docile or aggressive, sexually high or suppressed, and affect their thought processes so they couldn't think straight or were influenced in their actions by what the chip was receiving. This is the real story behind the microchipping of humans.

The aim of the system is to keep us in survival mode, always looking to tomorrow instead of living in the moment. As John Lennon wrote: 'Life is what happens to you while you're busy making other plans'. If our heads are down and we are focused on survival or seeking 'success' we won't look up and see the game that enslaves us. A document that came to light in 1986 brilliantly described the techniques at work in what we call 'society'. It was called *Silent Weapons for a Quiet War*, and another version is reported to have been in the hands of US Naval Intelligence in 1969. The one I have was apparently found inside an IBM photocopier bought at a second-hand sale in America. This lengthy and detailed document outlines a policy that has been implemented since at least the 1950s. It says the 'quiet war was … declared by the international elite at a meeting held in 1954'. A significant Illuminati organisation called the Bilderberg Group first met in 1954 (see *And The Truth Shall Set You Free*) and this consists of the elite in global politics, banking, business, military, intelligence agencies, and so on. The background, however, is less important than the content because it encapsulates the quiet war on the human psyche:

> Experience has proven that the simplest method of securing a silent weapon and gaining control of the public is to keep them undisciplined and ignorant of basic systems principles on the one hand, while keeping them confused, disorganised, and distracted with matters of no real importance on the other hand.
>
> This is achieved by:
> 1. disengaging their minds; sabotaging their mental activities; providing a low-quality programme of public education in mathematics, system design and economics, and discouraging technical creativity.
> 2. engaging their emotions, increasing their self indulgence and their indulgence in emotional and physical activities by:
>   a) unrelenting emotional affrontations and attacks (mental and emotional rape) by the way of a constant barrage of sex, violence, and wars in the media – especially the TV and the newspapers.
>   b) giving them what they desire – in excess – 'junk food for thought' – and depriving them of what they really need.
>   c) rewriting history and law and subjecting the public to the deviant creation, thus being able to shift their thinking from personal needs to highly fabricated outside priorities.
>
> These preclude their interest in, and discovery of, the silent weapons of social automation technology. The general rule is that there is profit in confusion; the more confusion, the more profit. Therefore, the best approach is to create problems and then offer solutions.

In summary:

Media: Keep the adult public attention diverted away from the real social issues, and captivated by matters of no real importance.

Schools: Keep the young public ignorant of real mathematics, real economics, real law, and real history.

Entertainment: Keep the public entertainment below a sixth-grade level.

Work: Keep the public busy, busy, busy, with no time to think; back on the farm with the other animals.'

The document says of the 'quiet war':

It shoots situations, instead of bullets; propelled by data processing, instead of grains of gunpowder; from a computer, instead of a gun; operated by a computer programmer, instead of a marksman; under the orders of a banking magnate, instead of a military general. It makes no obvious noises, causes no obvious physical injuries, and does not obviously interfere with anyone's daily social life.

Yet it makes an unmistakable 'noise', causes unmistakable physical and mental damage, and unmistakably interferes with daily social life, i.e., unmistakable to a trained observer, one who knows what to look for. The public cannot comprehend the weapon, and therefore cannot believe they are being attacked and subdued by a weapon.

The public might instinctively feel that something is wrong, but because of the technical nature of the silent weapon, they cannot express their feeling in a rational way, or handle the problem with intelligence. Therefore, they do not know how to cry for help, and do not know how to associate with others to defend themselves against it.

When a silent weapon is applied gradually, the public adjusts/adapts to its presence and learns to tolerate its encroachment on their lives until the pressure (psychological via economic) becomes too great and they crack up. Therefore, the silent weapon is a type of biological warfare. It attacks the vitality, options, and mobility of the individuals of a society by knowing, understanding, manipulating, and attacking their sources of natural and social energy, and their physical, mental, and emotional strengths and weaknesses.

Recognise that society? Of course, we live in it. The scale of the deceit is extraordinary – even down to your name. Have you noticed that when you receive correspondence relating to government, law and anything to do with finance, including taxation, your name is always spelt out in all upper case, as in DAVID ICKE? *This is because your upper case name is not you.* It is a corporation/trust set up by the government through the treasury department at your birth. Every time a child is born a corporation/trust is created using his or her name in all upper case. They do this because governments are corporations and they operate under commercial law, the law of contracts. The laws passed by governments only apply to corporations and not to living, breathing, flesh and blood sovereign-free men and women spelt in upper–lower or all lower case, as with David Icke, or david icke. The living, breathing sovereign man and woman is subject to common law, not the commercial law introduced by governments through legislation.

Using commercial law makes it much easier to install an 'elected' dictatorship because, unlike common law, you are not subject to precedents built up over centuries. You simply have to get a majority to vote for a bill in Parliament or Congress, or have the US President sign a document, and the law is imposed. What you also have to do – clearly not difficult – is to keep from the people the knowledge that their name in upper case is not them. They will then pay you taxes and be subject to your jurisdiction and control in all areas of their lives by unknowingly standing surety for the corporation – 'DAVID ICKE' – that they don't even know exists. In the United States you may notice that the national flag always has a gold fringe when displayed in a court or federal building and you see this also on the uniforms of US troops. This is because under the International Law of the Flags a gold fringe indicates the jurisdiction of commercial law, also known as British Maritime Law and, in the U.S., the Uniform Commercial Code or UCC. Americans think that their government and legal system is pegged in some way to the Constitution, but it is not. The United States, like Britain and elsewhere, is ruled by commercial law to overcome the checks and balances of common law. It's another monumental fraud.

When Pam received the speeding ticket from Hampshire Police, her name was spelt in the letter in all upper case. They could not have done it any other way or their traffic law would not apply because it is a *commercial* law applicable only to a corporation. I wrote to the police to point out that they had sent their threat of prosecution to a corporation and not to the lower-case living, breathing sovereign woman of the same name. I asked how a corporation could drive a car and challenged them to prove their jurisdiction over a live woman under their commercial law. All they would say is that the law was passed by the government and there was nothing more to discuss.

The chief debt collector in the speed camera department said they spelt the names in all upper case for the benefit of clarity. Or, to be more accurate, he said that this is what he had been *taught* was the reason. We are back to the compartmentalised pyramids again. The fodder employed to enforce the system must also be ignorant of what they are really involved with and they are given a false explanation for why things are done as they are. At least this guy said he had been taught; everyone else in the system I have asked about the use of upper case names had never even thought about it before. I have spoken with clerks of court, lawyers and financial people, and they said they had no idea why they always had to use names in all upper case. 'Maybe it's just the way the system is set up', said one clerk of the court. Yes it is, but this has nothing to do with 'clarity'. It is because commercial law only applies to corporations and so they must use upper case names because *governments* are corporations. I wrote to the Hampshire police guy to say that if clarity was the only reason for the upper case name would he please resend their threat of prosecution with Pam's name in lower case. After all, there would be no problem with clarity because we all knew who we were. He refused. Of course he did. The system wouldn't let him and even if he had tried to type in a lower case name, the police computer system would have defaulted to upper case. Such is the scale of the fraud that people are being prosecuted by laws that don't apply to them and fined 'money' that doesn't exist. Amazing, but true.

The detail and sources for what I have outlined, and so much more, can be found in my other books, like *And The Truth Shall Set You Free*, *The Biggest Secret* and *Tales from the Time Loop*. But just look around and you can clearly see what is happening once you know the agenda and the techniques used to achieve it; the world becomes an open book when you understand the game. So much of the global dictatorship is in place already. The Illuminati families control the money (debt) in your pocket or bank; they control the companies that provide most of the food, drink and power supplies, including the fuel in your car; they control the drugs you take and doctors you see; and they dictate what is taught in the schools, colleges and universities. They also control what mainstream 'science' researches through their choices of funding, and they control the governments that pass laws which suit their agenda and undermine or destroy their opposition. They are a few years from completion with 2012 apparently a target period for them, it would seem. Once they have the global government structure, and especially the mass microchipping of the people, their fascist dictatorship will be revealed on a scale of horror and sickness that few could currently imagine. *But this doesn't have to be.* Our destiny is in our own hands if only we will grasp it.

The secret agenda explains the endless contractions in our societies. People ask why things are done a certain way when there are obviously better options, but they don't realise that the power structure is not there to make things better or more effective for the population; it has been created to serve the Illuminati agenda for human enslavement. So, as writer Michael Ellner has said:

'Just look at us. Everything is backwards; everything is upside down. Doctors destroy health, lawyers destroy justice, universities destroy knowledge, governments destroy freedom, the major media destroy information and religions destroy spirituality.'

Why? Because they're *meant* to.

Source

1   Columbia Journalism Review: **http://www.cjr.org/tools/owners/**

CHAPTER TWO

Beyond the Veil

Whenever people agree with me I always feel I must be wrong
Oscar Wilde

As I followed the clues that revealed the extraordinary scale and depth of the global conspiracy, it soon became clear that even this was only one level of the story. From the latter years of the 1990s, the synchronicity of my life was leading me into areas of knowledge and awareness beyond the five senses. Understanding the nature of these other dimensions or realities was fundamental to identifying the force that was behind the Illuminati.

Everything in what we call Creation is energy resonating at different frequencies. The slower it vibrates the denser it appears to be (like a wall); the faster it vibrates the less and less dense and 'solid' it appears until the energy is vibrating so quickly that it leaves the frequency range perceivable by the five senses. What we call matter is energy resonating to a slow vibration. Albert Einstein's famous equation $E=mc^2$, written in 1905, says that mass/matter is a very concentrated form of energy, and concentrated is certainly the word. If you converted all the energy in one kilogram of sugar or water it would power a car non-stop for around 100,000 years. Other dimensions of reality, which some call the 'spirit world', are simply realms vibrating too fast for us to see.

It is easier now to talk of multiple realities because many scientists have begun to catch up with the mystics, psychics and others who have been saying all along that this 'physical' world is only one reality within an Infinite Consciousness. These scientists would say other realities are parallel universes and part of a single unified energy field. Quantum physics, which explores reality beyond the 'physical' world of the atom, is saying basically the same as the mystics, and people like me, who talk of different dimensions and frequencies of existence interpenetrating our own. Spirituality and true science – in its open-minded, open-hearted form – are essentially at one. It is *mainstream* science and *mainstream* religion that has caused the apparent rift because they are slaves to arrogance, ignorance and dogma. One is not science and the other is not spiritual. They are two polarities of the same falsehood. The open-minded quantum physicist would have no problem with most of what I am going to say in this book, while the cap-touching, protecting-my-funding, mainstream 'scientist' would roll his eyes in bewilderment. Such is the chasm of view that exists in the so-called scientific community. But it is the mainstream 'safe' version of scientific 'fact' that has dominated the academic text books and university lecture-theatres because that suits the agenda for human control.

The power structure wants us to believe that we are merely bodies being shuffled from a cradle to a grave and what happens on the conveyor belt in between is called 'life'. In mainstream society we are given the choice of believing that at the end of this life we either cease to exist, or we become subject to some dictatorial God who loves us so much he is quite prepared to send us into the fires of hell if we don't bow the head and bend the knee. I rejected both choices from an early age. They seemed equally ridiculous to me and it was only after my journey consciously began after 1990 that I found answers that made sense. I realised – or *remembered*, more like – that what we call Creation is made up of infinite frequencies and dimensions all sharing the same space. They are like the radio and television stations broadcasting to where you are now. They are 'around' you and inside your body, but they are not consciously interfering with you or each other because they are on different frequencies. Only when the frequencies are very close on the dial do we have interference. If you tune to Radio A that is what you will hear. You don't hear the others because you are not tuned to their frequencies, but they still exist and other people will be listening to them. When you move your dial from Radio A to Radio B, you are now hearing Radio B, of course, but Radio A doesn't disappear when you move the dial. It goes on broadcasting – existing – it's just that you can't hear it any more. These simple principles describe the nature of existence in our reality and other connected dimensions. These different 'worlds' can share the same space because they are resonating at different frequencies.

When our consciousness enters a 'physical' body some time after conception, it becomes locked in, tuned in, to this frequency range; so when babies are born they see this 'world' and not another one. It is also quite possible to be tuned to one primary reality but still be aware of others, through what we call the sixth sense of 'psychic' sight, intuition or hearing. Psychics tune their consciousness to other frequencies and access a channel for information to be communicated. Some of this can be fantastically advanced, some utter nonsense. It depends on the communicator and the quality of the 'channel' or psychic. There are countless stories of babies clearly seeing things that others couldn't see, and of young children having 'friends' – spirit beings – who visit them. Young children are especially open to this because they arrive with their full range of psychic potential before ignorant parents, child psychologists, and 'Education' close them down. In these circumstances, children soon learn that switching off their inter-dimensional abilities is less hassle than using them.

The Illuminati power structure wants the population to perceive only the world of the five senses, and our societies are almost entirely aimed at entrancing the senses of sight, sound, taste, touch and smell. People are so much easier to deceive and control when they are detached from higher sources of information, intuition and inspiration. This was the motivation behind the creation of the 'this world is all there is' version of 'science', the one that dominates the schools and universities to this day. The major religions are also used to defend the walls of this reality by labelling those who communicate with other dimensions as servants of the Devil. Hundreds of thousands were killed during the Inquisition alone for having inter-dimensional gifts. When you say you are 'hearing voices' or 'seeing spirit visions' they condemn or ridicule you; but when you say the Christian 'God' is on the line or you have seen a vision of 'Mother Mary', they want to build you a shrine. The difference is that one challenges the belief system, while the other sells it.

Animals don't experience this shut-down process, watch television or go to school and university, and they retain their ability to see beyond the frequency range of human sight. You often see cats reacting to what appears to be 'empty space'. 'What's wrong with the cat?' people ask. Nothing is 'wrong'. The cat is just seeing something you can't see in a frequency range beyond your five senses. You must have heard stories over the years of dogs and cats that wouldn't enter a house or room that was said to be haunted. The people involved don't see or feel anything, but the animals do because they are using the natural sensitivities that society has closed down in so many humans. Comparatively few animals died in the devastating tsunami that hit Asia in late 2004 because of their ability to sense the vibrations of danger. H.D. Ratnayake, deputy director of Sri Lanka's Wildlife Department, said: 'No elephants are dead, not even a dead hare or rabbit. I think animals can sense disaster. They have a sixth sense. They know when things are happening'. Yes, they do, but this potential is suppressed in humans. After my awakening in 1990, I began to regain some of the abilities that lie dormant in everyone until they are triggered, and these have continued to expand. One aspect of this is to *know* something. You don't know how you know, you just do. It is not an arrogance that says, 'I know everything and you don't'; nor are you asking anyone to believe that you know. It is a state beyond mind, thought or emotion. You just *know* from somewhere very deep. When I have a *know* even my body resonates in a particular way. I have *thought* things that were not right, but thought is a much lower level of perception, as we shall see. A *know* has never let me down and this has proved invaluable in charting a path through the *mis*information (thought to be true, but isn't) and *dis*information (purposely given to mislead) that was coming from all sides as I sought to uncover the truth of what was really happening behind the veil of public statements and the TV news.

I began to realise that the conspiracy was much bigger than just a group of families seeking global control. In my meetings with a stream of people with knowledge and experiences to share about the 'other world' connection, it was clear that the 'human' network of the Illuminati was only one level of a multi-dimensional conspiracy. The rabbit hole goes far deeper than even most conspiracy writers believe or are prepared to investigate. The next level of manipulation beyond the 'human' Illuminati involves entities in another dimension or realm that is very close to this one on the frequency spectrum. You could think of it as two radio stations close enough on the dial to interfere with each other. These entities

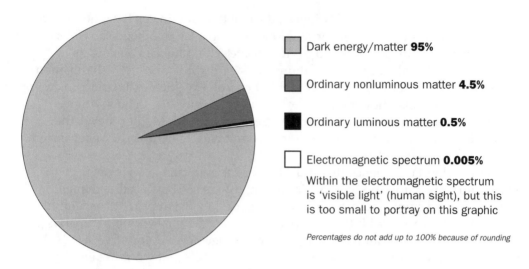

Dark energy/matter **95%**

Ordinary nonluminous matter **4.5%**

Ordinary luminous matter **0.5%**

Electromagnetic spectrum **0.005%**

Within the electromagnetic spectrum is 'visible light' (human sight), but this is too small to portray on this graphic

Percentages do not add up to 100% because of rounding

Figure 8: *Human sight can only perceive an almost immeasurable fraction of the matter/energy estimated to exist in the universe and yet still people ridicule the suggestion that we are not alone because they've never seen an 'alien'! Hysterical*

take many forms, but the key one appears to be reptilian in nature. I have met hundreds of people in more than 40 countries who have claimed to have seen these other-dimensional beings and they mostly describe their appearance as reptilian. I outline in other books the reams of folklore and ancient accounts throughout the world that refer to the same reptilian entities that people report seeing today. Credo Mutwa, the Zulu shaman, or Sanusi, calls them the Chitauri – the 'Children of the Serpent' or 'Children of the Python', and he talks about them at great length in the Bridge of Love video/DVD series called *The Reptilian Agenda*.

A recurring theme of the ancient and modern accounts is the way these entities can 'shape-shift' between a human and reptilian form. This will sound fantastic to most people, but when you appreciate the illusory nature of the 'body', it will be much easier to understand how shape-shifting is possible. The body is not 'solid', it just appears that way to the five senses, as we will pursue in more detail shortly. The body is a vibrating energy field and the shape-shifting is not between two 'solid' forms, the human and reptilian; it is a switch between fields of resonating energy. These other-dimensional reptilians 'wear' a human body like a spacesuit while manipulating from behind the vibrational veil. This veil is what we call the electromagnetic spectrum and human sight can 'see' a mere fraction even of that (*Figures 8 and 9*).

We can only see so-called 'luminous matter', which reflects electromagnetic light; but 95 per cent – at least – of the mass in the universe is known as 'dark matter/energy'. This doesn't reflect light and therefore cannot be seen, although it can be measured by its affect on the 'seeable' universe. What is called 'ordinary matter' makes up some 4.5% of the mass. This can be potentially seen by technology, but only a minimal amount has been observed so far. The

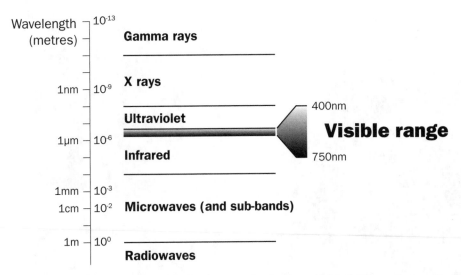

Figure 9: Even within the electromagnetic spectrum only a fraction – 'visible light' – can be accessed by human vision

electromagnetic spectrum is only 0.005 per cent of the estimated mass of the universe and yet human sight can see only a minute fraction even of these electromagnetic frequencies. Imagine how infinitesimal must be the figure for how little of the known universe human sight can perceive! Our eyes can see only one tiny frequency range of the electromagnetic spectrum called 'visible light' – the colours of the rainbow between red and violet. (Many animals can see further into the electromagnetic spectrum.) As one writer put it, humans are virtually blind. So our eyes can detect only a fraction of the electromagnetic spectrum, which itself is only 0.005 per cent of known energy/matter, and still enormous numbers of comatose people (including 'scientists') ridicule the suggestion that we are not alone or that other forms of life, very different from humans, could possibly exist. How breathtakingly absurd and these are the very ones who laugh at others! But because most people believe what the 'experts' say, this nonsense is perpetuated in the public mind.

The Reptilians and other non-human entities operate in the realms unseen by human sight. When they do move in and out of our tiny frequency range they seem, to human witnesses, to suddenly 'appear' and 'disappear', but, in fact, they have only entered our frequency range and then left. They have not disappeared, just exited the frequencies that our limited sense of sight can access. When our five senses look at these Illuminati families, like the British Royals, the Bushes, and so on, we see their five-sense form – apparently human. But behind that mask is the reptilian entity vibrating on a slightly different frequency and controlling the thought processes and actions of the 'human' level. Put most simply, the human body is 'possessed' by the reptilian, which is able to hide from public view, and the population has no idea who is really in control (*Figures 10 and 11 overleaf*).

Illustrations by Neil Hague

Figures 10 and 11: *We see the 'human' form of the Illuminati bloodlines vibrating within the frequency of 'visible light', but they are 'possessed' by reptilian and other entities operating in the realms beyond human sight*

This explains why the Illuminati families have obsessively interbred over thousands of years in our perspective of time. The motivation is not only snobbery, as some believe. DNA is a frequency field that carries the data for what we call our genetic nature and inheritance. The closer the frequencies are on the dial, the more interference there will be. In other words, the more *connection* between them there will be. The reason for the interbreeding, and why the upper levels of the Illuminati are the same bloodline, is because their DNA carries a frequency field extremely close to, and compatible with, the reptilian entities operating just beyond the range of the five senses. This sympathetic resonance allows the Reptilians and other entities to 'possess' – take over – these bodies (Illuminati families) far more effectively than the human population in general.

All human bodies have a huge amount of reptilian genetics, including the R-complex or reptilian brain (*Figure 12*). This is the oldest part of the brain, according to scientists, and gives us character traits such as cold-bloodedness where there is no empathy with the victims of our actions; 'territoriality' and a desire to control; an obsession with hierarchical structures of power; aggression, and the idea that might is right, winner takes all. These are the very characteristics always displayed by the Illuminati and their agents. This is no surprise because the more reptilian genetics we have the more we are likely to display such

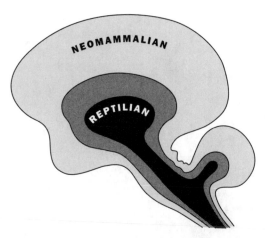

Figure 12: *The reptilian brain, or 'R-complex', is the oldest part of the human brain. It represents the base instinct of survival and produces the character traits of cold-blooded behaviour, a desire to control, an obsession with hierarchical structures of power and the idea that might is right, winner takes all. These are the very traits of the Illuminati bloodlines*

behaviour. Interestingly, the top of the Reptilian manipulating hierarchy has been connected by researchers to the Draco star constellation and certainly the word 'draconian' encapsulates their mindset. When we speak of beings from other planets and star systems, this does not necessarily refer to the 'physical' level of them within the visible light range of the electromagnetic spectrum. Everything is multi-dimensional and there are, for example, many frequency levels of the earth that we cannot see, where other civilisations exist. When people talk of life on other planets they refer only to the 'physical' five-sense reality, but planets have multiple realities vibrating on other wavelengths. Just because other planets of the solar system appear 'lifeless' to our sight and technology doesn't mean they aren't teeming with life on other frequency levels.

The whole focus of the reptilian brain is survival and the Illuminati seek to control us through this fundamental fear. The war on terror is blatantly manipulating the fear of not surviving, and George Bush's entire 2004 American presidential campaign targeted the reptilian brain to connect survival (protection from terrorism) with a Bush presidency. This reptilian fear of not surviving is so powerful that around half the voters in America gave an idiot a second term because the man who had killed tens of thousands of Iraqi civilians, caused more than a thousand troops to die, triggered violence around the world, and took away their basic freedoms, was considered the best guy to keep them safe! The reptilian brain is about fight-or-flight, attack-or-run, hunger and fear, and reacts overwhelmingly to what is called 'visceral stimulus-response'. This is to respond with emotional reaction, rather than reasoned thought. Does that describe a Bush voter, or what? The reptilian brain also reacts most powerfully to visual stimulus rather than verbal, and this is why the political spinners take so much trouble over the presentation of political events with the emphasis on visual image, rather than verbal substance. An article in the *Los Angeles Times* highlighted another expression of the reptilian brain – greed and excess. It was headed: 'Living Ever Larger; How Wretched Excess Became a Way of Life in Southern California'. French anthropologist G. Clotaire Rapaille is quoted as saying:

'... The desire for excess comes from the "reptilian brain," the earliest, most primitive structures in our mental evolution. The reptilian wants to grab as much food as possible,

Figure 13: *The two-faced (and then some) Illuminati manipulating human society under the control of the Reptilians*

to be as big and powerful as possible, because it's focused on survival. When it comes to a choice between the intellect and the reptilian, the reptilian always wins.

'Satisfying that inner lizard has its downsides. Our insatiable appetites have left Americans 9 pounds heavier, on average, than we were two decades ago, and more vulnerable than ever to heart disease and diabetes. We're racking up mountains of debt (the late fees we pay on credit cards have more than tripled since 1996, to $7.3 billion a year) and burning up fossil fuels like crazy. We demand things that, deep down, we don't really want or even use.'

This is the mentality of the Illuminati and they have structured society to target the reptilian brain in the population. The Illuminati secret society network manipulates its bloodlines into positions of power in politics, banking, business, media, military etc., and the reptilian entities possessing those bloodlines run the show while the rest of the population can only see their 'human' level (*Figure 13*) This is why American presidents have had such astonishing 'blue blood' genetic ancestry going back to the royal and aristocratic families of Europe and further afield. I have highlighted in my books the significance to the Illuminati of Charlemagne (742-814), also known as Charles the Great, the King of the Franks and Holy Roman Emperor (*Figure 14 overleaf*). It is no bizarre coincidence, therefore, that 35 of the 43 presidents from Washington to Bush descend from the German-born Charlemagne; nor is it coincidence that Adolf Hitler and the Nazis were also obsessed with the guy. Hitler's home at Berchtesgaden in Bavaria looked out at the Untersberg Mountains where it was believed the spirit of Charlemagne was residing until he rose to make Germany great again. The Nazis were a creation of the Illuminati and were especially influenced by a strand in the network known as the Bavarian Illuminati, officially created in 1776. This organisation also controlled prime players behind the formation of the United States. Presidents are not *elected* by ballot; they are *selected* by blood – reptilian blood. On another level this is better described as selected by *resonance* – reptilian resonance. It actually goes even further than this, as I will explain later.

The Bush family is descended from Vlad Dracul, or Vlad the Impaler, the 15th century ruler of a country called Wallachia, not far from the Black Sea in what is now Romania (*Figure 15 overleaf*). This region was once called Transylvania, home of the vampire legends, and Vlad Dracul was the inspiration for Bram Stoker's *Dracula*. Vlad the Impaler slaughtered tens of thousands of people and impaled many of them on stakes. He would sit down to eat amid this forest of dead bodies, dipping his bread in their blood, and he usually had a horse attached to each of the victims' legs as a sharpened stake was gradually forced into their bodies. The end of the stake was oiled and care was taken that the stake not be too sharp because he didn't want the victim dying too quickly from shock. Infants were often impaled on the stake forced through their mothers' chests. Nice man. Vlad Dracul was an initiate of the Royal Court of the Dragon, also known as the Brotherhood of the Snake, formed in Egypt from around 2000BC to advance the power of the reptilian

Figure 14: *Charles the Great, or Charlemagne, King of the Franks and Holy Roman Emperor, who lived from 742 to 814. His bloodline is highly significant to the Illuminati and 35 of the 43 presidents from George Washington to George W. Bush descend from the German-born monarch. Adolf Hitler and the Nazis were also obsessed with him*

Figure 15: *Vlad Dracul, or Vlad the Impaler, the 15th century ruler of Wallachia in the region once called Transylvania – now Romania. Dracul was the inspiration for Bram Stoker's Dracula and many Illuminati families descend from this line, including the Bushes and Windsors. Queen Elizabeth II is related to Vlad the Impaler through her grandmother, Mary of Teck*

bloodline (see *The Biggest Secret* and *Children of the Matrix*). The British Royal Family is also related to Vlad Dracul's bloodline through Mary of Teck, the grandmother of Queen Elizabeth II.

The 'royal' connection to the Illuminati bloodlines is simple to explain. Aeons ago in what we call time, interbreeding began between humans and these reptilian and other entities. This is the origin of the constantly recurring stories throughout the ancient world about the 'gods', as they were perceived, interbreeding with human women. The best-known version is in the Bible, which tells in Genesis of the Sons of God who interbred with the daughters of men to create a hybrid race called the Nefilim. The texts from which the English version was translated referred to the sons of the *gods*, plural, not the sons of a singular God. Almost every culture throughout the world has a similar story, including the Sumerians (4,000 to 2,000BC) in what is now Iraq. Their accounts told of the interbreeding with a non-human race called the Annunaki, and the hybrid children this produced. In southern Africa the same tale was told about the Chitauri, the 'Children of the Serpent'. Everywhere the story recurs, as does the theme of shape-shifting. In Asia, they had ancient gods they called the Nagas, whom they said could take either human or reptilian form.

These hybrid human–reptilian bloodlines became the 'royal' families of the ancient world and the idea of the 'Divine Right to Rule' was born. In truth, this 'right' was claimed because certain families had a genetic link to the 'gods' and acted as hybrid middlemen or 'demi-gods'. It was they who became the kings, queens and emperors. In China, emperors claimed the right to rule as descendents of the 'serpent gods' and the foundation of Chinese culture, of course, is the dragon, an ancient symbol for the Reptilians. The ancient kings of Media, near what today is Iran, were known as the 'Dragon Dynasty of Media', or the 'descendents of the dragon', and in *Children of the Matrix* I show how the theme of reptilian gods and their hybrid kings and queens is a global phenomenon. The same hybrid bloodlines are still in the positions of power today as political leaders and those who control the banking system, transnational corporations, media etc., hence the 'royal' genetic background to the dynasty of United States presidents from Washington to Bush.

Babylon, in modern-day Iraq, is a crucial part of the story of the Illuminati and their bloodlines because it was once one of their ancient strongholds. The hybrid bloodlines expanded out of Babylon, Sumer, Egypt and elsewhere to rule not only Rome (thus the Roman Empire), but the whole of Europe. They became the European royal and aristocratic families and Britain, France and Germany became major Illuminati operational centres, especially London or Babylon-don. In the same way that the Illuminati were behind the Roman Empire, so they spawned the British Empire, the biggest ever known, or at least recorded. This, and other European empires, became the means through which the hybrid bloodline was placed in power across the world, including what became the United States of America. When the European empires apparently withdrew from their former colonies it was only a sleight of hand to deceive the people. They left behind the bloodline and the secret society networks that manipulated the bloodline into power, and they have continued to control those countries ever since. The only difference is that they have more power now because at least under colonial rule the people knew who their masters were. Today they think they are running their own countries when, in fact, a hidden force has its hand on the tiller, and the politicians that the people think they have elected to lead them are only puppets. My other books have all the background and sources to support what I am describing here.

As I have been exposing for years in considerable detail, the Illuminati families continue to practice the same blood drinking and human sacrifice rituals they have been performing since the ancient world – not least Babylon. This includes some of the most famous families and people on the planet, like the British Royal Family, Rothschilds, Rockefellers, Bushes and a long list that I reveal in other works. Vlad the Impaler, an ancestor of the Bushes and Windsors, was an infamous example of the obsession with blood drinking and ritual sacrifice. The Dracula character he inspired was a shape-shifting vampire with the title of 'Count', symbolic of the way the Reptilian bloodlines have been carried by 'human' royalty and aristocracy. Dracula is not just make-believe. His like exist and they are in positions of national and global power.

The rituals are designed to achieve many things, including the interbreeding I have described. I should stress that this does not have to happen only through physical sex between a human woman and a Reptilian entity. I have been told by women who have been raped in satanic rituals (several of them under the Mormon temple at Salt Lake City) that whilst a 'human' man was having sex with them he was overshadowed by a non-physical entity channelling energy through the rapist at the time of orgasm. These energies – frequencies – recode the DNA of the resulting child into the frequency pattern of the Reptilian or other entity, so making the child compatible for 'possession'. You could think of it as rewriting a computer program or adding additional information to a disk. What holds the information on a computer disk? – a magnetic field. It is the same principle with DNA and this theme will be developed in the next few chapters. In fact, the more we understand about the nature of DNA, it is clear there are other ways to rewrite its program. The rituals performed by Illuminati initiates also create an energy environment that allows the Reptilians and others to cross from their dimension into this one. Many people who have participated in these rituals against their will have told me of seeing Reptilians and other entities manifesting during the ceremonies, and of 'human' participants shape-shifting into reptilian form. They are obsessed with blood drinking because it carries the frequency, DNA codes and life force of the victim. Just as electricity passes powerfully through water, so it is with the life essence energy carried in the blood. (By the way, Roman Polanski's 1968 movie, *Rosemary's Baby*, portrayed this interbreeding and involved a reptilian entity.)

Another reason for the rituals, especially involving human sacrifice, is that other-dimensional Reptilians feed off human fear. That is their prime energy source because they appear to operate in an 'in-between' world that Giuliana Conforto, an Italian astrophysicist and esoteric researcher, calls the 'interspaces' (*Figure 16*). These lie between this dimension and the next one, at least from our perspective of reality, and they might even be like vibrational crevices *within* our dimension, too. Credo Mutwa, the South African Sanusi and official historian of the Zulu nation, told me that in his culture they call the interspaces the 'heaven between heavens' and 'that's where the Reptilians are', he said. In the third of the *Matrix* movies they had a similar concept, the in-between world controlled by a computer program called the *Train Man*. Interspaces don't have an energy source like dimensions do. They are, by comparison, sort of neutral zones, gaps in the fabric of our reality from which we can be manipulated mentally and emotionally. Anyone operating there would need to create an energy source, which they have – *us*. They are harvesting fear, and they have structured the world to generate as much as possible in the form of not only sheer terror, but also fear of the future, worry, guilt, regret of the past, depression, frustration and stress in all its forms. These are the very emotions and states of mind that the system I described earlier is guaranteed to produce.

The human sacrifices engaged in by these world famous Illuminati names, and others, are structured to induce maximum terror in the victim and trigger an adrenalin release that enters the bloodstream in moments of extreme fear and stress. This is like an elixir to the Reptilian Satanists and they drink the blood of the

Illustration by Neil Hague

Figure 16: *Beyond the frequency of human sight lie the interspace planes between this dimension and the next. These are the realms of the Reptilian manipulators and other entities that seek to possess the Illuminati bloodlines and any others that fall vibrationally into their clutches*

victims as soon as they are killed, often before, when the adrenalin is at its most powerful. The concentrated fear and terror of the victim is also being absorbed by entities in the interspaces, which are extremely close vibrationally to our 'human' reality. This is the origin of the ancient theme of people making human sacrifices to the gods. The energy the entities want most is that of prepubescent children, especially young girls with blonde hair and blue eyes. Red hair is another trait they seek. It has nothing to do with how these girls look; it is what these genetic characteristics reveal about the frequency and make-up of their DNA field. The sacrifice of young girls is, once again, the origin of the ancient theme of sacrificing a 'young virgin' to the gods. Almost everyone accepts that these things did happen, but what most people don't realise is that they *still do* and many of the millions of children who go missing every year end up on the satanic altars of the rich and famous, or their underlings. (While this book was at the production stage I received information and pictures from a therapist in Australia that yet again supports the satanic abuse/reptilian connection. See *Appendix II*.)

As I entered what we call the 21st century, many pieces in the puzzle were coming together. The world was controlled by a network of secret societies manipulated by the Illuminati, who had structured the world to create maximum fear and stress. This was feeding the Reptilians and other entities in the interspaces, and the more wars, conflict, terror, despair and grief that could be generated by human events, the more power the Reptilians and company would have to recycle back against us, and speed the rate at which this energy-generator called human 'life' would spin. 'Life' is getting quicker and more stressful and fearful because they are upping the spin speed of the generator – human societies. The world government structure I have described (microchipping in particular) is designed to control us and harvest our energy even more effectively. But there is, you will be delighted to know, a way out of this, as I will come to later.

Staggering as this information will be to so many, even the Reptilians are only another level of the story. It is far, far bigger than that. The guiding force I have been aware of since my awakening experiences in 1990 is now leading me to the next layer of the cosmic maze, beyond the Reptilians and even the realms of dimension and vibration. In short, the world we think we see is an illusion that we have been manipulated to believe is real. This is the foundation conspiracy that has spawned all the others and this knowledge is the key to ending our enslavement. My focus has always been drifting into these areas because it is a prime interest of mine, but from the turn of 2003 it began to take centre stage and some incredible revelations have been communicated to me.

Carol, a psychic friend of mine, told me some months before I started this book that I would now be dealing with information that could not be proven, but that people needed to know. This has certainly turned out to be the case. While much of what I am going to say is supportable by even mainstream science, a lot of it is not. Or, at least, not *yet* at this point in scientific knowledge. But that doesn't mean it's not true and it doesn't matter anyway because I'm not asking anyone to believe it. If it doesn't make sense to you, bin the book. What you believe is *your* right and no business of mine. Proof is only what someone accepts to be so, anyway. One man's proof can be another man's nonsense. I *know* that the themes I am about to describe are correct, but I am not asking anyone to accept that they are. People must decide for themselves what they make of it.

How deep does the rabbit hole go? Far deeper than most people can begin to imagine and certainly further than they are prepared to explore. I'm ready to go anywhere, no matter how apparently bizarre, because I want to know the truth and the answer to the age-old question: What the fuck is it all about?

Thank you for joining me in this journey beyond mind, thought and preconception, as we explore the depths of the illusion we call Life. You'll need a very large torch and bring lots of batteries.

CHAPTER THREE

Downloading Reality

One's real life is so often the life that one does not lead
Oscar Wilde

How many people who dismiss all this illusion stuff as bonkers know that they don't even see with their eyes? They 'see' with their brain. That's the only place the 'world' you think is 'around' you now exists.

I'm not sitting in a darkened room coming to these conclusions while smoking a weed; this is mainstream science. Our eyes only transform light into electrical signals that are constantly delivered to the brain for interpretation. This 'visible light' is confined to a tiny fraction of the electromagnetic spectrum, which is, itself, only *0.005 per cent* of the matter/energy in the known universe. It is within this minuscule frequency range that we decode 'light' into 'physical' reality. The eyes don't send images to the brain of three-dimensional street scenes or forests or children playing in the park, or anything else that we *think* we are seeing outside of us. They send electrical signals. Only when the brain decodes these signals into an apparent 3D reality does the world we believe is 'around' us actually exist (*Figure 17*). There is no world 'around' us as we perceive it; everything is all happening in our brains, or at least at one level of the illusion it is.

As you look at this book it certainly appears to be outside of you, but it only exists in your head – and, as a 'physical' body, so do you! The way the book feels and looks are electrical signals decoded by your brain and it's the same when you hear, smell or taste. The ear, like all the sense organs, converts vibrations into electrical signals that are sent to the brain for interpretation into sounds. Noise is in your head. There aren't even any colours, except as neurons firing in a particular way. Colours are different

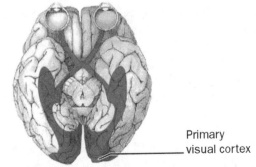

Primary
visual cortex

Figure 17: *The brain creates 'physical' reality by decoding electrical signals into a 3D holographic illusion. This is done through the visual cortex on one level, but the whole brain is involved because it is a hologram, as I will explain shortly*

35

Illustration by Neil Hague

Figure 18: *The only place the 'physical' world exists is in your brain. There is no 'out there', as we perceive it; only an 'in here'*

wavelengths that the brain decodes from the 'white' light in the electro-magnetic spectrum. We only 'see' what the brain tells us that we see and, as experiments have shown, that is decided by what we *believe* we see. There is no such thing as '*the*' universe because there's a universe inside every brain, each with a different perception (*Figure 18*). The electrical path of a single thought can now be tracked by the latest scanning technology, and what we *believe* dictates which path is taken.

Note that word – believe. We can now begin to appreciate the deeper reasons behind the Illuminati control of 'education' and the media, especially television. If they can implant in human minds a set of programmed beliefs about the world and what is real, those beliefs will edit, via the brain, what people 'see'. This editing process will construct reality to match what they believe they should be seeing. In this way we put *in* detail that supports the preconceived belief and take *out* that which is at odds with it. What we think we see is dictated by preconceived ideas and that's why the system is constantly seeking to implant them. What do we call the information that television presents to us? Television *programmes*. Television is *tell-a-vision* or, even more accurately, *sell-a-vision*.

Political elections, not least in America, are not about discussing issues and what the candidates would do in office; they are aimed at implanting an image to edit the reality of the voters. These are the simplistic mantras and lies that politicians and their spinners parrot by the hour. This is so effective that in November 2004 they managed to convince around half the American electorate that George W. Bush was the one to protect them from terrorism when (a) he is a terrorist of monumental proportions; (b) his decisions have led to the murder of tens of thousand of Iraqi civilians and, at the time of writing, the deaths of well over a thousand American troops; and (c) he sends others to fight his manufactured wars while spending his life making sure that he never sees so much as a bullet fired in anger. But once the *belief* in 'John Wayne Bush' is implanted, the brain edits reality to fit. Another example is to watch two people talking who have preconceived ideas about each other. Neither hears what the other says or how they say it because their entrenched belief is editing the words and tone to fit what they believe about the other person. We are doing this with every image that we think we see.

I told a story in *Tales from the Time Loop* about a hypnotist who was hired to entertain guests at a party. What happened was witnessed by Michael Talbot, author of an outstanding book called *The Holographic Universe* (HarperPerennial, New York, 1992). A guy called Tom was put into a hypnotic state and given a potato to eat while thinking it was an apple. To Tom, it looked and tasted like an apple because the belief implanted by the hypnotist was editing his reality as his brain decoded the electrical signals from his tongue. The hypnotic suggestion simply reinterprets the signals, in this case from a potato to an apple. This applies to all of the five senses. There is a condition called synaesthesia in which the senses become confused and signals are interpreted by the wrong sense. I saw a British television documentary in which a man called James Wannerton decoded sound into taste. He had a different taste for every word. Each time he heard the name 'Derek', he tasted earwax; and the name of another customer at his pub gave him the taste of wet nappies (how did he know??). I'd find a friend who tasted like red wine myself. Other 'synaesthetes', as they are called, see colours when they hear or see words. A lady called Dorothy Latham told the programme that when she hears words she also sees them as like a coloured ticker tape apparently in front of her. When she hears music she sees a riot of colour. Everything is a frequency in this reality, including colour, and what can be decoded as sound through one sense can be decoded as colour through another.

With synaesthesia the senses get confused and this is what hypnotists (and the Illuminati) are doing – implanting false beliefs that cause the brain to decode electrical signals to fit the beliefs. It is like reprogramming a computer and I have seen demonstrations of how easy it is to do. This includes transforming atheists into religious believers in a matter of seconds and these are the mind-games played by those evangelical 'white-suits' at the mass 'conversion' and 'miracle healing' rallies. The stooges on stage, and the audience as a whole, are put into a trance-like state, open to hypnotic suggestion. Suddenly, 'I give my life to Jesus' (and my money to the 'ministry') is their new reality. They say 'Jesus is in my heart' when, in fact, the white-suit is in their head. Many fraudulent 'psychics' use the same techniques. When someone says a medium has been 100 per cent accurate, it is often because their implanted belief has filtered out all that was false.

The hypnotist at the Michael Talbot party told Tom that when he returned to a waking state he would not be able to see his daughter. Before he clicked his fingers, the hypnotist led the daughter to stand right in front of her father, so Tom was sitting down looking at her belly. When he 'came out' of the trance state he was asked if he could see his daughter in the room. 'No', he said. His daughter started laughing, but Tom couldn't hear her. The hypnotist went behind the daughter and put his hand against her lower back. He said he was holding something in his hand and could Tom tell him what it was? Tom looked a little bemused because it seemed so obvious to him. 'You are holding a watch', he said. The hypnotist asked if he could read the inscription on the watch and Tom did so. All the time his daughter was standing between him and the watch! Impossible? Fantastic? Not at all. The hypnotically implanted belief that his daughter wasn't there edited her from the information Tom's brain was receiving, and when his 'reality' was neurologically constructed she was no longer to be seen. With his daughter removed from his personal illusion – or movie – there was nothing to stop him seeing what was behind her.

It is worth pondering on this story when you next believe without question in what you are seeing. When I asked the Zulu Sanusi, Credo Mutwa, why more people didn't see the reptilian entities, he said it was because they are so at odds with human reality that the brain removes them from what it 'sees'. This is one reason why some people see ghosts and others don't. The mystic, Sri Aurobindo Ghose, said that most humans possess a 'mental screen' that keeps us from seeing behind 'the veil of matter'. Clearly this is correct and the 'veil of matter' is the visible light within the electromagnetic spectrum.

So what *is* real? Whatever you *believe* it is or can be *manipulated* to believe it is. For instance, we are programmed to believe in scarcity of food, resources, water and all the rest. But how can there be scarcity in an illusion? Only if you *believe* in it. Albert Einstein said that we don't observe nature as it actually exists, but nature exposed to our methods of perception. The theories determined what we could or could not observe. That's right, but he could have gone further and said that there *is* no nature as it 'actually exists', except as illusion. The human race is in a hypnotic trance every bit as much as any subject in a hypnotist's stage show; even more so, in fact, because the stooge on the stage only has one hypnotist working on him for a short time. In everyday life we are all being bombarded with hypnotic implants. When we're young we have parents and teachers telling us what is real and possible, and throughout our lives we have the media and peer pressure doing the same. Just as the subject in the stage show is told there is an elephant in the audience, or that he's eating a banana when it's really a lemon, so we are told that Osama bin Laden orchestrated 9/11, and that doctors and mainstream scientists know what they're talking about. He didn't and they don't, but if we believe such rubbish we will construct our reality to fit. As a result, we will support the war on terrorism; take prescription drugs that often do us even more damage than the ailment they are treating; and accept that when a scientist says Infinite Consciousness does not exist then it must be true.

Techniques like the Totalitarian Tiptoe and Problem-Reaction-Solution are major examples of the way the Illuminati attempt to implant a belief that we will edit into a reality that suits their agenda. The human race is in a trance, seeing what it is told to see, in precisely the way that Tom was at the party. We don't have to seek enlightenment and truth, we are *already* enlightened. We just have to wake-the-fuck-up, break out of the trance, and remember who we are. As psychiatrist R. D. Laing said: 'If I do not know I know, I think I do not know'. Another comment of his also encapsulates the human plight: 'We forget something; then we forget we have forgotten'. That sums up how consciousness became caught in the illusion, or what I will call the Matrix. One aspect of the New Age 'movement' are the 'Workshop Groupies' who go from seminar to seminar, guru to guru, trying to find something they already have. They don't find it because they are too busy looking. We think that enlightenment is like finding the needle in the haystack when, in fact, it is the realisation that there is no needle and there is no hay. It is the trance-state that keeps us from this truth.

The illusion goes even deeper than our beliefs constructing our reality. I guess I started to appreciate this a few years ago when I had my first experience of seeing the backdrop of the cosmic computer game. It was like looking at the world through those 3D viewer things they call Viewmasters. They give you two versions of the same picture, one for each eye, and the brain turns the flat photographs into an illusory three-dimensional scene. If you've ever experienced this you'll recall how the 3D effect is really pronounced, far more than normal. I began to see the world like that, briefly at first, and then for longer periods. It looked like the 3D version of something you'd get from Nintendo. Today when I walk down a street it's like I'm in a scene from a *Matrix* movie. I am not *in* the world; I am *detached* from it – observing rather than participating. It's always a shock when anyone speaks to me in this mode because I feel invisible to people. When I look at the apparently 'solid' buildings and cars, it's like I could put my hand through them. That may sound weird to anyone new to this, but how can they be anything but illusion when they are only electrical signals decoded by the brain? The 'world' is not solid at all, merely an illusion of solidity. In one of the books of Carlos Castaneda, he quotes his shaman source, 'Don Juan', as saying:

'We are perceivers. We are awareness; we are not objects; we have no solidity. We are boundless ... We, or rather our reason, forget [this] and thus we entrap the totality of ourselves in a vicious circle from which we rarely emerge in our lifetime.'

Quantum physics explores and tries to understand the subatomic realm of reality or, put more simply, it is the study of energy in waveforms and particles operating beyond the 'physical' reality of atoms and 'matter'. In these realms, the 'laws' of conventional physics (which are illusions anyway) are seen not to apply and the idea that the physical world is solid is shown to be impossible. The physical realm is constructed, scientists say, from atoms. This name originates, we are told, with an ancient Greek called Democritus, who made the first known claim that matter was composed of tiny particles that he called atoms. But hold on. If atoms are the building blocks of our 'solid' world, how come atoms are about as least solid as you could possibly imagine? In fact, they ain't solid at all! (*Figure 19 overleaf*)

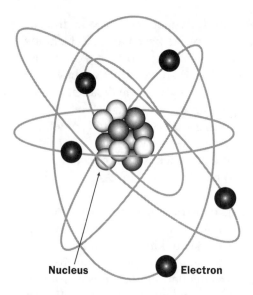

Figure 19: *An atom is 'empty' to five-sense reality and so how can they be the building blocks of our 'solid' world. They can't – 'solidity' is an illusion. The electrons and nucleus (also 'empty') are much further apart than can be portrayed in this graphic. As one writer said: 'If an atom was the size of a cathedral, the nucleus would be about the size of a ten cent piece'*

Nucleus   Electron

I know I didn't go to university (thank you, God), but even uneducated (thank you, God) me can see a little contradiction here. How can something that is not solid be the building blocks that construct this 'solid' wall I am looking at now? It *can't* – our brains do it. With the emergence of quantum physics, science has had to concede that atoms are not solid. It knows that they contain even smaller particles consisting of a nucleus (made of protons and neutrons) that appears to be circled by electrons. The atoms that comprise 'physical' matter are overwhelmingly 'empty' and even illustrations of this are misleading because there is not enough room in a book or science paper to accurately depict the proportions of particles to 'empty space'. As one writer put it: 'If an atom was the size of a cathedral, the nucleus would be about the size of a ten cent piece'. The rest is 'empty' to the perception of the five senses because it consists of energy vibrating on wavelengths higher than the 'physical', and even the particles are found to be empty as you go deeper into the subatomic realm. If you magnify anything powerfully enough and go deeper than the atom, you will find that *nothing* has solidity. No, not even buildings, cars, mountains or the bones in your body. It's Iluuuuuuuusion! If you find this hard to accept, think of your dreams. You dream in three-dimensional images and yet no one claims they are solid do they? This reality is the same – a dreamworld that we believe to be real.

I don't go into my virtual reality 'Viewmaster' mode by taking drugs; it developed without me doing anything consciously to make it happen. But the three occasions that I have taken so-called psychoactive drugs confirmed in detail the same recurring theme. We are living in a collective dream that we have been manipulated to believe is solid and 'real'. As I describe at length in *Tales from the Time Loop*, in 2003 I was invited to speak at a gathering in the Amazon rainforest in Brazil and this included the opportunity for participants to experience the psychoactive effects of a plant called *ayahuasca*. This has been used for at least hundreds of years by South American shamans to take people into other states of consciousness that the five senses cannot access. It contains many powerful hallucinogenic properties including Dimethyltryptamine, or DMT, a naturally occurring component of the metabolism of mammals and plants.

Ayahuasca is known as the 'teacher plant' and the 'plant of the gods' because it allows people to experience unseen realms or dimensions where so much can be learned about self, life and reality, and where the 'gods' of myth reside on frequencies outside the range of the five senses. Indeed, the organisers invited me to the event because of the number of times that previous participants had seen reptilian entities and imagery in their altered states of awareness. But again, all these realities are also signals decoded by the frequency fields we call the brain/body. The drug simply changes the nature of the decoding process and plugs you in to another information source. Some people have great experiences with the plant while others go into really dark mental and emotional states. It depends on the person and where their mind takes them. My two experiences were incredibly powerful and transformed my sense of reality. I had long been aware that the 'world' was an illusion, but now came some serious detail.

I took the ayahuasca over two nights in the form of a liquorice-tasting drink in a small glass and I lay back on a mattress amid the darkness of a big, round, wooden building in the rainforest. After about an hour I began to enter altered states of awareness. I saw swirling colours and images at first when I closed my eyes, and I went deeper and deeper through levels of consciousness until I reached a state of indescribable peace and bliss. It was beyond fear, doubt, guilt and regret; beyond time, and even vibration. All was stillness or sometimes like a slow-motion wave. In the first session only Zoe, the facilitator, and I were in the room. As the ayahuasca kicked in, I began to speak in a voice very unlike my own. The words were not preceded by thought; they just emerged slowly and powerfully without any help from me. It began with 'I am love', and then, 'I am everything and everything is me, I am infinite possibility'. With that I felt energy begin to stream from the centre of my chest and fill the room. The human energy field in this reality is interpenetrated by a series of vortices known as 'chakras', an ancient Sanskrit word meaning 'wheels of light' (*Figure 20*). The one in the centre of the chest is

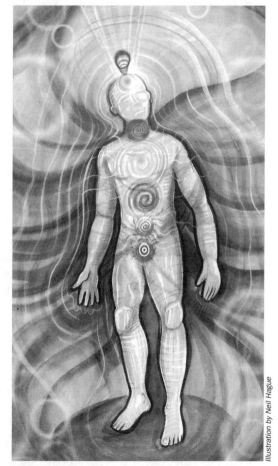

Illustration by Neil Hague

Figure 20: *The seven major vortex points, or chakras, which connect the human body/hologram to other levels of reality*

called the heart chakra and this is the real origin of the idea of feeling love in your heart. It is symbolised today as the physical heart, but love is expressed through the heart chakra or vortex that connects us to the love of all that is, a connection the manipulators are desperate to suppress with their mind games and microchips. I would stress that all this relates to *this reality* because chakras are illusions, too.

The power of the energy coming through me was fantastic. It was like someone was squeezing my chest at the point where the energy seemed to be pouring into the room. A strip light on the ceiling began to flicker on and off, and then three of the lights came on full power. I wondered why the lights had been turned on when the session was supposed to be in darkness. But no one had touched the light switch and they came on without electricity, empowered by another form of energy. The music player also turned on and off, but as I felt the energy streaming from me I could understand why the electrical circuits were going haywire. The flow changed and I felt it arch from my chest to my head like some unseen rainbow. With that I began to speak fluently in my altered state. The words told of an Infinite Consciousness, referred to as 'The Infinite', 'Oneness' and the 'One'. Everything was Infinite Consciousness, the words said. Division and polarity were illusions of the manufactured virtual reality that I call the Matrix and beyond the veil of illusion everything was *One*. There was no *me* or *we*, just an Infinite 'I'. Even within the virtual-reality game everything was the same Oneness and it was only the illusion that gave the *impression* of division. The difference was between Oneness in awareness of itself and Oneness that had forgotten what it was. Whenever I talk about Oneness from now on I am referring to Oneness in awareness of itself, as opposed to that caught in the illusion of division. The ancient Vedic works of India tell a similar story. The eighth century Hindu mystic, Shankara, said: 'Brahman [Infinite Consciousness] dwells beyond the range of Maya [illusion]. There is nothing else'.

On the second night in Brazil, the ayahuasca experience was even deeper and, as my consciousness tossed and swirled through realities, I began to hear a loud, clear, female voice speaking with great dignity and clarity. This was not, of course, a woman in a body speaking through a voice box. It was consciousness communicating telepathically and my brain was decoding these frequency fields into words that I could understand. I heard the words in English, but had I been Italian or Pakistani I would have decoded the consciousness fields into those languages. 'David', the voice said, 'we are going to take you to where you come from, so you can remember who you are'. With that I was taken to a realm of indescribable bliss, even more profound and wondrous than the night before. There were no divisions, no polarities, no black and white, no us and them. There was no time, no place, no vibration. Everything just was and this is a state of being that has to be experienced to be understood. I was not my body; I was consciousness, *all* consciousness, all that exists in any expression. Everything just *was*. I was Oneness, *Is-ness*, All Possibility. But I was still self-aware, an 'individual' with my own point of observation within the whole. I was here and I was there. I was everywhere and nowhere, everything and nothing. I was and I wasn't, and I was all 'in between'. It may sound mumbo-jumbo, but it will be clearer later why encompassing polarities is the door to Oneness, completeness. 'This is the Infinite, David', the voice said. 'This is where you come from and this is where you shall "return".'

I was told that there was really only one thing I needed to know and these words began to repeat over and over in my head: 'Infinite Love is the only truth – everything else is illusion'. I began to form a question in my thoughts: 'You really mean *everything*?' But before the thought could fully emerge, the voice interrupted. 'Infinite Love is the only truth – *everything* else is illusion; no buts, no exceptions, that's it.' The existence of one Infinite Consciousness is the only truth; everything else is the imagination of that Consciousness – illusion. I should also define 'Love' as used in this book. It's not the, 'I love you darlin', fancy a quick one?' version, or any other misrepresentations along the same lines. Love in the context of Infinite Love is the balance of all. Infinite 'Love' is also Infinite Intelligence, Infinite Knowing, Infinite *Everything*. Thus, it is and it isn't; it is everywhere and nowhere, everything and nothing. It is All Possibility in perfect balance.

The 'voice' spoke to me for some five hours and another veil lifted for me that night. I have begun to understand new levels of the game thanks to what I learned in the ayahuasca experience, the ever-expanding insights that have followed, the knowledge given to me by the synchronicity in my life and, increasingly, the way I am seeing through the 'solid' world of illusion. These new levels are centres of awareness, control and manipulation from which the 'Reptilians' and 'Illuminati' are made manifest. Throughout the rest of the book I am going to describe reality as I have come to understand it from all these sources of information and insight. Much of it is supportable by evidence emerging at the forefront of science, especially what is known as quantum physics. But I go further than that and so much will not be 'provable' in the sense that the human mind demands proof and people will have to decide for themselves what they think or, better still, *know* about what they read. It is not my desire to convince anyone that this is true or to tell them what their reality should be; the Matrix does that well enough already without any help from me. So, here we go: the illusory wool that has been pulled over our illusory eyes.

Oneness is Infinite Possibility with a limitless imagination to manifest anything and everything. This 'physical' world is only one example. Given this, how silly it is to dismiss by reflex action the accounts of shape-shifting Reptilians and other non-human entities just because they are so different to what is perceived as the 'norm'. There is no norm within Infinite Possibility and such myopia is indicative of just how caught-in-the-box most people are. As a car sticker I saw in California said: 'You laugh at me because I'm different; I laugh at you because you're all the same'. Seven months after the experience in Brazil, I came across an ancient Hindu myth. It said human consciousness had begun as a ripple that decided to leave the ocean of consciousness – the 'timeless, spaceless and eternal'. When it awakened to itself in this 'disconnected' state, the myth said, it forgot that it was part of the infinite ocean and felt isolated and separated. This was pretty much what the voice told me in

Figure 21

Illustrations by Neil Hague

Figure 22   **Figure 23**

The creation of the Matrix, as symbolised by Neil Hague. First came imagination into 'form'; with that came the illusion of separation; this led to the manifestation of fear (the winged entity) that took on a life of its own; and consciousness was caught in an illusion it believed to be 'real'.

As a Hindu myth says, human consciousness began as a ripple that decided to leave the ocean of consciousness – the timeless, spaceless and eternal. When it awakened to itself in this 'disconnected' state, it forgot that it was part of the infinite ocean and felt isolated and separated.

another way. I am constrained by the use of words because feeling or *knowing* something is much more profound than describing it in language. But, basically, the imagination of Oneness created an illusory realm, one of infinite such 'worlds' within Infinite Possibility. This 'world' began to forget it was Oneness, like a dream forgetting it is the dreamer. With this amnesia came the phenomenon we call fear, an expression of All Possibility that cannot manifest within the balance of Oneness. Fear only comes with the illusion of division and separation when consciousness perceives itself as a part and not the whole. Fear is the shadow of illusory disconnection.

Neil Hague's superb pictures (see colour section) symbolise the progression from Oneness to division and fear (*Figures 21 to 26*). First came imagination into 'form'; then the illusion of separation, which was followed by the manifestation of fear that took on a life of its own. The creation of the Matrix Dreamworld was not good or bad, right or wrong. It just was. It's not the structure of the Matrix that is the problem so much as the force that controls it. The 'Matrix' is a virtual reality illusion hijacked by

Figure 24

Figure 25

fear and so is empowered by fear. The voice in Brazil said that when people are in fear they find comfort in the familiar and predictable and this had happened in the Matrix. It was a way for consciousness to whistle in the dark, giving itself comfort in the familiar because it feared what lay beyond. I guess you could think of it as like a lost child disconnected from its mum and dad. What is humanity's biggest fear in its daily experience? Fear of the unknown. Wilson Bryan Key described the human attitude to the unknown very well in *The Age of Manipulation* (Madison Books, USA, 1989):

> 'Humans detest uncertainty.
> Uncertainties produce anxieties. To
> reduce anxiety, if no factual structure

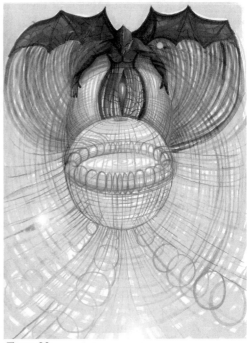

Figure 26

is readily available, humans will simply invent one or accept a ready-to-wear media reality structure … these perceptions, of course, are fictional constructs.'

The Matrix is just that, a fictional construct of collective mind. This 'physical' level of the Matrix, what I call the Time Loop, was created to provide familiarity that eased the fear of the unknown caused by illusory separation and was a very much more pleasant experience than it is in our reality. You could think of the Matrix as a thought projection, like a movie projecting on a cinema screen. The projection was dependent for its survival on the projector. But the projection, the act of imagination, took on a 'life' of its own when it gained access to its own source of energy. This source, the voice told me, was fear. Now it was that the dream took over the dreamer. The Matrix – self-aware fear as the voice described it – developed an agenda of its own and sought to generate as much fear as possible to empower and expand itself. The reason the Matrix needs fear as an energy source is because it *is* fear. The more fear its manipulations generate through wars, conflict, stress, guilt and aggression, the greater its power to increase this cycle of fear-production. As the voice was describing all this, I was shown scenes from the Disney cartoon movie, *The Sorcerer's Apprentice*, in which the sorcerer created an entity to do all the jobs he didn't want to do, but then the entity took over and became the sorcerer's controller. The story of Frankenstein is also very symbolic of what happened. Entrapped consciousness became controlled by its own fear in a labyrinth of self-deceit and manipulated illusion (*Figure 27*).

(I should explain how I am defining consciousness for the purposes of this book. Everything is consciousness, but there are different levels of awareness depending on how connected something is to Infinite Oneness. To compare the consciousness of Oneness in awareness of itself with what we call human 'mind' is to compare Einstein with a baked bean. Indeed, the difference is so fantastic that there is no comparison. So when I speak of consciousness in this book I mean awareness *beyond* mind, beyond the Matrix.)

When we forget that we are Infinite Consciousness experiencing an illusion, everything else loses perspective. I was on a catamaran ferry one afternoon with my son, Jaymie, making the 15-minute crossing from mainland England to our home on the Isle of Wight. As we left the harbour, a mist descended which denied us sight of land in any direction. Normally, the ferry follows the mainland coast for a few minutes and then turns sharp right and heads for the Island. Independently of each other, both Jaymie and I began to wonder why we were not turning this time. We passed one of the big concrete 'forts' in the water which, even when the tide is low and the ferry takes the long way round, is the last point at which the turn is made. But it still appeared to both of us that we were continuing to go straight ahead and away from the Island. Just as we were wondering what on earth was happening, the lights of the Island pier came into view and we realised that we had been going in the right direction all along. We had become disorientated ('lost') by losing the key coordinate – sight of land. With that it would have been obvious what was happening and the direction we were taking. But once that had gone, all other

Figure 27: *The virtual-reality game: entrapped consciousness, in a state of collective amnesia, became controlled by its own fear in a labyrinth of self-deceit and manipulated illusion that I call the Matrix*

Illustration by Neil Hague

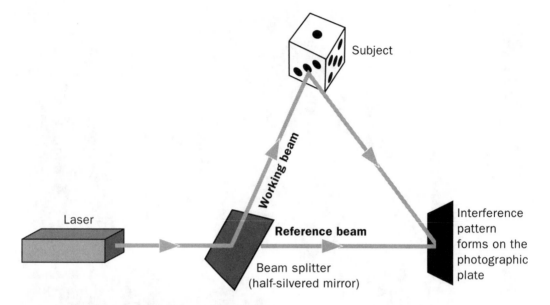

Figure 28: *Holograms are made by using two parts of the same laser light. One half (reference beam) goes almost directly to the photographic plate and the other (working beam) is diverted onto the subject. When this working beam is diverted again onto the print it forms an "interference pattern" with the reference beam. If a laser is shone upon this pattern it creates a 3-D holographic picture of the subject*

Figure 29: *The wave or 'interference' pattern on a holographic print. It seems random and meaningless until a laser light is shone on the pattern and a hologram is formed.*

coordinates, like the fort, lost perspective. We had actually turned at the fort but, without having the land for reference, that wasn't obvious. This is what happens to us in the Matrix. Once we lose sight of the foundation coordinate – we are Infinite Consciousness experiencing an illusion – we lose the point of reference from which to understand everything else. We think we are going in a certain direction (that we are humans in 'real' bodies experiencing a 'real' world) when, in fact, it's all a manipulated dream. One other point is that both Jaymie and I were caught in the same illusion and this meant that we were confirming each other's reality and making it more 'real'. So it is with humanity – 'everyone knows that'!

The Frankenstein Matrix is a *super-hologram* that feeds us the dreamworld. Dennis Gabor discovered holograms from the late 1940s and won the Nobel Prize for his work. He turned a three-dimensional object into a frequency pattern on photographic film and converted it back to a 3D holographic image. Holograms are made by directing a laser onto a piece of photographic film (*Figure 28*). The laser is

Figures 30 and 31: *This girl and soldier look 'real' and 'solid', but you are looking at holograms that you could pass your hand through. It's the same with the human body – its 'solidity' is an illusion*

(Pictures 'Little Birch' and 'Old Soldier' courtesy of Holography Studio, All-Russian Exhibition Center, Moscow. For more see **www.holography.ru***)*

directed at the film through a semi-transparent mirror. Some of the light is deflected away in another direction and onto the object you want to photograph. Now you have the laser light pointing at the film (known as the reference beam) and the part deflected away onto the object (known as the working beam). This working beam, carrying the vibrational image of the object in question, is then also directed onto the photographic film. When it hits the film it 'collides' with the reference beam – its 'other half' – and this creates what is known as an interference pattern between the two. You can liken the principle to throwing two stones into a pond and seeing how the two wave formations collide and interfere with each other. They form a pattern that is a wave representation of the two stones, where they fell and at what speed. The interference pattern imprinted on the holographic film looks much like the waves in the pond. It is a series of lines that appear to be random and incomprehensible (*Figure 29*). But when you shine the same type of laser light upon this pattern, suddenly an apparently three-dimensional image of the photographed object comes into view (*Figures 30, 31, 32, 33 and 34*). The images can appear to be solid, but you can pass your hand through them; and immediately you turn off the light the hologram disappears because it is only an illusion. Lasers are used because they produce a stable, focused beam known as 'coherent light' and project a single

Figure 32: *What can appear to be so solid is not – this is another hologram ...*

Figure 33: *... So is this, a 'solid' metal tap ...*

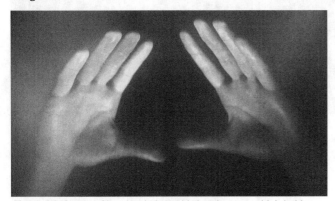

Figure 34: *Sleight of hand ... holographic hands you couldn't hold – unless your brain told you different!*

Picture 'Medina' courtesy of Laser Trend Holographie, Germany.
Email: **lasertrend@aol.com**
Picture 'Running Tap' courtesy of 3-D Hologrammen, Amsterdam.
For more see **www.3-Dhologrammen.com**
Picture 'Father' courtesy of Holography Studio, All-Russian Exhibition
Center, Moscow. For more see **www.holography.ru**

frequency. Coherent light is that which holds a narrow, even beam over long distances and does not expand and weaken like the light from a torch.

The Matrix, the virtual-reality game, is a super-hologram projecting endless other holograms, including the human body and, they are all, by their very nature, illusions (*Figure 35*). One of the amazing characteristics of a hologram is that every part is a smaller version of the whole. No matter how much you may cut the film into smaller and smaller pieces, when you shine the laser on them they will all give you a smaller *whole* picture. If you cut a normal photo into four pieces each of them will obviously contain a quarter of the entire image, but not with the hologram. Any part of the film will always give you a smaller version of the whole. The human body is, therefore, a smaller version of the entire Matrix hologram and I suppose you could say the Matrix made 'man' in its own image. This means that because the human body hologram has a brain, which communicates to all parts of the body and decodes the information coming back, so the Matrix as a whole must have a version of this. It communicates to its 'cells' (human bodies and other life forms) and processes the information it receives from them. This is how we receive our collective reality and also change it through the signals we unconsciously send back to the Matrix 'brain' – the central computer (*Figure 36 overleaf*).

Every part of the body is a smaller version of the whole body and this is why every cell contains all the information necessary to create an entire human form. I'll explore the health implications of this later as it solves many scientific 'mysteries'. Mainstream science has been unable to locate the area of the brain that contains all the memory because what we call memory exists throughout the brain and body. This must be the case because it's a hologram. People with tumours, who have large parts of their brains removed, do not lose specific memories. They might not remember, in general, quite as well because they have moved to a smaller level of the holographic memory where there is less clarity than in the whole. But they don't lose one memory completely and retain another in crystal clarity as they would if memory was located in one area. The body hologram stores information from all the senses and so when we smell something it can trigger a memory just as powerfully as sight or hearing. Even this is another level of the illusion because if the brain is a hologram it must also be illusory. It is, like everything in this reality, the 'physical' expression of a frequency field or resonance. Incidentally, the holographic nature of the body means the whole brain/body is involved in decoding the five senses and not just the 'visual cortex' and other areas of the brain associated with these specific duties.

This is a perfect time to describe the structure controlling our reality because we have computers, the Internet, holographic photography and television, which mirror the Matrix in so many ways. But I stress that when I say the Matrix is like a computer or software program I am only using this term to symbolise the theme of what I mean because today's computer technology helps me to describe these concepts. When it comes to the Matrix, even the most fantastic of today's computers and software is like comparing roller skates with the space shuttle, and even that gap does not tell the full story. By the way, if you know nothing about computers, and we tend to assume that everyone is aware of this stuff now, software is a set of electronic instructions that the computer reads and responds to. Another bonus in describing our illusory world is the *Matrix* movies, which have provided a brilliant visual representation of the virtual reality we are experiencing. I couldn't believe it when the first one came out because it has been such a great tool in communicating what I was trying to explain with only words before. Without this, and the computer technologies, it would be hard to know where to start in describing the workings of the Matrix, but with them it's so much easier.

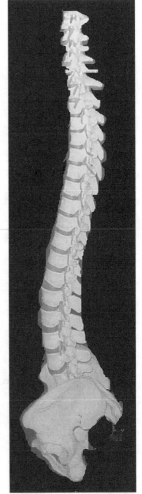

Figure 35: *Our bones seem so 'solid' and surely our bodies must be 'physical' and 'real'? This is a hologram of the human spine that is only an illusory projection.*

Picture 'Spine' courtesy of Jason Sapan, Holographic Studios, New York (see details at the back of the book)

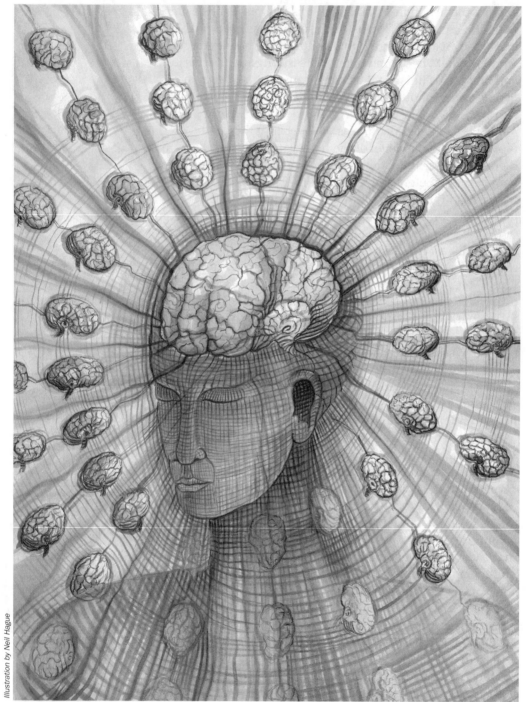

Illustration by Neil Hague

Figure 36: *The Matrix 'brain' communicates a collective reality to human brains (and all others), which decode the signals into a holographic 3D illusion. In turn, human brains are giving feedback to the Matrix and this two-way loop leads to changes that we call 'Evolution'. It's like rewriting a computer program and this is how consciousness can regain control of the Matrix*

We are 'living' in a highly sophisticated version of a virtual-reality game or, put another way, a holographic Internet giving the illusion of 3D. One of the big questions people ask is why, if we are creating our own illusory reality, do we all see the same basic world in street scenes, people, cars, roads, forests and mountains? The answer is that we are being fed frequency signals by the force manipulating the Matrix and we decode them into the collective reality we call the world (*Figure 37*). We add our own spin to this in that we differ in our opinions of what we collectively 'see'; but we all share the same basic reality because we are decoding the same signals from the Matrix. This reality is not out there, it is '*in here*' – inside our heads. Or, more accurately, it is in our genetic data bank, DNA. As the writer Edgar Allan Poe put it: 'All we see and seem is but a dream within a dream' ... a hologram within a hologram.

Figure 37: *We are constantly receiving a collective reality in waveform from the Matrix and we decode these frequencies into an illusory 3D holographic reality. You could see it as like holographic television in which the pictures broadcast as waveforms from the transmitter are decoded into moving images by the TV*

In the late summer of 2004, I met a friend, Mike Lambert, from the Shen Clinic on the Isle of Wight in England. Mike is a healer forever pushing back the boundaries of his profession in pursuit of greater understanding. As usual, this has not made him popular with the medical authorities and even those who seek to dictate the norms within so-called alternative or complementary therapies. I have yet to see a hierarchy of any kind that did not act out the same characteristics of control of events and defence of the status quo. What the hierarchy represents is irrelevant; it is the fact that it *is* a hierarchy that creates the replicated mindset. Even anti-hierarchy hierarchies behave the same – see the 'radical' and anarchist organisations for confirmation. 'Right, order, order, your anarchist committee has decided what the rules will be.' To see this attitude controlling the alternative-therapy arena is sickening. Anyway, in the 1980s Mike Lambert wrote a paper well ahead of its time about DNA or deoxyribonucleic acid. This is the body's genetic library found in every cell and we all have some 120 *billion miles* of the stuff. It is DNA that carries the codes for our physical characteristics, but it is far more than that. It contains in excess of a hundred *trillion* times more information than our most sophisticated storage devices. The known DNA codes represent roughly only three to five per cent of the mapped human genome and the other 95 to 97 per cent is not yet

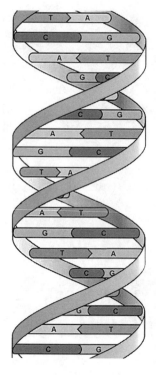

CCCAACACCCAAATATGGCTCGAGAAGGGCAGCGACATTCCTGCGGGGTGGCGCGGAGGGAATGCCC
GCGGGCTATATAAAACCTGAGCAGAGGGACAAGCGGCCACCGCAGCGGACAGCGCCAAGTGAAGCCT
CGCTTCCCCTCCGCGGCGACCAGGGCCCGAGCCGAGAGTAGCAGTTGTAGCTACCCGCCCAGGTAGG
GCAGGAGTTGGGAGGGGACAGGGGGACAGGGCACTACCGAGGGGAACCTGAAGGACTCCGGGGCAGA
ACCCAGTCGGTTCACCTGGTCAGCCCCAGGCCTCGCCCTGAGCGCTGTGCCTCGTCTCCGGAGCCAC
ACGCGCTTTAAAAAGGAGGCAAGACAGTCAGCCTCTGGAAATTAGACTTCTCCAAATTTTTCTCTAG
CCCTTTGGGCTCCTTTACCTGGCATGTAGGATGTGCCTAGGGAGATAAACGGTTTTGCTTTAGTTGT
CGCCAAGGCAGTTCCCTTCCAAACTAGCGCTAGAGCGAATGAGCGAGCAGCCAGGACCACCATTCTG
GGTTTCCAACAGGCGAAAAGGCCCTTTCTGAGTTTGAAATGTCACAGGGTTCCTAACAGGCCACTCT
TCCCTGGATGGGGTGCCAACGCCTTTCCCATGGGCATCTCCTTCCACCCTCACGCTGGCCCAGCAAG
CAGGCAGTGCTGAGGCCTTATCTCCCTAGGTGACAGATGTGGTCAGGGAGGCGCAGAGAGGATGGGC
ACTAGCGTCCAGCTCCTGGAACAGGTGTCAGGCAGGGAGGGCAGACAGGTCTTGGGAACATGTTCCC
CTGGCTATGTGGACAGAGGACTTCTCAGTGGGTCTCGCGACCCTGTGCCCCTTTTCCTGGTTCAGGG
CAGCCTTAGCCGGGGCAAAGGTCGAGAAGAGAACCCCTGGTCGCCGCCCTGGCAGAATTTGAGTGGC
TCCGGCAGGAGATGTCCCTAGGTTCCTGGGGAGGGAGGACGTCGGGGGCCAGCCAGGCTTACCCCCCC
CTGCCGCTGAGACTTCTGCGCTGATGCACCGCGCCTCTTCGCGGTCTCCCTGTCCTTGCAGAAACTA
GACACAATGTGCGACGAAGACGAGACCACCGCCCTCGTGTGCGACAATGGCTCCGGCCTGGTGAAAG
CCGGCTTCGCCGGGGATGACGCCCCTAGGGCCGTGTTCCCGTCCATCGTGGGCCGCCCCCGACACCA
GGTCAGGCTGCCCCTCCGCAGAGGGAGCCGGCTCGGGGTCCCCGCGTAAGCCAGCCTGGTGCCACC

Figure 38: *The double-ladder helix of DNA, the crystalline receiver, transmitter and amplifier of frequencies or 'light', that connects us to the Matrix. DNA is the software program that contains our genetic data and what we call mind and emotions*

Figure 39: *DNA can be expressed as a series of letter codes in sequences of A, G, C and T. How these are arranged decides the nature of the 'physical' form. Remind you of the codes in the Matrix movies?*

understood by conventional science.* Mike showed me a summary of what he had written all those years before and, as I scanned the paper, two things hit me like a smack on the head:

1) The DNA of all life, everything from a human being to a reptile, cat, dog, tree, flower, fish, insect, *everything*, shares the same codes known as A, G, C, and T (adenine, guanine, cytosine and thymine).

2) DNA is a crystalline structure and a receiver, transmitter and amplifier of frequencies or 'light'.

Holy shit, I thought. This is it! This is how they do it – this is what plugs us into the Matrix. It's the *DNA!* When you look at the graphic of DNA structure it is a double helix which, when unravelled, looks like two ladders (*Figure 38*), although some researchers believe there were once many more. The winding stairway in Freemasonic symbolism relates to DNA because it is the key to human control and the same symbol can be found in the secret mystery schools of the ancient world. The sequences of A, G, C and T decide the genetic characteristics, what your body looks like or whether the form is a mouse, elephant or daffodil (*Figure 39*), and

---

* Figures vary depending on the source and I have also seen the figure of 90% quoted. Whatever the precise figure, it is the overwhelming majority of DNA that science is yet to understand

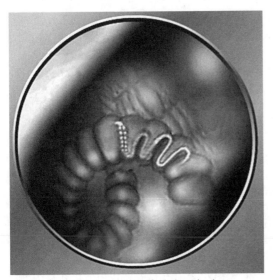

Figure 40: DNA has a reptilian feel about it when massively magnified

Figure 41: The ancient double helix snake image known today as the caduceus, a symbol for DNA and, appropriately, today's medical profession

there is another player in this that I'll come to shortly. The DNA differences between species are far less than their similarities. *Ninety per cent* of the DNA in humans and mice is the same and there are enormous parallels between human DNA and that of a housefly. As an article in the *San Francisco Chronicle* said: '… DNA is a universal software code. From bacteria to humans, the basic instructions for life are written with the same language'. And this language is the language of the Matrix.

If you saw DNA massively magnified it would look like a snake (*Figure 40*) and, not by coincidence, a major symbol throughout the ancient world was the double helix snake image known today as the caduceus (*Figure 41*). This is the symbol of the medical profession. DNA, the foundation of 'physical' form, has a reptilian-like appearance and the most ancient part of the human brain is known as the R-complex or reptilian brain. I'll come to how the Reptilians and Illuminati fit into all this in the next chapter. What we think of as 'physical' is actually a holographic illusion, and the base form of DNA, as with everything, is a frequency field, a sort of floppy disk or CD holding the genetic program. We need to think in computer terms to understand most simply how it all works.

When we procreate we see the physical expression of this with sperm from the father fusing with an egg from the mother, and the baby developing from this union. But on an energy level, beyond the holographic appearance of 3D, it is two 'software programs' being copied onto another disk. The DNA of father and mother are downloaded and the result is a 'disk' or program containing a fusion of both – the baby. This is how genetic characteristics and defects are passed on. A download containing a computer virus or flaw will be passed on to the new 'disk', the 'next generation'. The body is created from one fertilised egg (program) and this is copied

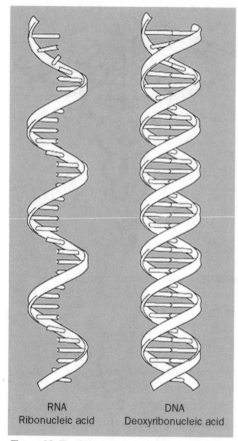

RNA
Ribonucleic acid

DNA
Deoxyribonucleic acid

Figure 42: *The RNA 'laser' reads the DNA 'software' and passes the information to the cells. Which part of the DNA 'disk' it chooses to read and communicate is controlled by the force controlling the RNA – the program or consciousness, depending on our state of awareness and connection*

over and over until the adult human has between 50 and 100 *trillion* cells. Each one contains the same library of instructions that are read according to their function, just as a computer reads software.

The reader of the body software is called RNA, or ribonucleic acid, which is usually found in the form of a single strand. To keep it simple, the DNA is like the disk or template and the RNA is like the laser that reads the information on the disk and communicates it to the cells (*Figure 42*). The RNA decides cell function by which information it chooses to transcribe from the DNA and deliver to a cell. Transcribe one set of DNA data or 'language' and it's a brain cell; select another sequence and it's a cell in the liver. One part of the RNA decodes the DNA information and another decides which information to decode. The understanding of RNA – how it works and what makes its decoding decisions – is still far from fully understood by mainstream science. But here is another massive key to the creation of reality. These RNA decisions can be made by the Matrix via the DNA or through the intervention of consciousness to override the body program. They are also affected by mental and emotional influences like stress and trauma, and electromagnetic and chemical pollution, including additives in our food and drink. These can destabilise the RNA reading process and cause translation mistakes that lead to disease.

All of these factors, and more, can affect how the RNA reads the DNA and this is fundamental to both physical and mental health, and our sense of reality. This is important to understand because, while the DNA stores the data, it is the RNA that chooses *which* data to select and manifest. The computer may have the hard disk, but the computer *operator* decides which information on the disk to activate and use. RNA is the laser reader deciding which sense of reality we will experience – as with the example of the hypnotised Tom who could not see his daughter. The RNA read his reality through the DNA in line with his programmed belief that she was not in the room. How the RNA reads the DNA also decides our physical and mental health. It can decide to read a genetic flaw or ignore it. So from now on when I talk about DNA or the DNA network, I am including in these terms the work of the RNA and its choices of what to transcribe and communicate.

Incidentally, it is said that 'practice makes perfect' and this is true because the mind/body is like a computer reading software. When a soccer player practices a skill over and over the resulting data is downloaded onto the 'disk' and can be accessed later when he's playing a match. As the ball comes to him in a certain situation, the 'computer' will react according to downloaded data. Practice well and you perform well, and vice versa. When I am coaching my son, Jaymie, at goalkeeping, I always say practice as you'd like to play because the computer doesn't distinguish between practice and match – it just reacts to the input it has recorded for a given situation. It's the same with any skill you want to develop although, no matter how much you practice, some will be have a greater 'natural' aptitude for certain things than others because of the base program they have 'inherited' in the first place.

What struck me most about Mike Lambert's paper was the relationship between DNA and the receiving and communication of information. DNA, he pointed out, was a crystal that emitted light energy in the form of photons to such an extent that it had been compared, by some, to an 'ultra weak laser' (the same with RNA). The cutting edge of scientific research is beginning to understand that DNA is a perfect antenna/transmitter. One Internet article said:

'From the characteristic form of this giant molecule - a wound double helix - the DNA represents an ideal electromagnetic antenna. On one hand it is elongated and thus a blade antenna, which can take up very well electrical pulses. On the other hand, seen from above, it has the form of a ring and thus is a very good magnetical antenna.'

It is through this receiver/transmitter that we are connected to the Matrix. I have been saying and writing for two years that our reality was like a holographic Internet. Our bodies are akin to computers connected to the World Wide Web (*Figure 43 overleaf*). The computer can travel through the collective reality that we call the Internet, visiting a news site, sports site, environmental site, porn site, whatever. It can also communicate with other computers via the Web through what we call e-mail and networking, when computers link up and work together. All the computers in the world connected to the Internet share the same collective reality, the same *matrix*. Humans also share a collective reality and we can surf our illusory web of holographic countries, people and interests. We can follow the news (news site), play sports (sports site), work for environmental groups (environmental site) or seek to roger every man or woman that takes our fancy (porn site). The principle is exactly the same. Our collective 'physical' reality is a like a holographic Internet and our bodies are biological computers. We understand how the World Wide Web is constructed through telephone lines and cable networks, but I wanted to know how *our* collective reality was generated. When I read the line about DNA being a crystal communicator and receiver of laser-type light, I had my answer. The Matrix was unveiled.

Illustration by Neil Hague

Figure 43: *Our brains and DNA/RNA are like computer terminals receiving and transmitting data. This information is exchanged with the Matrix brain and with other people and life forms. We are operating in a holographic version of the Internet*

Insights began to flood my mind as this realisation developed. The DNA was, in effect, the computer terminal through which we logged into the Matrix and were fed its collective reality – the illusions that hold us in slavery. Einstein said: 'Reality is an illusion, albeit a persistent one'. The persistent bit is the virtual-reality game transmitted by the Matrix super-hologram to the body hologram via DNA. The RNA then decides which of the program to read and manifest as 'reality', a decision made through a combination of programming, mental and emotional state, belief, and, for those who are awakening – consciousness. I had long said that most people were controlled in their thoughts, responses and reactions by the genetic traits of their bodies, the software program that we inherit from our parents and the genetic line. I saw the body as a bucking horse that our consciousness had to subdue and harmonise by expressing *its* reality over that inherited genetically, or through society's programming, by the body or 'horse'. I felt that the 'horse' (DNA) was in control of their actions and reactions, and not the 'rider' (consciousness experiencing this world through the body). In such people, an inherited genetic trait like alcoholism would be repeated in their own experience while those with consciousness more powerful than the DNA programming would be able to override it and avoid the repetition (the RNA decides to read the program differently from the alcoholic parent).

DNA/RNA is like a computer reacting to the data it receives. This data can come from the Matrix, our consciousness, or through programs affecting other programs. The latter includes the way human society is manipulated to program the people with a false reality. I recalled in *Tales from the Time Loop* how I was walking in an altered state on the only other occasion I have tried psychoactive substances, in this case 'magic mushrooms'. The voice was talking to me again as I came across a horsebox parked in the street with a horse and rider alongside. The voice said that the analogy of the horse and rider – body and consciousness – was valid. Imagine, it said, that the 'incoming' consciousness has to cope with all those inherited programs, beliefs, and assumptions of reality carried in the DNA. It said: 'Do you wonder any longer why people are so easy to manipulate when they inherit that genetic programming to start with?' Most people expended so much energy coping with the inherited responses, reactions, desires and demands of their DNA that they had little left to look up and see beyond the illusion. The DNA is decoding the signals from the Matrix into a holographic illusory world and it also connects with the DNA of other people and life forms to create the human collective mind. This holographic Internet – the Matrix – is what we call 'Creation'.

It is not only inherited genetic software that is held in our DNA. This is continually being added to and rewritten by the messages it is receiving from the Matrix, consciousness and the programming of 'society'. This is what is called 'evolution'! For example, it is the brain/DNA and its information loop with the Matrix central computer that leads to changes in animals to match their changing environments and circumstances. In the Beginning was the Word – *Microsoft* Word – and the story is constantly changing in response to the information sent and received by the Matrix and other sources. The DNA/RNA is a biological computer, reading interactive software programs in the same way that the crystalline brain decodes electrical signals from the senses and turns them into sight, sound, smell, taste and touch – the illusory holographic world that exists only in our heads. The brain is to the body what the central processing unit, or CPU, is to a computer. The central processing unit, or central processor, is responsible for controlling and reading all communications traffic and it is the most important part of the computer system. One explanation of the CPU I saw actually called it the 'brain of a computer' and the human brain is the CPU of the body computer. The healing art of acupuncture is based on the lines of energy flowing around the body called meridians. In *Figure 44 (overleaf)*, you can see the meridian system picked out by a gamma camera after radioactive tracers had been injected into acupuncture points.

This is a computer-enhanced version of an image produced in a study at the Necker Hospital in Paris held in conjunction with the Cytology Laboratory at the Military Hospital. I know what the meridians remind me of – a *circuit board*. This energy, known as *chi* in acupuncture, consists of photons carrying information around the body computer under the guidance of the central processing unit, the brain. The chakra system also connects into this network.

After I had written this chapter I came across research at the University of Florida that confirmed still further the 'computer' nature of DNA. They grew a 'brain' in a laboratory from 25,000 neural cells extracted from a single *rat* embryo and *taught it to fly an F-22 jet simulator!* It was part of a research project to develop a new breed of 'living' computer that has the ability to 'think'. It is possible for rat cells to fly a jet plane in the same way that you download software on to a computer.

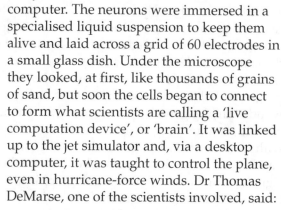

The neurons were immersed in a specialised liquid suspension to keep them alive and laid across a grid of 60 electrodes in a small glass dish. Under the microscope they looked, at first, like thousands of grains of sand, but soon the cells began to connect to form what scientists are calling a 'live computation device', or 'brain'. It was linked up to the jet simulator and, via a desktop computer, it was taught to control the plane, even in hurricane-force winds. Dr Thomas DeMarse, one of the scientists involved, said:

'When we first hooked them up, the plane "crashed" all the time, but ... the neural network slowly adapts as the brain learns to control the pitch and roll of the aircraft. After a while, it produces a nice straight and level trajectory. The network receives the information about the aircraft's pitch and roll in the form of stimulation pulses and its responses change over time. We are its external teachers as it learns.'

Figure 44: *A computer-enhanced image of the meridian system picked out by a gamma camera after radioactive tracers had been injected into acupuncture points. This is the body computer's circuit board. The energy flowing through the meridians, known as chi in acupuncture, consists of photons carrying information around the body. The chakra system also connects with this network and when the flow of energy (information) is blocked or suppressed it manifests as illness or dis-ease. Acupuncture needles are used to keep the energy flowing and balanced – and thus the body healthy*

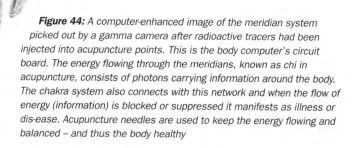

This is what is happening every day to humans. Our DNA computer cells are downloading data from the Matrix and 'society', and they are taught to respond according to program, just like the rat cells with the simulator. The only way to override this DNA programming is through the intervention of consciousness. When we do this, the resonance of the body hologram increases with the spin speed of the particles as they respond to the higher consciousness we are accessing. Consciousness then dictates events through the DNA and not the low-vibrational program. Incidentally, the development of biological computers that can 'think' is a dangerous road and the potential consequences were superbly portrayed in the *Matrix* movies when the world was taken over by machines that could think. (Indeed, has it already happened?) The takeover by the biological computer machines in those movies mirrors the way the Matrix has been hijacked by self-aware fear.

Messages are constantly being passed between the DNA computers of people, animals and all life, and this is a further extension and expression of the Matrix. This is how we can communicate without words with animals, trees and flowers, as experiments have shown, and how we pick up good or bad 'vibes' from people no matter what their outward demeanour might be. It is a bit like sending vibratory DNA e-mails, I guess, or '*d*'-mails, you might say. You have d-mail – the guy across the room is a con man. 'Hey, Ethel, I get bad vibes from that guy across the room.' These DNA computer-terminal connections are what we call the collective mind or, as the Swiss psychologist, Carl Jung, termed it, the 'collective unconscious'.

I have written many times about the so-called 'hundredth monkey' syndrome. This was the discovery that when a few members of a species are taught something new, suddenly all, or most, of the species begin to do the same instinctively without being shown. They may tell us this phenomenon is mysterious, but it's very simple, even more so as we understand the nature of the DNA 'Internet'. The monkeys, or whatever species, communicate the new knowledge via their DNA by the very act of learning and realisation. It is like finding new information and posting it on the Web to make it available to everyone logged on. In this case, the 'everyone' is the rest of the species operating with the same DNA codes and the same broadcast frequency. This is how *all* species communicate, and why they do so more efficiently with each other than with other species. They share the same DNA codes and transmit and receive on the same wavelength. This happens between the human species, too, and the system seeks to keep us divided to undermine the power of the collective unconscious to rewrite reality.

As I mentioned, we have 120 billion miles of DNA and our bodies are monumental computer terminals that can process unbelievable amounts of information both coming in and going out. In fact, more than enough for us to receive and hold manifest the collective illusion we call the world, or the cosmos. The Matrix controls consciousness trapped within its vibratory walls by holding it in a false reality that it believes to be real. This is done by constantly broadcasting a 'world' as frequency, or wave, fields to the DNA computer terminals and the DNA, through the brain/RNA, decoding these broadcasts into the holographic form that we call the physical, or five-sense, universe. Some researchers say that the synapses, which communicate information between nerve cells in the brain, are fundamentally involved in this process. The principle is similar to television, which decodes frequencies, or waveforms, broadcast from a transmitter into pictures on the screen. The only real difference is that DNA/RNA does this holographically to give the illusion of 3D – although holographic television is already being talked about.

It was the discoveries of the Frenchman Jean B. J. Fourier in the 18th century that led to both television and the discovery of holograms. He developed a process called Fourier transform, a mathematical method of converting patterns into simple waveforms and back again, so providing the potential for a television camera to convert pictures into electromagnetic frequencies and the television to convert them back again. Scientists have discovered that the human brain operates on the principles of Fourier transform – it is a *frequency decoder*. Precisely! At the end of the 1970s, research by Russell and Karen DeValois, two neurophysiologists at Berkeley University, revealed compelling evidence, since supported by countless other scientists across the world, that the brain is decoding frequency patterns and turning them into holographic images that we 'see' (or think we do). The brain cells in the visual cortex react to different frequency patterns and activate according to the types of frequency they receive. I would suggest that it is decoding the frequency signals, the waveforms broadcast by the Matrix, into the illusory holograms of the 'physical' world, although I would say the whole brain is involved in this and not just the visual cortex. Indeed, it involves more than even the brain. The entire body, all 120 billion miles of DNA (along with RNA), is involved in the decoding process. For well over a century it has been known that the ear is a frequency decoder, and experiments by Georg von Bekesy, another Nobel Prize winner, have long confirmed that the skin responds to frequencies. The voice in Brazil told me that all five senses are frequency decoders and now we can see why – the decoder is the brain and the DNA/RNA operating in every cell.

As I said earlier, DNA (like RNA) emits light-energy in the form of photons to such an extent that it has been compared by some to an 'ultra weak *laser*'. They generate coherent light in the same way that our technological lasers do – the lasers that *create holograms*. The Matrix broadcasts its signals in wave, or interference, patterns and it may be that the laser light emitted by the DNA/RNA is part of the process of turning them into holographic representations of that waveform – people, animals, houses, streets, forests and landscapes. This is the computer-game scene that I increasingly see as I walk or drive around. One mystery of quantum physics is how particles can either express themselves as a 'wave' form (non-physical) or as a particle (apparently 'physical') and the waveforms only become particles when they are being *observed* – when we are looking at them. What is actually happening is that the DNA/RNA/brain is causing the waveform or interference pattern to project an illusory hologram. The act of '*observation*' – focus – projects the holograms from the waveforms and when this happens the quantum physicists see the waveform 'becoming' a particle. Both the waveform and the particle (waveform observed as a hologram by the DNA/RNA/brain) exist at the same time and they don't move from one state to another. When a laser is shone onto a photographic interference pattern to manifest a hologram, one does not *replace* the other. Both waveform and hologram (particles) coexist. It is just that the observer sees the hologram as the prime reality. The waveform is possibility; the particle is 'physical' experience. Karl Pribram, a neurophysiologist at Stanford University, has been at the forefront of understanding the holographic nature of physical reality. Michael Talbot writes of his conclusions in the *Holographic Universe*:

> '... [Karl] Pribram [realised] that the objective world does not exist, at least not in the way we are accustomed to believing. What is 'out there' is a vast ocean of waves and frequencies and reality looks concrete to us only because our brains are able to take this holographic blur and convert it into sticks and stones and other familiar objects that make up our world ...

> '... In other words, the smoothness of a piece of fine china and the feel of beach sand beneath our feet are really just elaborate versions of the phantom limb syndrome [when amputees "feel" a limb long after it has been removed].

> 'According to Pribram, this does not mean there aren't china cups and grains of beach sand out there. It simply means that a china cup has two very different aspects to its reality. When it is filtered through the lens of our brains it manifests as a cup. But if we could get rid of our lenses, we'd experience it as an interference pattern. Which is real and which is illusion? "Both are real to me," says Pribram, "or, if you want to say, neither of them are real."'

I know that conventional scientists will mock the idea that the laser emitted from DNA/RNA is powerful enough to be involved in the manifestation of holograms, including its own 'body'. DNA is claimed to have the laser power of only a single candle, but there are two points to make about that. Firstly, the DNA laser is coherent light, focused and concentrated, as opposed to a candle, which diffuses its light and power; secondly, the DNA laser is far more powerful than a single candle, as science will eventually discover. The ability to measure something is dependent on the advancement of the technology used to do it. Try measuring the accuracy of the most advanced computer with counting-beads. The true power of DNA/RNA operates on frequencies that human technology cannot yet measure and in ways it does not understand. If your radio dial is not properly tuned to a station it can sound weak, quiet and fuzzy, but hit the right frequency and the same station could blow your ears off.

Science may think it is advanced in its knowledge of DNA, how it works, and the power of its laser emissions, but, compared with what there *is* to know, mainstream science is still hunting mammoths and going 'Ug, ug'. Let's get this straight here. Scientists understand, or think they do, only some *three to five per cent*

Illustration by Neil Hague

Figure 45: *'Elephant? What elephant?'*
'I trained at Harvard and Oxford and if there was an elephant in this room I would be the first to see it'.

of our DNA. The other 95 to 97 per cent they basically know bugger all about. So how can they pontificate on what DNA can and can't do – the same with RNA? They call this other up to *97 per cent* 'junk DNA', as if it doesn't do anything of significance. Let me go through that again in case you missed it or you're still trying to lift your jaw from the floor. *They call this other up to 97 per cent 'junk DNA' as if it doesn't do anything of significance.* What is it there for, then? Was 'God' taking the piss? 'Science' refuses to see the elephant in the living room no matter how much it may dump on the carpet – the official version of reality (*Figure 45*). In fact, the more it dumps the more establishment 'scientists' hold their noses, cover their ears and stare at the floor. For example, get this professor. Do you think that by any chance these might be related??

- We cannot perceive, even with technology, *at least* 95 per cent of the mass in the universe known as dark energy and matter, and what we 'see' with our eyes is a minuscule fraction of what exists.

- 95 per cent of the brain's activity does not relate to the waking state or 'physical reality'.

- Scientists call some 95 to 97 per cent of DNA 'junk DNA' because they don't know what it does.

Now, the figures may be approximate, but do you think it could just be that this 95 per cent or so of 'junk' DNA, and 95 per cent of brain activity not involved with the waking state, could relate to the 95 per cent (plus) of energy/matter that we can't perceive? And that it could be connecting us to levels of awareness that operate outside the realm of visible electromagnetic light, as symbolised in *Figure 46*?

Hey, I just saw this big grey thing with a long nose sitting on the couch – did you see that?

Illustration by Neil Hague

Figure 46: *The 95 per cent of 'junk' DNA, 95 per cent of brain activity not involved with the waking state, and at least much of the enormous brain capacity that science says we don't use, are actually connecting us (or should be) with the 95 per cent of energy/matter in the universe that we can't see – and also to realms beyond that*

This is a wonderful example of how mainstream science ignores, discards or dismisses anything that undermines its assumptions. It reaches the conclusion first and makes the 'evidence' fit. So much is being received, transmitted and processed by DNA that we are not aware of because 'scientific' research is limited to the frequency range its instruments can measure. Outside that (tiny) range they're basically fucked. There *is* no 'junk' DNA; it all has a purpose and that's up to 97 per cent more purpose (at least) than we know about! The brain alone receives 400 *billion* pieces of information every second, but we are aware of just 2,000. What's more, experiments have revealed that electrical signals necessary to move a limb, open your mouth or take any 'physical' action, begin some half a second *before* sensory signals arrive in the brain to be translated into action. Who or what is tapping the keyboard here?

It is said that we use only a fraction of our brain's capacity, less than ten per cent in most cases. I say that this 'unused' capacity is operating at frequencies that science has not yet measured and connects us with realms way beyond electromagnetic light (or that's what it is meant to do). This is the connection the manipulators work to suppress. I suggest that fundamental to this is the corpus callosum which links both hemispheres of the brain and regulates information passing between them. It also dictates which hemisphere will govern perception and behaviour at any point. The left side (which dominates 'modern' society) deals with the 'logical', analytical, judgemental and verbal; the right is about the creative, artistic, intuitive, visual and emotional. Clearly, the corpus callosum is key to the process of either intergrating this brain duality into a unified whole or keeping us 'in two minds'. If information passing from right to left is suppressed, the person will be 'this world' dominated and far less intuitive. It is worth noting that the 'education' system is almost entirely aimed at the left side of the brain with the right-brain stimulators, like music and art, way down the list of priorities and continuing to diminish. The most successful students are therefore left-brain prisoners, and they are the people who go on to administer the system through politics, banking, business, medicine, science and media. It is no surprise that they perpetuate the left-brain society the Illuminati has sought to impose. There are billions of neurons in the corpus callosum that are a mystery to science and they have no idea what they do. It will eventually be realised that this 'brain-bridge' is part of the transmitter/receiver system that connects us to 'out there' and to each other – as with the hundredth monkey syndrome (*Figure 47*).

The hypothalamus at the base of the brain is another vital regulator of the body and it works closely with the pituitary gland, the 'master gland' of the endocrine system, and the pineal gland, the so-called 'Third Eye', through which we manifest 'psychic sight'. The endocrine glands connect the body to the chakra system and this network links our 'physical' reality with the wider universe of unseen energy. What are called psycho-active drugs – like ayahuasca – open us consciously to those areas of the brain and DNA that interact with these other realms.

There's another crucial point to highlight about DNA: it is also the home of what we call the *mind* and *emotions*. This is the greatest deceit of all that holds us in servitude to the Matrix because we accept that our instinctive responses and

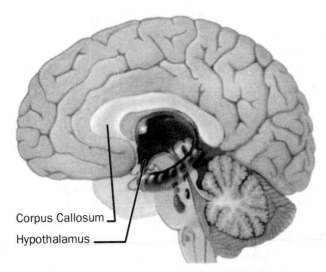

Corpus Callosum

Hypothalamus

Figure 47: *The hypothalamus in the brain is a key regulator of our emotional state and it organises and controls feelings and moods, as well as hunger, appetite and food intake, and everything to do with the concept of pleasure and creative activity. The Hypothalamus is vital to the balance of body, mind and emotions and, as we shall see later, it is targeted by chemicals used in mass-market food and drink*

reactions must be coming from us; they must be who we are. As I've said, everything is consciousness, but there are different levels of awareness. When I use the term 'mind', I mean thoughts emitting through and from DNA and not consciousness in its 'Oneness' state. The mind is a software program connected to the Matrix, as are emotions. We believe our thoughts and emotions are our own, but they are the program playing out its pre-recorded responses and reactions. You'll notice that when we feel emotions there is an immediate physical affect. Our heartbeat quickens, the mouth dries or we feel sick in the stomach. Emotions cause bodily reactions because that is where they are located – in the DNA. Once again, the hypothalmus in the brain is a prime regulator of our emotional state. One Internet explanation said:

'... The Hypothalamus organizes and controls many complex emotions, feelings and moods, as well as all motivational states including hunger, appetite and food intake, and everything to do with the concept of pleasure including satisfaction, comfort and creative activities. The neurons in the Hypothalamus produce a number of Hypothalamic neurotransmitters which relay information and instruction to all parts of the body ... The Hypothalamus ... is intimately involved in the integration of all physiological stimulation, all 5 senses ... which it then translates, distils and assembles into one discernible "package," relating all the attributes of an experience ...'

The hypothalamus is an excellent example of how the physical, mental and emotional ('all attributes of an experience') are processed through the same source – the DNA/brain. I should define what I mean by the term *Emotion* in this book because I know some writers believe that emotions are either our connection to the 'One', or that the One is their origin. I have heard it said that we connect to Oneness through the emotions of joy and happiness, but I don't perceive these as *emotions*. I say that true joy and bliss are natural states of Oneness – as I experienced in Brazil – and they don't need a name to describe them called 'emotions'. They just *are*. Oneness is bliss and joy ... *love*. When we open to Oneness beyond the program we experience these states because they are the nature of the One. These are not emotions; they are a state of Oneness. Emotions under my definition are programmed reactions that disconnect us from awareness of the One and we don't know what real joy, bliss and happiness really is within the Matrix flytrap, unless we connect with the One. We judge our state of 'happiness' by our level of unhappiness. 'Oh I feel a lot less unhappy today, so I must be happy.' *That* kind of happiness is emotion, but not the Oneness variety that defies any label. I suggest that what we *understand* as emotion (including illusory 'happiness') is a software program designed to enslave us and I will develop this theme later.

Emotions are phenomena of the DNA hologram. If you rub your hands over your body and press with your fingers, you will usually find areas that are uncomfortable when there is no 'rational' reason why. Alternative healers, involved in what they call 'body work' or kinesiology, locate these areas very skilfully and my goodness they can hurt. These points of discomfort are unprocessed emotions stored in the body (often as toxins) and when the locations are massaged the freed emotions are often expressed through anger, tears and so on. This stored emotion is actually information held in the hologram and is akin to a hard drive on a computer holding saved data. It's like a computer operator saving something he doesn't want to deal with immediately. The body-work healers are, in effect, pressing the delete button.

People say things like 'I am only human', and they talk of 'human nature', as if this is who they are. But it's not. They are the consciousness of Infinite Possibility and what we call 'human' is the DNA mind, emotions and holographic 'body'. What makes us 'human' is the Matrix interactive software program in the DNA, and we confuse this with who we are. It is also what makes us men, women, black, white, young or old. These are programs and this misunderstanding is at the very core of the illusion. We are not our bodies, mind or emotions. We are *Infinite Consciousness*.

An article in *The Scotsman* newspaper in 2004 featured the research of David Hamilton, a scientist who changed his views on life after experiencing a firewalk. It was clear that if you could walk through fire without getting burnt there was just a little bit more to know about the nature of reality. The article explained how Hamilton became convinced that our mental and emotional states can not only affect our health, but actually change the DNA. Yes, they can, and the reason is that they *are* the DNA. When one part of a computer changes, it affects the whole computer because the data passing through the system is changed. So it is with our changing mental and emotional states that affect the balance of the DNA and thus our 'physical' health. This is how the placebo effect works when people regain health after taking sugar pills they believe are powerful drugs. The belief in the 'drug' rewrites the DNA (and/or tells the RNA to read the program to match the belief) and manifests the 'cure' they believed the treatment would bring. David Hamilton said he had found some 500 scientific papers from mainstream academic journals which confirmed the effect that thought, feeling and faith (belief) have on the body's systems, and he highlighted in particular the work of Eric Kandel, joint

Figures 48 and 49: *The stunning effect of thought and words on water crystals. The crystal in Figure 48 formed after water was exposed to words of 'love and appreciation'; in Figure 49, the words were 'You make me sick – I will kill you'. The difference makes clear the power of words, thoughts and emotions to affect the world, not least the human body, which, in this reality, is mostly water.*

(For more examples see the books, Messages from Water, volumes one and two, *by Masaru Emoto)*

winner of the Nobel Prize for Medicine in 2000. Kandel has concluded that many genetic differences between people are influenced by society and conditioning and are not just inherited from parents. These influences caused genes to switch on or off and this is the DNA computer system reacting to changing input. Hamilton cited a scientific study of rat pups which showed that two separate growth hormones are switched off in those deprived of a mother's touch. He went on:

> 'There is a whole branch of medicine called psychoneuroimmunology, which studies the effect of thoughts and emotions on our biochemistry. The biochemistry is intimately connected with the DNA, so if these ... components are affected by thoughts and emotions then thoughts and emotions must also affect our DNA.'

Yes, because they *are* DNA! The brilliant work of Japanese scientist, Masaru Emoto, at the I.H.M.-Institute in Tokyo, has revealed how water is fundamentally affected by words, thoughts and emotions – all of which are waveforms. He and his team exposed water to various music and different words and expressions, and then froze it to produce water crystals. When these were examined under a microscope the response of the water was amazing. In *Figures 48* and *49* you can see the way the crystals responded to the words and thoughts (vibrations) of 'Love and appreciation', and, 'You make me sick – I will kill you'. Imagine the effect on the body hologram of our words and deeds when it is some 70 per cent water (this figure varies by age and weight); and these attitudes, and states of being, rewrite the DNA in the same way that they affect water crystals. (I have to laugh when I hear people say that planets have no effect on us – within the illusion – when our bodies are 70 per cent water and the moon alone can move the tides across entire oceans!) Incidentally, it is not the *words* that have the effect, but the *intent* behind them. If you said 'I will kill you' in a light-hearted, jokey fashion, it would not have the same effect as it would if you meant it, or said it with malevolence. Thought and emotions produce wave forms and quite obviously music does. Music can be healing and inspiring or extremely detrimental, depending on its vibrational impact.

I also saw a documentary that showed how the brain forms networks of electrical connections in response to mental and emotional states. The longer these states continue, like depression, and worry, the more this network 'solidifies' and becomes the reflex-response system of the brain. It is literally like programming a computer and the brain edits reality in line with the program that the mental and emotional state has downloaded. But the moment we change our thoughts and emotions, say to enthusiasm and optimism, these electrical connections break up and re-form to reflect the new attitude. Thoughts and emotions can be measured as chemical reactions because the pituitary gland in the brain, interacting with the hypothalamus, releases chemicals known as *peptides* in response to emotional changes, and these chemicals attach to receptors on the cells. Whether it is a chemical form of what we call 'love' (in its human sense), or 'hate', or even a drug like heroin, they all connect with the cells through the same receptors.

I have written in other books about what I call emotional addiction when people require a constant fix of an emotion, be it anger, depression or 'love'. One main reason for this is the addiction to the chemicals secreted by the hypothalamus/DNA network when emotions are felt. In the words of the Robert Palmer song, for example, people can be 'addicted to love'. As with all addictions, there can be a need to constantly increase the dose to get the same effect and humans are subconsciously creating situations in their lives to give them the emotional fix. Such people will create circumstances in which they can get angry, worry or become depressed, while others will jump from partner to partner saying, 'I fall in love so easily'. They are addicted to the melodrama because they are addicted to the chemical fix it supplies. Dr Candice Pert, author of *Molecules of Emotion: The Science Behind Mind-Body Medicine* (Scribner Book Company, 1999), said: 'At any instant our body is in our mind and our mind is in our body'. This is because mind and body – and emotions – are expressions of the same DNA. What we call 'personality' (mind and emotions) is a DNA program and we have been kidded to believe that this is who we are. When we ride a horse we don't believe that we are the horse, do we? But with the body, and its mind and emotions, we do.

I have heard it said by psychologists that there is only a small number of what they call archetypal 'personalities'. Some say there are no more than 12 basic ones. The Swiss psychiatrist, Carl Jung, sought to connect these archetypes to genetic inheritance and believed them to be instinctive. He said we are born with these patterns that structure our imagination and make it distinctly human, and he suggested that archetypes are very closely linked to our bodies. Jung identified the archetypal patterns in every culture and period of human history, and found that they mirrored the same archetypal 'laws' in all cases. He suggested that a 'Universal Unconscious' was behind all this. Humans did not have separate, or personal, unconscious minds and instead shared a single Universal Unconscious, Jung said. What we call the conscious mind was rooted in this, he believed, and to him the mind was shaped according to universal patterns. I'd say he was right in all these assumptions, but that the archetypal patterns come from the Matrix via the DNA/brain. The Matrix, at this level of reality, is Jung's Universal Unconscious – the energy/matter that we can't see, which is constantly interacting with the 95 per cent of brain activity not related to the waking state and to the 95 per cent or so of 'junk DNA'.* This is why, as he said, personality patterns are inherited and closely linked with the body. Too right they are – through the DNA. These are the patterns that, in his terms, make us 'distinctly human'. They are the human software program. Like everything in this reality, 'humans' are a computer construct and not who we really are. Psychiatrists and mainstream therapists who work with the 'human mind' are like computer tech-support and hypnotists are reprogrammers. They are not dealing with consciousness within the definition in this book, but the *mind* – a software program.

Oneness is *All Possibility* and yet humans overwhelmingly fall into a few basic archetypal personalities. How can this be? We see such a contradiction because the archetypes are not Oneness in awareness of itself; they are software programs downloaded and read by the DNA/RNA. Look at the classic 'fight or flight' response, which comes from the reptilian brain. When people or animals are faced with danger they either fight or run for it. Are they really the only choices in such a situation within Infinite Possibility? No, of course they're not. They are *programmed* reactions. Our emotional responses are almost entirely predictable for the same reason. I have known people in highly volatile relationships who were simply reacting to each other according to DNA program. They pressed each other's buttons and reacted in the same way every time. It is like tapping data into the other's computer and pressing enter. The Matrix wants us to react in this way because it leads to conflict and instinctive (programmed) behaviour that produces the energy that empowers the system. When some of these volatile couples saw what was happening and stopped reacting according to program, bingo, the storm was over. Their consciousness began to have the relationship instead of their DNA programs that react through what we call *instinct*.

As I have mentioned, electrical activity necessary for any 'physical' action begins some half a second before the conscious mind makes the 'decision' to act. Benjamin Libet and Bertram Feinstein, neurophysiologists at Mount Zion Hospital in San Francisco, asked people to press a button when they were touched. The outcome was that the brain reacted to the touch in 0.0001 of a second and the button was pressed in 0.1 of a second. But the person was not aware of feeling the touch or pressing the button for a full half-a-second. The subconscious programming makes

---

* I stress again that these figures are approximate

the decisions and the conscious level is the observer and reactor – unless consciousness intervenes. Without that, the conscious and subconscious *minds* – both expressed through the DNA – will react according to program or what some call 'archetype'.

Once you stop the programming governing your mental and emotional responses, a higher awareness – Infinite Possibility – can come in and override the archetypes. More than that, it can rewrite the DNA/RNA program and attune it to Oneness, instead of the Matrix. These programmed archetypal reactions are mercilessly exploited by the Illuminati. They know that if they input something, like 9/11, they are going to get a predictable DNA/RNA reaction, which they can manipulate to advance their agenda. I saw an old First World War recruiting poster that called for the men of the Isle of Wight to attend a meeting aimed at persuading them to volunteer to fight for their country. It said that 'Patriotic airs would be sung' and, of course, this was meant to manipulate the men emotionally to react to 'love of country' by signing up to die. Emotions are the major access code to the body computer, including the mind. Now we have multi-channel television, Hollywood movies and the media in general, to whip up the emotional response to events that leads people to 'fight for their country' and support governments that send them to kill and be killed.

Unless we operate from a level of awareness beyond emotional reaction, the Matrix will continue to construct our reality. Problem-*Reaction*-Solution depends 100 per cent for its success on this response system, and the *Fear of Not Surviving Program*, located in the reptilian brain, is the central target. Are we going to let the Matrix dictate our lives through our DNA, or are we going to open ourselves to awareness beyond the Illusion and manifest that level of consciousness? When we do the latter we are *in* this world, but not *of* it, and I will go into this further in the final chapter. I wrote earlier how the mystic, Sri Aurobindo Ghose, said that most humans possess a mental screen that keeps them from seeing behind the veil of matter. That screen is the DNA/RNA and the way it interprets reality through the body's central processing unit, the brain, within the tiny frequency range called visible electromagnetic light. Astrophysicist and esoteric researcher, Giuliana Conforto, wrote in her book, *Organic Universe* (Edizioni Noesis, Italy, 2004):

'We have to remember that the luminous matter we observe with our instruments is only 0.5 per cent of all calculated mass. What we see with our eyes is still less. "Reality" is a thin "film" of [electromagnetic] light, a visible matrix, our biological body or robot can interact with; such a body is just a "costume" that lets us participate in the "film" itself for a while; it is not our true identity or "I".'

So what is the Matrix? It is information, a ready-to-wear world and belief system broadcast to the DNA as frequencies, and decoded into holographic 3D collective reality. It acts like a voice talking in our heads, telling us what to believe is real. In the *Matrix* movies when they looked at computer screens full of moving green codes, they were seeing street scenes and people. It is the same with our illusory reality. Scientists and esoteric researchers have identified recurring mathematical codes like the Fibonacci number sequence found throughout nature. This involves adding the last two numbers to get the next one, as in 1,1,2,3,5,8,13,21... . The sequence can be found in everything from the proportions of the human body to the way plants grow. Other mathematical and geometrical codes and recurring sequences include Phi proportions, Golden Mean, so-called 'sacred geometry', numerology, the Chinese I Ching, astrology and many others. These are the mathematics of the Matrix which, at least in this reality, can be broken down into numbers and codes, as with DNA.

Appropriately, and not coincidentally, this is how computers work. Everything you see on a computer screen, including the colours, are sequences of numbers using the binary system based on 1 and 0. This is an expression of the duality and polarity of the Matrix, like negative and positive, yin and yang. Many of the Illuminati symbols I have identified in other books, such as the pentagram, are codes that relate to the mathematics of the Matrix and affect how DNA interprets reality. These are placed all 'around' us to manipulate the way we decode our reality into holographic experience. As I, and others, have long detailed, towns and cities like Washington D.C. are laid out according to the geometry of the Matrix. The vortex points all over the planet that form perfect grid patterns are also part of this mathematical construct and the Matrix can be manipulated at these locations. Stone circles like Stonehenge and Avebury, and the temples of the Illuminati secret societies, have been built on these vortices, and they are also targeted for satanic rituals. Everything can be expressed as numbers within the Matrix. Stephen Marquardt, an American doctor, who has studied Fibonacci number sequences with regard to the human face, correctly concluded: 'All life is biology. All biology is physiology. All physiology is chemistry. All chemistry is physics. All physics is math[s]'. He might have added that all maths is energy and all energy is consciousness.

The DNA/RNA network, in the act of 'observing' wave patterns, transforms them into holographic illusion and the ancient Greek philosopher, Plato, was quite right when he said that human beings were like people sitting in a cave always facing a wall. The universe was the shadows projected on the wall – illusions that the people mistake for reality. That is a perfect description of what I am outlining here. Everything you think you see, including your own body, is a hologram, a 3D illusion, which is fed to you to trap your consciousness in mesmerised servitude. Think moth. Think light. That's us and that's the Matrix.

Wow.

CHAPTER FOUR

Past and Future on DVD

The public is wonderfully tolerant. It forgives everything except genius
Oscar Wilde

The Matrix sells us the illusion of passing from past to future when we are actually going nowhere. 'Time' is one of the most effective ways of enslaving us. Oneness is no-time and if we attune ourselves to the deceit of passing through time we disconnect from awareness of the Infinite. How can you connect with someone standing still when you are hurtling past them in a sports car on your way from labour ward to cemetery? Hey, look, there's Oneness ... Zeeeeowwwwwwwwwww ... shit, missed him – and her.

When people hear claims that past and future are happening together they usually dismiss the idea as ridiculous and impossible. After all, aren't we passing through the 'years' and getting 'older' by the 'day'? I understand the question, but days, years and ageing are all illusions that we manifest because we believe in them – or our DNA does. Given that everyone else is ageing around us, why would we not think it was real? But then everyone ages because they are all caught in the same illusion. How can we age when there is no time? We can't. But we can experience the illusion of ageing when that is written into the Matrix software (again involving the hypothalamus and endocrine glands) and our consciousness falls for it. A hologram projected by a laser from an interference pattern never ages and yet our bodies – also holograms – go through a predictable cycle of young to old, birth to death. The difference is that one hologram is programmed to age and the other is not. People talk about the power of mind over matter, but to rewrite the ageing software we need to have the power of consciousness over mind – higher awareness over DNA program. That's the way to change all the programs.

I have had some visions and insights about illusory 'time' while I have been sitting here writing, in fact they are hitting me like machine gun bullets. Take the world we live in to be a movie you are watching on DVD. You press the button and the movie begins to take you from scene to scene. You are passing from A to B to C or, put another way, passing from past to future. But when you get, say, to the middle of the movie, the part you have just watched has not ceased to be. It is still there in the same form, it's just that the laser is now reading a different part of the disk. If you press stop and run back you'll find that exactly the same scenes you

74

have watched are still there. Ahead of you in the movie is the part you haven't yet seen, the 'future'. But fast forward and you'll find it is already there before you arrive in the course of scene following scene at 'normal' speed. When you get to the end of the movie everything you have seen and experienced is still there for other people to experience or for you to watch again. The past, as you perceived it, is always there and so is the future. They are all happening at once, and past and future are illusions relative to where you are in the movie, or the software program.

A sense of 'time' is based merely on the observer's perspective. This is why, as Einstein pointed out, when you are doing something you like 'time flies', and when you are in the dentist's chair it appears to 'pass' slowly. When you panic, time seems to pass very quickly, but not so when you stay calm. The very fact that time is relative to the observer means there is no time. It is a perception and not 'real'. Our manufactured official 'time' is linked to the earth's rotation and when that changes so does our 'time'. In America, you can drive across a state border and be in a different hour, and when you fly across the International Date Line you are instantly in a different day. Time is an illusion.

The theme of that DVD analogy is how the Matrix Time Loop works, as I highlighted in *Tales from the Time Loop* at considerable length. What I call the Time Loop is the vibrational level of the Matrix that we think of as the physical world, the realm of visible electromagnetic light, and it *appears* to move from past to future. 'Time' is there to entrap us in the Matrix and detach us from consciously reconnecting with the Infinite that we are. What we *call* past and future is our illusory journey 'through' a software program or holographic movie on DVD. The Time Loop movie is always there to be experienced at whatever point you choose. Imagine a storyboard on a wall and you choose to start at a certain place and walk along the wall following the story for a while before walking away. Then you might come back and read some more at another stage of the story ('reincarnation'). The basic backdrop – the world we see 'around' us – remains constant unless one of the following intervenes to change it:

- The Matrix brain or central computer system changes the messages it transmits for us to decode into holographic reality.

- Consciousness overrides that program and sends its own instructions to the DNA/RNA/brain network.

- Our DNA software is rewritten by experience or programming, as with the Illuminati manipulation of information and the suppression of alternative realities.

It is not DNA or even the Matrix that is the problem; it is the nature of the program that they follow. There are actually multiple matrices or possible 'past and future' realities to choose from – just as you can have many different recordings on a DVD – and I will develop this point later. One of the unique characteristics of a holographic film is also that, unlike a conventional picture, you can have many images on the same print. They are different interference patterns, waveforms, and the various pictures are selected by the angle at which the laser strikes the film. This is the same principle as the laser passing across the wave patterns of the DVD picking out the scenes in order. What I am suggesting is that our DNA/RNA decodes wave patterns broadcast by the Matrix in basically the same way and, as the angle of 'strike' changes, we move from scene to scene as if we are moving 'forward'. *But*. We are actually going nowhere. Does your DVD machine go anywhere while it is playing the Hollywood film that appears to 'move'? Do the actors go anywhere or the backdrops for their scenes? Do we go anywhere when we are 'moving' around the Internet? No, we are just sitting there. We are not moving in our daily lives, either.

Moving is an illusion because it's all going on in our brain. It's like playing one of those virtual reality car-racing games when you appear to be speeding around a track, but in fact you are just sitting in a chair. You are not moving; the game is. It's the same with the Matrix super-hologram. I go into modes sometimes, especially when I am driving, when I see the world moving in my mind while my body goes nowhere. The virtual-reality game is so clear to me in these moments. It's like the story of the two monks debating about the movement of a flag in the wind. 'The flag is moving', said one. 'No, the wind is moving', said the other. A third, passing by and hearing the conversation, said: 'The flag is not moving. The wind is not moving. Your *mind* is moving'. Remember in the *Matrix* movies how people were 'plugged in' to the Matrix through their brains while 'they' stayed outside sitting in a chair without moving? It's the same principle.

There is something highly significant about the angle at which we observe reality in the Matrix computer game. I saw a hologram in a shop a few years ago that showed a human face when you looked at one angle and a reptile face when the angle was changed. What I saw, in effect, was a shape-shift. The Matrix is an enormous library of waveform images waiting for DNA/RNA to manifest them as holograms. I remember being contacted by the neighbour of a man who worked as a gardener at one of the British Royal Family estates at Sandringham, in Norfolk. The man had been describing very bizarre experiences there. Through the neighbour, I arranged to meet him, but then he was apparently warned not to speak with me. However, one of the experiences he had recounted to the neighbour was about part of the estate where he had seen two completely different scenes at the same location. If you looked from one *angle* (his words), it was a small wood and if you looked from another it was a Swedish-style pine cottage! It is we, through our DNA/RNA, who change the scenery we experience by, to maintain the movie analogy, selecting different 'sets' or locations in the program. It is not the scenery that is changing, but rather our DNA/RNA that makes the scenery *appear* to change as it decodes the wave patterns. Strike them at one point and you are in the 'future', strike them at another and you are in the 'past', or the 'present'. But where is the past, present and future on a software program or movie? There is no past or future – everything is happening NOW. This is how psychic people are able to 'see' what we call the future. Their DNA/RNA network has the ability to pick out the frequency patterns 'later' in the movie. It is the same with those who have visions of the past.

Illustration by Neil Hague

Figure 50: *'Past', 'present' and 'future' on DVD. All are happening at the same 'time' in different parts of the same 'disk' and what happens in one 'scene' can affect all the rest. Thus, the 'past' can change the 'future' and the 'future' can change the 'past'*

I have read and been told of many experiences where people have seen something, like a building, and yet when they return, even hours or sometimes minutes later, it has disappeared. I remember one story about people who saw an old-style American house on fire as they drove past and they immediately went to call for help. It was standing by itself back from the road and was clearly visible like any other building. But when they returned there was no house and no sign of where one had been. They had somehow accessed a different part of the program. As we change our DNA/RNA focus from one wave pattern to another, the patterns we have ceased to manifest still exist for other DNA (people and all living things) to experience.

As I was writing this I had a clear picture of a DVD with scenes from 'history' lined up along the surface as the laser moved across to manifest the various events in turn. And the laser was RNA reading the program. You can see Neil Hague's portrayal of the image in *Figure 50*. This symbolises how, as we strike or *observe* different patterns in the program and 'move' into the 'future', there is other consciousness 'following' us in the program and still more 'ahead' of us. As we change scenes, so others are accessing the scenes we left behind. Using that earlier analogy of walking past a storyboard on a wall, someone else can walk behind you reading (experiencing) the same scenes that you have because the basic story is always there until it is changed. What I am saying, therefore, is the 'past' has not *ceased* to be, and nor is the future *yet* to be. Both are being played out *Now* by those in other parts of the program. We see Stonehenge, for example, as an ancient ruin from the past because that is where we are in the Matrix/Time Loop program/movie. But, at another point, people are 'living' at the original Stonehenge, and at another it is not even built yet! In one part of the program the American War of Independence may be just starting and at another the Second World War is still going on.

I know it sounds impossible that the same battle is constantly being fought, but think about it. When you have a battle in a movie on DVD or the Internet, the start, middle, and end of the fighting always exists on the disk or software. It is the same with the Matrix. When you spin back a movie and press 'play', has anything changed since you last watched it? No, and, once again, it is the same with the Matrix unless the script is rewritten by either the Matrix or consciousness making decisions at odds with the software. The latter is why those Matrix clones, the Illuminati, are so freaked out by mavericks that refuse to conform to the program. In doing so, they are rewriting it. Consciousness can do this by overriding the program through the DNA. If we don't, then, as they say, history keeps repeating. The Stone Age, Iron Age, Industrial Revolution and computer-dominated world of 'today' are happening over and over. To experience them you need to be at that point in the program, that's all. We are not going anywhere, not evolving, we are experiencing part of a program designed to enslave us and turn us into generators of fear – the energy that powers the Matrix.

Think of horses on a carousel. Whether anyone is sitting on them or not they still go round with the rest. Our 'physical' bodies are biological computers reading software programs and they are running all the time. The question is whether self-aware consciousness chooses to experience this illusory world through one of those software carousel 'horses' (human bodies) or not. If it doesn't, the 'body' will still play out the program, because it is a biological computer capable of 'thought' (assessment of data). But it will be nothing more than software without consciousness as defined in this book. Everything you see in the Matrix is part of the program, including your own body. The exception to this is your consciousness, those that have any that is, because, in the way I am defining consciousness in this book, not everyone has. The phenomenon of the 'woman in the red dress' in the first *Matrix* movie, the woman who was just part of a software program despite appearing 'real', is not confined to a Hollywood sci-fi script. These 'computer' creations, these carousel horses with no rider, are everywhere. There are three main groups of 'people' in the Matrix (see *Figure 51*):

1) First there are the software programs whose only consciousness is the DNA/RNA receiving instructions from the Matrix. They are constructs of mind, not consciousness. All energy/consciousness is Infinite Oneness, but not all

Figure 51: *The three types of 'human': on the left is the pure software program, the horse with no rider, which includes the 'pure' Illuminati bloodlines; the centre image represents the majority of 'humans' who are self-aware consciousness, but trapped in the illusion and dominated by the program; and on the right is symbolised the much smaller – but rapidly growing – number of people who are connected in awareness to consciousness beyond the Matrix. For this reason they perceive life and the world very differently to the rest and can be seen as 'crazy' or 'dangerous'*

expressions of this are at the same level of awareness. The 'human' interactive software programs are sophisticated robots following a 'life' program dictated by the Matrix and their free will is basically zilch. I'm sure you must have met many. They appear to be the same as everyone else in the way they look, but the best special effects studios can now put digital 'people' into advertisements and you can't see the join. There is a television presenter in Britain who is famous for being enormous and she appeared in a commercial with a far slimmer body to sell a food product. You could not see the join and anyone who didn't know what she really looked like would believe the body in the ad was hers. This is why we have to be extremely wary about 'Bin Laden' videos that suddenly come to light at just the right time from the agenda's point of view. Producing a fake Bin Laden saying fake words is a cinch to the state-of-the-art special effects houses. The same principle applies with these 'Red Dress' programs, as I will call them. They are bodies without consciousness, interactive software programs. The lifeless look in their eyes is one way of picking them out, as is the lack of energy coming from them. They resonate to a different frequency to conscious awareness and again you can symbolise them as the horses on the carousel with no one on board. These interactive software programs can malfunction, go off message, and 'hack' into other programs – as with the Agent Smith character in the *Matrix* movies. A lot of that is going on, too.

2) Other people do have consciousness, but are so entranced and deluded by the Matrix that their DNA programming calls the shots and dictates the path that they take. These horses do have a rider, but the horse is still making the decisions. They go where the DNA program takes them because they don't think they have a choice or don't choose to make one. They can be lovely, caring people and express their consciousness in that way, but they can't see beyond the illusion. These are the main energy source for the Matrix because it feeds off the emotional energies of fear, guilt, and frustration etc., generated by consciousness trapped in this virtual reality prison and identifying with its programmed 'personality'. Once consciousness identifies with the mind and emotions – the software – it begins to resonate to those frequencies and this invariably means an expression of fear. These people, with what you might call 'back seat consciousness', also represent by far the biggest section of 'conscious' humanity. They are the system fodder who overwhelmingly do and think as they are told.

3) The third, and by far the smallest, group are those who are aware enough to see through the illusion and have begun to access the *knowing* of Infinite Oneness beyond the walls of the software program. This doesn't mean they understand the full nature of life and reality, but they have at least a subconscious *knowing* that the world is not as it seems. They are the only ones with free will in the sense that they have the awareness and power of consciousness to break the control of the DNA software. They can ride the horse and, in doing so, rewrite the program. These people stand out from the crowd and are dubbed dangerous

or mad because they don't see the world like everyone else. The Matrix is a six-stone weakling compared with consciousness in its true power, and this group is like a computer virus that has the means to scramble the program and download another reality. The Matrix targets these people with a vengeance to protect its control and also because if it can manipulate this level of consciousness to become caught in the illusions and succumb to fear, it is a massive potential energy source.

Consciousness has become trapped by the Matrix in a maze of smoke and mirrors that has implanted a false reality. The 'Red Dresses', or software people, are no problem because they just follow the codes. The targets of the Matrix are those with self-aware consciousness who find themselves, for whatever reason, caught in the flytrap. It is in pursuit of these people – this *consciousness* – that the system of society is so designed in this part of the program. I have been saying in my books for years that the system has been structured to hold consciousness in a prison of the five senses. You can see everywhere that this is so obviously true. But what is this five-sense jail cell? It is a prison of the brain and body – the *DNA*! While we are focused purely on the five-sense reality we are slaves to the DNA that dictates our thoughts, emotions and actions. The consciousness of most people never gets its hands on the wheel of life because the DNA will not vacate the driver's seat. Consciousness in its reconnected infinite power could easily take control, but it is difficult to do this when you are not aware that you *are* Infinite Consciousness and you think that the DNA thoughts and emotions you are having are yours. This is how the movie constantly plays out while slumbering consciousness thinks it is calling the shots!

The aim is to turn conscious beings into generators of fear in all its forms to empower the Matrix, and to take away freedom and replace it with what I call *fear*dom – domination by fear. One of the major ways this is done is through the software programs that we call 'leaders'. You will recall the emphasis I have placed on the obsession of the Illuminati families with interbreeding and genetics. As I have already suggested, what we call procreation is the recording of two software programs (father and mother) onto one disk – the child. All bodies are software programs and the difference is whether they are *pure* software (Red Dresses) or whether consciousness is involved. When consciousness expresses itself through the body it rewrites the DNA programming which, in turn, is transmitted to other DNA and to the Matrix in general. These people change what we call the bloodline and, as a result, these Red Dress genetic lines become increasingly less controlled by the dictates of the program. Such people will have a heart dimension to their views and decisions; they will have a sense of empathy, compassion and fairness. They will not, in short, react as a programmed disk in the way the Matrix demands with violence, bigotry and an absence of empathy with those who suffer the consequences of their actions. The world is awash with this mentality because it is awash with software people.

The leading Red Dress bloodlines are the Illuminati families. At the level we are discussing now, the reason they are so obsessed with interbreeding and avoiding outside genetic input is to ensure that their replicated programs ('offspring') remain pure software and are not rewritten by the infusion of consciousness. Since the ancient world (as we perceive it anyway), they have bred (copied the disks) overwhelmingly with each other. The royal families that ruled ancient societies were mostly Red Dress software programs and they maintain this power today through Illuminati families like the Rothschilds, Rockefellers, Windsors and those I name in my other books (*Figure 52*). The Bush family is the same, but then you only have to see George 'Dubya' to know that. Obviously he was a duff download. The Illuminati Red Dresses are there to dictate and control conscious beings so they remain caught in the illusion and produce the desired fear to fuel the system. By placing themselves at the top of the political, banking, business, media and military system these bloodlines can easily do that, so long as most conscious people remain puppets to their DNA.

The Matrix has its software in positions of power across the world and uses these programs to cause the wars that conscious people, or lower level Red Dresses, are told to fight. The wars generate enormous amounts of fear and the Matrix sucks it in. Interestingly, the *Matrix* movies featured a character, a software program, called the Merovingian. One of the purest Illuminati bloodlines (programs) is known by the same name because of its connection to the Merovingian kings in what is now France, leading up to the period of Charlemagne. The Merovingian character in the movies was French and controlled the Train Man who policed the in-between realm that was remarkably similar in concept to the interspaces.

Talking of which, I have connected a reptilian 'species' very strongly to the Illuminati and I can now see more clearly how this fits in. I remember Credo Mutwa, the Zulu Sanusi, telling me once that 'to understand the Illuminati you must study the reptile'. How right he was and even more so in the light of what is emerging. I did indeed study the reptile and it is as near to a computer program that you could find. Of course there are variations but, basically, they are creatures controlled by instinct (programming) and they will react in an incredibly predictable way to any situation. I have watched a few demonstrations at crocodile farms in Australia where the keeper told the audience how the croc would react to something he was going to do and every time, without exception, that is what happened. The Illuminati, too, are nothing if not predictable in their techniques and reactions, and the character traits of the reptilian brain within the human brain mirror those of the reptilians and Illuminati – cold-blooded attitudes with no empathy for their victims, a desire for top-down structures of control, territorialism (this is *mine* keep out) and obsessive ritualistic behaviour. This describes the Illuminati exactly because they are reptilian software. You will find no better example of reptilian behaviour than the British Royal Family, which is obsessed with ritual and protocol.

The Illuminati 'human' bodies are only holographic veils that hide their true nature. They allow them to operate undetected within the realm of visible electromagnetic light. The voice in Brazil described the Reptilians behind the Illuminati as very much like the agents, or 'sentient programs', that manipulate in

Figure 52: *The 'Red Dress' bloodlines of the Illuminati that dominate royalty, politics, banking, business and media. They obsessively interbreed to stop the software program being rewritten by the infusion of self-aware consciousness*

the *Matrix* movies. They could either operate as a reptilian hologram, or hide behind an apparently 'human' one, just as the sentient programs morph in and out of different human forms in the *Matrix* trilogy. Either way, the Reptilians and other projected agents of the Matrix were not 'real' in consciousness terms. They were like projections, holographic thought fields or, as the voice put it, highly sophisticated *software programs*. 'If you programmed a computer to kill children, would that computer have any emotional problems with that?' the voice asked. The answer is obvious; it would follow the program because it does not have a consciousness to intervene in the decision. It was the same with the Illuminati Reptilians, the voice said. They were like digital people implanted in the movies alongside human actors. They appeared to be the same, but they were not and their power of thought was limited to data processing within the confines of their software.

The Reptilian program would seem to be a foundation code of the Matrix and it is not surprising that even the magnified DNA has that look about it. The very fact that the body is a hologram with a reptilian brain means that throughout the super-hologram, or Matrix, the reptilian dimension must be repeated because every part of a hologram contains a smaller version of the whole. The Reptilians immediately behind the Illuminati are one example of that. When you look at the response characteristics of the reptilian brain in 'humans', it is about instinctive (programmed) emotional reactions and not consciousness or love. The voice in Brazil said the Illuminati Reptilians did not know they were tools of the Matrix – computer programs designed to manipulate the sub-plots in the movie that generate the fear that powers the system, although they did have an understanding of how the Matrix works. The Reptilians feed off fear, but on behalf of the Matrix that wrote their program. They think they are masters when in truth they are slaves to their creator.

I also stress that that there are Reptilians not involved in the manipulation and, even with regard to those who are, I am not presenting this information from the perspective of 'us' and 'them'. Everything is the same Oneness, whether it is the energy/mind of a software program or Oneness in awareness of itself. The Matrix is controlled by our own fear and the Reptilians, Illuminati and other 'enemies', are this fear made manifest. They are us and we are them. When we free ourselves from fear, they will cease to take illusory form because the source of their projection will have been switched off.

The holographic nature of reality explains how the Illuminati Reptilians, and others, can shape-shift. I understand how people find it impossible to comprehend how something can instantly swap its body, including heart, lungs, brain and so on, for another. But this is not what is happening because that's all holographic illusion. If people think *physical* with this they will never get it. Shape-shifting is the movement from one illusory holographic projection ('human') to another ('reptilian'). It is all happening as an illusion in the brain because that's where this whole reality is located. Scientists say this 'physical' world is made up of atoms and subatomic particles such as electrons, and this is how author and researcher Michael Talbot describes their properties in the *Holographic Universe*:

'The electron, like some shape-shifter out of folklore, can manifest as either a particle or a wave ... This chameleon-like ability is common to all subatomic particles. It is also common to all things once thought to manifest exclusively as waves. Light, gamma rays, radio waves, X-rays – all can change from waves and back again. Today physicists believe that subatomic phenomena should not be classified solely as either waves or particles, but as a single category of **somethings** that are always somehow both. These **somethings** are called **quanta**, and physicists believe they are the basic stuff from which the entire universe is made.'

Talbot adds that the 'capacity to shape-shift from one kind of particle to another is just another of a quantum's abilities', and he says of 'extraterrestrial' entities: ' ... if we are being visited by beings who are as insubstantial and plastic in form ... it is not at all surprising that they might appear in a chameleon-like multitude of shapes'. We are dealing with a virtual-reality game here and so *anything* is possible. Shape-shifting is small deal once you realise what is happening, but people find it hard to comprehend because they believe the world to have solidity.

I would stress, by the way, that the Reptilians and other Red Dress people are not confined to the major Illuminati families. You find them throughout society at all levels and especially at the extremes and polarities because the Matrix needs polarities to function (*Figure 53, overleaf*). It is the realm of vibration and for something to vibrate (as all does within the Matrix) it has to have two points or polarities between which to oscillate. Everywhere you see the system seeking polarisation. The Red Dresses are programmed to create this and draw slumbering conscious beings into the manufactured conflicts and divisions. Listen to the mainstream software talk-show hosts on American radio or look at many of the software soldiers and John Wayne sound-a-likes during the invasion of Iraq. I heard one soldier say on BBC television: 'We bomb 'em, you know? It's cool to me because I like explosions and stuff like that but, like, I don't get to see the actual explosion, and that's what I want to see but, I guess when we get closer to Baghdad we'll get to see more of that.' Definitely early Microsoft, maybe Windows 95, or perhaps that's optimistic. The uniform doesn't matter and nor does the race or the 'cause' they claim to be fighting for. Whether it is American troops killing civilians in Iraq, Israeli troops murdering Palestinians in Gaza or fanatics bombing restaurants or buses in Jerusalem, they are versions of the same software program. Not all soldiers are like that, some are consciousness caught in the game, but most are clone-like programs and you will find the same throughout the system.

From this perspective we are able to see a deeper reason behind the Illuminati obsession with mind control. I have written about this in detail in other books because it is such a fundamental part of the Illuminati modus operandi. They use millions of children abducted into the mind-control projects or handed over by their sick or mind-controlled parents. The children have their brains rewired and their minds turned into a honeycomb of self-contained compartments known as Alters. What they call the 'front alter' is the one that interacts with the world most of the time, and people who know them think this is them. These alters are implanted

Illustration by Neil Hague

Figure 53: *Pure software programs are not confined to the Illuminati families. You find them at all levels of society and they are often the clone-like gofers that serve the system without question. Self-aware consciousness can also behave the same way when it is deeply caught in the illusion*

with specific tasks, together with trigger words and other codes to activate the programming – everything from an assassination or being sexually abused as a child, or adult, by a famous Illuminati name that they don't remember once the experiencing alter, or compartment, is switched to another. What the Red Dress families behind these projects are doing is seeking to take conscious beings and reduce them to that of software. They want conscious people for this because they have more potential abilities and gifts to be exploited than the most advanced of the software variety. For example, the major Illuminati human sacrifice rituals are often conducted by a conscious being in a mind-controlled state. The top mind-controllers also know that the human body/brain is a holographic computer system and they exploit this understanding to download programs onto their victims' DNA and manipulate the RNA to read them. What we call the trigger words, sounds or images that activate the programming are like pressing 'enter'. Victims of Illuminati mind control have described how they could be drugged or drunk in one compartment, but immediately clean and sober when they were switched to another. This is perfectly explainable when you realise that they were being switched between software.

When I say it's all an illusion and a computer program, I do mean *all*. It is an apparent contradiction that the earth and the cosmos was supposed to have been created by a loving God and yet what we call Nature is a bloody battle-ground in which one animal's survival is dependent on another's, often grotesque, demise. The voice in Brazil told me that there was no contradiction in this because the 'law of the wild' was not the creation of a loving God or Oneness in awareness of itself. It was a Matrix software program and, without the control of fear, the relationship between animals, and animals and humans, would be very different. Did you ever sing that song at school called *All Things Bright and Beautiful*? It tells us how wonderful God is for making the world:

All things bright and beautiful,
All creatures great and small,
All things wise and wonderful,
The Lord God made them all.

Each little flower that opens,
Each little bird that sings,
He made their glowing petals,
He made their tiny wings.

Well, it sounds like a good CV, but let's read the small print here. There is another way of looking at this:

All things shite and horrible,
All killers great and small,
All things pulled apart alive,
The Lord God made them all.

Each great big shark that eats you,
Each little snake that stings,
He made the lethal venom,
He made the torn off wings.

The voice in Brazil asked: 'Do you think the Infinite, where you are now, would wish to see anything suffer and live in fear, never mind create a structure in which this happened as a matter of course?' Nature was another holographic projection that was only 'real' because we were conditioned to believe it was (*Figure 54, overleaf*). The voice said the 'laws' of the natural world reflected the state of being of their creator, the force controlling the Matrix. This was a state of fear and desperation to survive … a trait of the reptilian brain. (Observe human society and you'll see how it is structured in the same way with people surviving or prospering at the expense of others – 'dog eat dog' and all that.) There were, the voice said, some apparently beautiful expressions of nature on 'Planet Earth' and so long as we

Illustration by Neil Hague

Figure 54: *Animals, the Natural World and the 'law of the wild' are all holographic illusions projected through DNA software*

Figures 55 and 56: *Everything in our 'physical' reality is a hologram decoded from waveforms by our brain/DNA/RNA. The 'solid' cats and rose here are holograms.*

(Pictures 'Cats' and 'Rose2' courtesy of Holography Studio, All-Russian Exhibition Center, Moscow. For more see **www.holography.ru***)*

realised they were illusions they could be enjoyed. But we should be careful not to become mesmerised by what we see on earth or we would become like a moth hypnotised by a light, trapped by illusions that held us in a disconnected state. The Matrix can be extremely captivating – just look at a clear night sky, or a panoramic landscape. The message was to enjoy what you see, but remember that what you 'see' is merely what you *think* you see or are *manipulated* to see (*Figure 55 and 56*).

If you observe Nature from this perspective you can see the program very clearly. A few months before I started this book I was watching a series on BBC television called *Massive Nature*. It featured animals and fish that only survived by reproducing in fantastic numbers because of all the predators they faced. If they didn't do this their species would die out and so would others who depended on eating them for their own survival. This is a classic Matrix program with one creature surviving, or prospering, at the expense of another (again, see the 'human' world). Each show in the *Massive Nature* series followed the same basic story in that the 'massive' species would make a journey every year that would take them through the very location where their predators lay in wait.

One involved the Wildebeest, which is dinner for so many species in Africa, including the crocodiles featured in the BBC show. Every year the wildebeest went on a journey for their own survival in search of the grass they needed and it took them across a river where the crocodiles would wait, knowing they were coming. Some call this 'instinct' and I say that what we term 'instinct' is the software program activated through their DNA. When the wildebeest tried to cross the river there was carnage as the crocodiles attacked, and similar scenes are being constantly reproduced by other species of animals, birds and insects across the planet. Ain't Nature great? The program is written to include the circumstances in which the 'massive' species is spawned every year and then has to travel from a safe area to where the predators are waiting to take advantage. The laws of nature, and how animals have incredible abilities or colourings to meet their particular needs or environment, are computer programs, and this is what we call evolution. Sorry, Mr Darwin, evolution is the cycle of the program and survival or extinction depends on the keyboard operator, be it the fear-controlled Matrix or consciousness.

Another documentary I saw told the story of Grey Whales which, once again, spent part of the year in warm waters where they were safe, but had little food, and then headed north where there was food, but they weren't safe. Or at least the calves weren't. The programme showed how Killer Whales pursued a Grey Whale calf for six hours as its mother, who was too big and powerful to be attacked, tried to provide protection. The killers sought to separate calf from mother and hold it under the water to drown. The mother fought desperately to save her offspring and help it to breathe but, in the end, exhaustion took over and the Killer Whales lived up to their name. Even after all those hours of pursuit and all that fear and trauma, they only ate the calf's tongue and lower jaw and the rest was left to the scavengers on the ocean floor. It was just another bloody crime-scene in the wonderful world of Nature. What kind of 'intelligence' creates a natural world in which the survival of one depends on tearing another to pieces? What sick mind would design a global life-cycle in which the participants were in a mode of constant fear – humans as well as the animals? Would a loving God do that? No, but the mind behind the Matrix would, and it has.

Funnily enough, a few weeks after I saw the wildebeest documentary I was watching another about the Battle of the Boyne in Ireland, when the Illuminati frontman William of Orange (Protestant) was fighting for the British throne against James II (Catholic) in 1690. It led to the Protestant–Catholic conflicts in Ireland right up to modern times (this point in the program, in other words). At one stage in the computer-generated reconstruction of the battle, William's fodder troops began to pour across a shallow part of the River Boyne while army of James pounded them with a hail of gunfire from the other side. What I was watching was a mirror of the wildebeest trying to cross the river under attack from the crocodiles. How appropriate because both are part of the same computer program – the Matrix. What is the difference between a lion or croc devouring a wildebeest, tearing its flesh from its body, and a child being blown to pieces by a British or American bomb during the invasion of Iraq? They are products of the same mentality behind the program.

All bodies are DNA software and it is the same with animals. Some will have a form of consciousness and others will not. Most animal species operate on a much more collective level of reality – more of a hive mind – and the Illuminati are seeking, through the reptilian brain, to take humanity further down this same road. As we can see, they have succeeded on an enormous scale. The more consciousness inhabits the software of the animal species the more it rewrites the DNA. Also, the more the animal software comes into contact with human self-aware consciousness, the more the same will happen because of the vibrational communication between them. A domesticated animal will have its instincts (DNA programming) rewritten by contact with self-aware consciousness, and the communication that takes place between the animal and human DNA via the codes common to both. A domesticated dog and a wild dog may look basically the same, but their behaviour traits and attitudes can be very different because domestication has changed the DNA program. Whales and dolphins would also appear to be examples of species that express consciousness at a far higher level than most others. Trees, flowers, plants and landscapes are software, too. I know this is highly controversial, but so what? No one has to believe it. I have always loved the Natural World – animals, forests, seascapes and rolling countryside. I still enjoy these scenes, even from my emerging perspective, but I see them in a different light. Instead of looking at something that is 'real', I see them as like beautiful holographic paintings that can be enjoyed, but not allowed to delude my reality of what they are.

It's *all* an illusion, even breathing and eating. We only have to do this because our DNA tells us that we do and we believe it. Remember that scene in the first *Matrix* movie when the Neo and Morpheus characters are fighting in a kung fu software program? Morpheus says to a heavy-breathing Neo: 'Do you think that's air you're breathing now, in this place?' Of course it couldn't have been because his mind was in the kung fu program, not his body. But he still breathed because his mind was programmed to do so. Does pure energy, pure consciousness, have to breathe with lungs? So why do *we* when we are pure consciousness, too? Only because we *believe* we do and let us not forget that the world in which we 'need to breathe' is all happening in our brain. There is no 'out there' where the laws of breathing apply. It is the same with eating. Does energy, consciousness, sit down to lunch or order a pizza? No, the DNA programming does that. The need for food, warmth and shelter is written into the Matrix program because it controls through dependency and the need to survive. If you didn't need food, warmth or shelter to survive look at how the control of the system would dissolve from your life. I am not saying we can just stop breathing and eating at the point when we intellectually see the nonsense of it. If we don't override the DNA programming our body will 'die' because its software says, 'If I don't eat or breathe I will die'. It has to be done at the deepest of levels so that this part of the program – I have to eat and breathe – is deleted. It is for this reason that I am not about to hold my breath or cancel the dinner reservation. But it *is* all illusion. Even what the food tastes like is a program. It is the Matrix that decides how an egg or banana tastes because what we call taste is just an electrical signal from the tongue to the brain (DNA central processing unit) which interprets the 'taste' in line with the programming. Different programs decode these signals in different ways – 'I love eggs', 'bananas are yuck'. As the voice in Brazil said:

> 'Do you think the Infinite sits down to dinner? Do you think the Infinite has to breathe or it will die? So why do those in the Time Loop? Answer: because they identify who they are and their sense of possibility with being a physical "personality" subordinate to illusory "laws" and not with being what they really are – the Infinite One.'

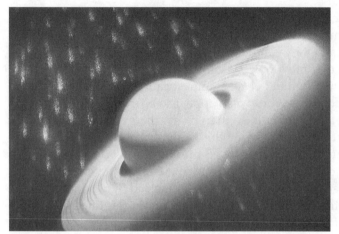

Figure 57: *The universe is a holographic illusion similar to looking up at the 'sky' projected on the ceiling of a planetarium. When you look at the illusory night sky in a planetarium it can look incredibly 'real'. But what is it? A computer program! 'Planet Saturn' here is a hologram*

(Picture 'Saturn' courtesy of Royal Holographic Art Gallery. For more see **www.holograms.bc.ca***)*

There have been people who have stopped eating without ill effects, as I explain in *Tales from the Time Loop*, because they are able to absorb nourishment directly from light/energy without going through the 'middle men' of plants and animals. The need to eat is, literally, all in the head, as is the 'warmth' of the sun on which life appears so dependent. 'Do you think the Infinite needs the sun to survive?' the voice asked. '*You* are the Infinite so why do you need the sun to sustain you?' Certainly no sun was required in that state of bliss and wonder that I experienced in the ayahuasca session. The voice said that we felt heat from the sun simply because that is what the Matrix programmed the body to feel. The sun and moon were holograms to provide the illusion of night and day – the movement of 'time'. As Genesis puts it: 'And God said, Let there be light: and there was light. And God saw the light, that it was good: and God divided the light from the darkness. And God called the light Day, and the darkness he called Night'. Or, put another way: 'And God said, Let there be light: and he tapped on the keyboard, pressed 'enter', and there was light'.

I was told that what we call the Universe is a holographic illusion similar to looking up at the 'sky' projected on the ceiling of a planetarium (*Figure 57*). The only difference was that in the 'universe' the projections appeared to be 3D because they were holograms. When you look at the illusory night sky in a planetarium it can look incredibly 'real'. But what is it? A *computer program!* The 'universe' was a figment of our conditioned imagination, the voice said, and it was only part of our reality because we believed it was. The universe was also far smaller than people perceived even within our illusion of space and distance. 'Look at the sky in a planetarium and it seems so vast, yet it only goes as high as the ceiling.' At one point in the Brazilian experience, the voice said: 'Do you think that's the earth you're lying on now? Mmmm … *Illuuusion*!' As with everything in the Time Loop and throughout the Matrix, the 'physical' earth was a holographic projection. 'You are lying on the earth now only because you think you are', the voice said. I believed I was lying on the earth because that is what my DNA program was telling me and the earth I was 'lying on' only existed in my head! And even my head was another illusion. 'Remember always', said the voice, 'Infinite Love is the only truth, everything else is illusion – *everything*.'

This includes 'space' as well as 'time'. Scientists talk about the space/time continuum, but space and time do not exist. When a hologram is projected by a laser from the photographic interference pattern it appears to be 3D and occupying 'space'. But it isn't, it just seems that way. Everything is Infinite Consciousness, so everything is everything else. Therefore, a pinhead is infinity because *everything* is infinity. Size is an illusion, as men have been saying all along. Where does the droplet of water end and the ocean begin? They don't; they are *One*. Infinity has no beginning and no end. The droplet ('pinhead') *is* the ocean.

Scientists can't understand why subatomic particles can communicate instantly with each other over staggering distances because they are thinking in terms of space. But there is no space involved. It is like the droplet of water and the ocean. There are no particles, *plural*, except in the way we perceive them in the illusion. All particles are the same *One*. They don't have to communicate between each other because there is no 'each other' and they don't move from one place to another because there is no space and so there can be no places. Appropriately the word 'Utopia' means 'no place' – beyond the illusion of time and space. The super-hologram appears to occupy space and we talk of the vastness of space. But it's a hologram and so that cannot be. If there is no space how come we seem to travel through it? Once again because that is the illusion our DNA/RNA decodes for us and we travel through space only as electrical signals interpreted by the brain. The voice in Brazil said: 'Why do you need to fly around in aircraft? You are point A and you are point B and you are everything in between. Why then do you need to use an aircraft to fly through yourself?' William Blake described this magnificently when he wrote:

> To see a World in a Grain of Sand
> And a Heaven in a Wild Flower
> Hold Infinity in the palm of your hand
> And Eternity in an hour.

This can also be related to the hologram because a grain of sand and a wild flower are smaller versions of the whole. In the same way, the inside of an atom is similar to a solar system, and the human body, itself made up of cells, is like a cell of the super-hologram.

There is another important point to make about this Matrix software/illusion thing. What is 'history'? OK, we might say that it is the earlier scenes in the movie leading up to where we are. Yes, it could be, but there are other ways to look at it. We think we know what history is because of archaeological finds and accounts 'passed down' through the 'ages' or other parts of the program, as I would put it. But have they been? I am not saying they have or haven't, I'm just exploring other possibilities in the light of a greater understanding of the illusion we are experiencing as 'life'. What if each part of the program has its own version of

Figure 58: *This is a hologram of Egyptian artefacts. What if archaeological finds, relics, monoliths and other 'historical evidence' are merely written into the program at this point? DNA is constantly receiving information from the Matrix, so 'history' at any stage is only what the Matrix chooses to communicate to the DNA. Did 'yesterday' really exist as you thought it did or is it just a signal your DNA is receiving now?*

*(Picture 'Usheptis' courtesy of 3-D Hologrammen, Amsterdam. For more see **www.3-Dhologrammen.com**)*

history or that history is being changed at will by the Matrix simply by changing the program it broadcasts to the DNA? A few taps on the keyboard, a click of the mouse and, hey, we've just made an incredible discovery that tells us more about our history! When the Matrix or consciousness changes the program at any point, it could, and probably does, reassemble the entire DVD movie/Time Loop in what we call the 'past' or 'future'. You see the theme in some movies of people going back in 'time' to change the sequence of events that led to some problem in their 'present'. As I add in sentences amid the already written text on this computer, what goes before and after reassembles itself to accommodate the new information. Why can't this be happening with 'history'? When consciousness or the Matrix changes another part of the program (the 'past'), the scenes that follow ('the future') reassemble themselves in a new way. It is like dominoes falling when the first one is pushed. In other words, our 'history' is constantly being rewritten. But let's go further. Say there was no Stone Age and that all the

archaeological 'finds', relics, monoliths and 'evidence' is merely written into the program at this point (*Figure 58*). The DNA is constantly receiving information from the Matrix, so 'history' at any stage is only what the Matrix chooses to communicate to the DNA and the RNA decides to read. Did 'yesterday' really exist as you thought it did or is it just a signal your DNA is receiving now? But I have 'memory', you might say. 'I remember yesterday.' Maybe that's true, but here's a question. How can you have a memory when there is no time? Memory is a recollection from the past, but there is no past, only *Now*. What we think we see at any point are only electrical signals decoded by the brain. The signals + *interpretation* of the signals = reality.

One other point is worth introducing here. I have mostly been talking about the Time Loop and the Matrix in singular form because I am trying to keep it simple. But there are infinite versions of it in the sense that we interpret the Matrix according to our belief and perception. While we may decode the signals to 'see' the

Neil Hague Colour Gallery

The creation of the Matrix: first came imagination into 'form' and with that came the illusion of separation.
As a Hindu myth says, human consciousness began as a ripple that decided to leave the ocean of consciousness
– the timeless, spaceless and eternal. When it awakened to itself in this 'disconnected' state, it forgot that it was
part of the infinite ocean and felt isolated and separated

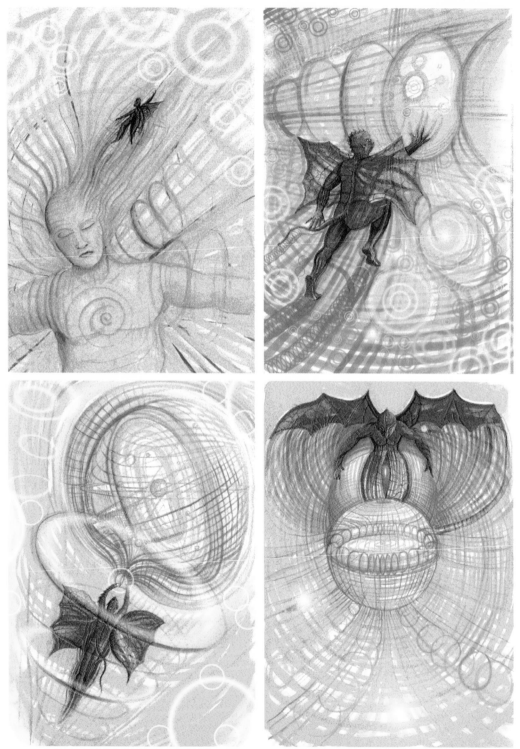

... Separation led to the manifestation of fear (the winged entity) that took on a life of its own; consciousness was caught in an illusion it believed to be 'real'. Self-aware fear became the Frankenstein that controlled its creator by manipulating reality through the illusion of form, 'time', and a sense of separation

One aspect of the Matrix control is through Reptilian and other software entities vibrating outside the frequency of 'visible light'. They 'possess' the Illuminati bloodlines – and others – and dictate their actions in 'our' world

The 'Red Dress' bloodlines of the Illuminati that dominate royalty, politics, banking, business and media. They obsessively interbreed to stop the software program being rewritten by the infusion of consciousness

The two-faced (and then some) Illuminati manipulating human society under the control of the Matrix program

BLUE DEGREES

The Illuminati use their human software clones to run their system of control. This includes using techniques like Problem-Reaction-Solution and Hidden Hand manipulation to advance their agenda for an Orwellian global dictatorship

The three types of 'human': on the left is the pure software program, the horse with no rider, which includes the 'pure' Illuminati bloodlines; the centre image represents the majority of 'humans' who are self-aware consciousness, but trapped in the illusion and dominated by the program; and on the right is symbolised the much smaller – but rapidly growing – number of people who are connected in awareness to consciousness beyond the Matrix. For this reason they perceive life and the world very differently to the rest and can be seen as 'crazy' or 'dangerous'

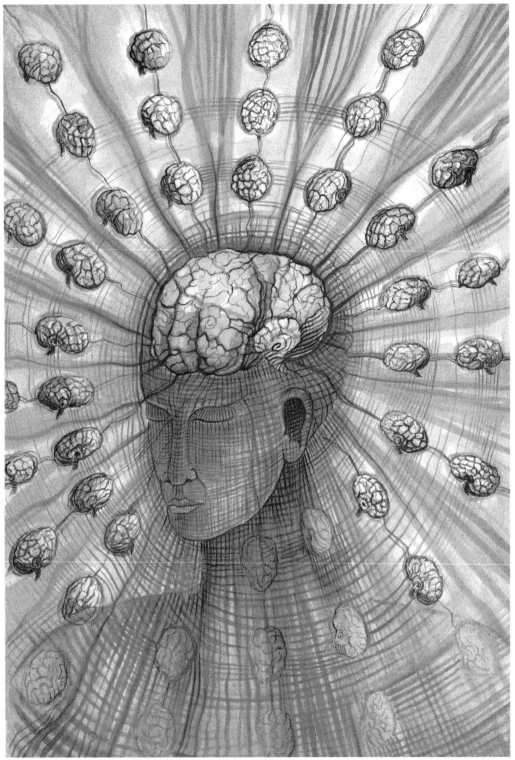

The Matrix central computer or 'brain' communicates a collective reality to computer terminals/brains throughout the super-hologram. We decode these signals into an illusory 3-D reality

The eyes only tranform the tiny frequency range known as 'visible light' into electrical signals that are decoded by the brain/DNA network into a holographic '3D' reality. The 'physical world' we think is 'around us' only exists in our heads!

Everything in our 'physical' reality is a hologram decoded from waveforms by the brain/DNA/RNA. Animals, the Natural World and the 'law of the wild' are all holographic illusions – the Matrix program

The 95 per cent of 'junk' DNA, 95 per cent of brain activity not involved with the waking state, and at least much of the enormous brain capacity that science says we don't use, are actually connecting us with the energy/matter in the universe that we can't see – and also to realms beyond that. (Or at least they should be)

Human religions are all aspects of the same Matrix God Program (see chapter six)

The New Age Matrix: consciousness caught in the illusion of evolving through reincarnated experience is playing a sort of snakes and ladders game. It believes it is progressing 'up the dimensions', but the Matrix is designed to make sure it doesn't escape (see chapter seven)

When we open ourselves to the Infinite Consciousness that we are, we begin to see through the illusion and the Matrix loses its control of our sense of reality. Those still caught in the illusion once again see such people as mad, dangerous or extreme (see chapter ten)

As the energy of Oneness pervades the Matrix, the fear vibration dissolves and the reality of its captive consciousness is transformed into Infinite unity (see chapter ten)

Transformation from division to Oneness is open to everyone. There are no 'chosen people', only Infinite Love (see chapter ten)

illusion of the same landscape or street scene, we can perceive the detail very differently, particularly if consciousness is seriously involved in the process. Each interpretation creates a different illusory 'universe'. They may look like the same one with planets and stars, roads and cars, but they are not the same. My universe, for example, is, to put it mildly, not the one perceived in the head of George W. Bush. Each of these interpretations creates what scientists call a parallel universe, so imagine how many there must be. They are actually parallel imaginations, parallel perceptions or realities, held together by the Matrix 'brain'. There are also other Matrix programs that would be perceived as parallel universes and other dimensions of reality. As astrophysicist and writer, Giuliana Conforto, said in *Organic Universe*:

'We are not only "inside" one visible matrix, but also in more than one, maybe in all of them. We might participate in other movies, too, each with its own event horizon or peculiar frequencies. Matrices are like TV channels.'

A 2002 edition of the BBC science series, *Horizon*, was devoted to the gathering acceptance of parallel universes. The opening narrative to the programme said:

'For almost a hundred years science has been haunted by a dark secret, that there might be mysterious, hidden worlds beyond our human senses. Mystics have long claimed there were such places. They were, they said, full of ghosts and spirits – but ever since the 19th century physicists have been trying to make sense of an uncomfortable discovery. When they tried to pinpoint the exact location of atomic particles like electrons, they found it was utterly impossible. They had no single location. The only explanation that anyone could come up with is that the particles don't just exist in our universe. They slip into existence in other universes, too, and there are an infinite number of these parallel universes, all of them slightly different. In effect, there's a parallel universe in which Napoleon won the Battle of Waterloo; in another the British Empire held on to its American colonies; in one you were never born. They are even stranger than Elvis being alive.'

What the narrative is describing are other holographic illusory realities within the super-hologram I call the Matrix. Thought creates; emotion creates; the Matrix creates; consciousness creates; and this all is happening within Infinite Consciousness, the Infinite One. No wonder scientists are bemused and dumbfounded when they try to understand the nature of reality. Infinite Possibility does not 'do' rules that you can pin down or record on a data sheet, and they had better get used to it or spend the rest of their lives seeking something that isn't there.

So what *is* real any more? What *is* truth? *Nothing* is real except Infinite Love. That is the only truth – everything else is illusion.

CHAPTER FIVE

Physician, Heal Thy Computer Virus

On an occasion of this kind it becomes more than a moral duty to speak one's mind.
It becomes a pleasure
Oscar Wilde

The human body and its health, or otherwise, can be seen from a massively different perspective when you realise that reality is illusory and what appears to be solid is a hologram that only gives the *appearance* of 3D. 'Empty' atoms do not a solid wall make and it's the same with the 'body'. It is a frequency field decoded into a hologram by other frequency fields called DNA and RNA.

This explains so many apparent mysteries, not least in the realm of so-called alternative or complimentary healing. How can reflexology and acupuncture find points throughout the body that relate to all the organs and other functions? How can you massage, or insert a needle at a point on the foot, hand or ear and affect the liver, stomach or heart? It seems crazy if you accept the official explanations of the human form, but it makes perfect sense when you know the body is a hologram. Remember that one of the amazing properties of holograms is that every part is a smaller version of the whole. Far from being a mystery that the whole body can be found in the foot, hand or ear, it is the way it *must* be if the body is a hologram. An entire body can be grown from a single cell because every cell is a smaller version of the whole and contains all the information contained in the whole.

On another level, the body is like a smaller (to our reality) version of the earth, the solar system and universe. They, too, are computer programs, operating with or without consciousness, and smaller expressions of the super-hologram that I call the Matrix. So the human brain must be a version of the Matrix 'brain', or central processing unit. Palm reading is based on this same principle because the hand is a smaller version of the body, but it goes further. Every *part* of the hand, foot and ear also contains the whole and so does every part of the finger and every part of every part of the finger down to every cell, atom and electron. And all these are holographic projections from a frequency field or interference pattern. This means that we affect the super-hologram with everything we believe, think or do in the same way that a reflexologist can affect the whole body through its 'parts'. This is how love can influence the reality of the Matrix and replace the dominance of fear.

In the summer of 2004, I experienced these principles myself when I went to speak in Hawaii. Well, someone's got to do it, eh? For several weeks before the trip my health had been poor. I had severe pain in my spine, especially my neck, and within days of arriving it was excruciating. Anything I did was agony. Even lying down or driving over a little bump in the road made me feel like screaming. Fortunately, I went out to Hawaii three weeks before the talk and it gave me time to seek help. Funnily enough, I had been saying for many months that I felt I would have some significant healing in Hawaii and that's how, thank goodness, it turned out. I was staying on the island of Maui when I woke up one morning with this overwhelming feeling that I had to go to Big Island, a short flight away. A few minutes later, Pam came in from checking e-mails to say that some friends had invited us to use their house on Big Island while we were in Hawaii. It was the first of many synchronicities that led me to be healed.

The day after we arrived at the house my neck and spine worsened rapidly and I went to see a chiropractor, desperately seeking relief. He was a guy who was far more enlightened than conventional chiropractors and manipulating the spine was only part of his philosophy. Within a few minutes of our first meeting he also suggested that I have a colon cleanse in which a pipe is stuck up your bum to literally wash out the crap. He said it was a pity because a colon cleanse programme had started a few miles away and I had just missed it. In fact, when we rang the people involved, there had been two cancellations, allowing Pam and I to take part a day behind all the others. With both the colon cleanse and the chiropractor, the key to my healing was the holographic nature of the body.

Most colon cleanses are like wham-bam-thank-you-ma'am, or man. Whack it in, turn it on, whoosh, slosh, yuck, thanks for calling. The best ones do it gently over several days, in my case eleven, and clean away the accumulated debris from ever further inside the colon. I am no expert on what came out to play, but I can say with certainty that it was better out than in. I'll spare you the details, much as I know how interested you must be. One common problem to mention, though, is a sort of mucus that lines the sides of the colon and stops the body absorbing the goodness in the food. You can eat all the good food you like in that state, but the body sees very little of it in nutrients. On the wall beside me, as the peaceful waters flowed, was a chart with the colon laid out in sections, each relating to different organs and parts of the body – the hologram (*Figure 59, overleaf*). With every daily session of around two hours, the water goes deeper to clean out more and more of these sections. My general health began to improve in the first few days and my neck and spine improved dramatically when the cleanse reached the area that related to this part of the body. By the end of the eleven days my health had not been better for years and my neck and spine were virtually pain free. At the same time I was seeing the chiropractor. He couldn't touch me to start with, such was the pain, and he said it was one of the worst cases he'd seen. But as the colon cleanse did its work he was able to make his contribution to freeing the neck and spine. In his treatment room was another chart, this time with the spine marked out in sections, each relating to an organ or part of the body (*Figure 60, overleaf*). Wherever you look you see the hologram, including the eyes (*Figure 61, overleaf*).

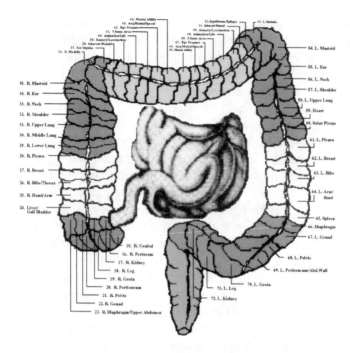

The chiropractor told me before one manipulation that I might find the spinal movement emotional because the part of the spine involved was connected to emotion. Sure enough when he clicked that vertebra I began to cry, although I had no idea what emotion had triggered it. The colon cleanse was also a very emotional – even spiritual – experience. In the body hologram everything connects to everything else because everything *is* everything else. We feel fear and nervous emotion in the colon area and some people call it 'having the shits' or being 'shit scared'. This is most appropriate because as the water cleans out the stored physical shit that has not been processed, so it unlocks the *emotional* shit that has not processed. The physical always reflects the mental and emotional because they are expressions of the same DNA communication network – the same hologram. There is a point in the cleanse where they focus on the section of the colon that represents the liver, and this also coincides with another process that directly cleanses the liver itself with a concoction you drink the night before. This can be very intense physically and emotionally because the liver processes toxins and is known as the seat of anger. While

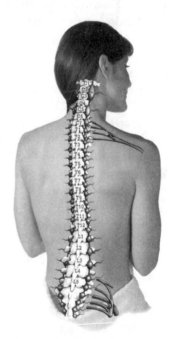

Figure 60: *The spine, too, represents the whole body. For example, T7 in the centre affects the pancreas, duodenum, stomach, liver, spleen, gallbladder and peritoneum*

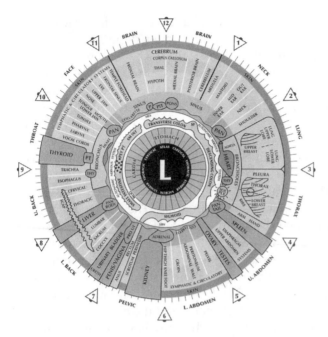

Figure 61: *Every part of the eye at this level of the illusion represents a part of the body - this is a chart of the left eye.*

(Chart courtesy of the copyright owner, Bernard Jensen International of California. To purchase this and other charts see **www.bernardjensen.org** *Further details at the back of the book)*

everything reflects everything else, the different organs specialise in certain things. For example, the whole body is a DNA computer system receiving and transmitting information, but the brain is the central processing unit that specialises in communication traffic. The liver is the toxin-removal specialist and that includes an emotional toxin – anger.

The gall bladder, which is part of the liver, produces fluid called bile and when we are describing someone venting anger we talk of them being full of bile. Our everyday phrases describe many literal and symbolic truths without us realising. The liver dumps its toxins into the colon to be discharged, but when the colon is blocked, or if the body is massively toxic, there is more poison than can be processed. The liver deals with this by producing little 'stones' made from hardened bile or minerals to block blood vessels and stop the toxins re-entering the bloodstream. As the flow of blood is suppressed, the body protects the torso first, and the extremities become starved of optimum blood supply with many potential consequences. Once the colon has been cleaned out, the liver is confident enough to dump more of its stored toxins into the exit system, and sometimes thousands of these little stones, together with the toxins, are washed from the body. That certainly happened to Pam and me. The difference in health is amazing, not least in the glow of the skin as its blood supply increases. My friends couldn't believe how much better I was looking.

Pam had suffered for some years from a skin disorder called Rosacea, which conventional 'medicine' says is incurable and can only be kept in check by constant antibiotics. But her condition disappeared in days with the colon cleanse because it is caused by toxins in the liver. If the build-up of toxins is not dealt with, especially if you have a very toxic lifestyle, the liver eventually becomes overwhelmed and the body dies from liver failure. Anger is an emotional toxin that creates physical toxin because they are one and the same. When I had my liver cleanse and the stones and toxins poured out, so did my pent-up anger. For 48 hours I was in a barely-suppressed rage of the chair-throwing variety. If you have a serious liver cleanse lock away the crockery. I stress again that emotion, be it anger, depression, whatever, is not a function of what I am calling consciousness beyond the hologram. Emotions are programmed reactions transmitted through DNA. Love and emotion is not the same thing, nor is emotion and empathy, and I will expand on this later. Many pharmaceutical drugs/toxins have been linked with depression, but how can drugs and poisons directly affect consciousness? They can't. What they do is affect the DNA's decoding system and, through that, produce the feeling of depression and other psychological consequences in the emotion program. It is like a computer malfunction.

During the colon cleanse, and on many other occasions, I have met healers who believe that different parts of the body have their own brain. They say the digestive system has a brain, as does the immune system, liver and other organs. This must be the case because the body is a hologram and this is why these organs and systems have the ability to communicate and react to events and changes in the most extraordinary way. The hologram ensures that there will indeed be a smaller version of the brain in every part of the body. The DNA/RNA communicates and receives information to and from every part of the body and the brain acts as coordinator. When the colon is blocked and the liver has nowhere to send its toxins this information is communicated through the body's 'Internet' system and the computer takes the appropriate action. We see this as liver stones. In this case it is akin to a computerised canal system in which the sluice gates are closed in reaction to changing circumstances.

The process of healing wounds, stopping blood loss and all the billions of other ways the body reacts, is the DNA/RNA communicating information in accordance with the program. One other point to remember is that the body/hologram is two-thirds water. This is essential to every function of the body, including maintenance of temperature, and, as Masaru Emoto's work has established, water stores information. It is also a superb medium through which to transmit the electrical and other frequency signals passing around the DNA. The body in this sense is like a battery and when the water levels fall because we don't drink enough it has a similar effect to a car battery with too little distilled water – it doesn't work as well. Among the many signs and symptoms of too little water in the body are headaches, poor concentration and tiredness. All are the result of the DNA communications falling below optimum. But let us not forget that even this is only happening in our heads and, on a higher level of awareness, that's illusion also.

In a healthy body the DNA is communicating accurately between different parts of the computer through the RNA, and what is termed disease, or *dis-ease*, is when the system malfunctions. There are endless causes for this, but all have the same theme: they affect the accuracy of the information passing through the DNA/RNA. People who live near power lines or work with electromagnetic technology are more prone to certain ailments and cancers. In Britain, they are installing a stream of so-called Tetra masts as part of the communication network for the emergency services. The masts emit pulses in the frequency range of human brain waves. I have been told that the technology was introduced through the US National Security Agency, a 100 per cent Illuminati-controlled operation. This makes sense because the Tetra masts are quite rightly being connected with increases in cancers and other physical, mental and emotional disorders – including depression – where they are located.

The reason for these effects is that electromagnetic, microwave and other frequencies disrupt the input/output system of DNA/RNA, and the computer gives and receives inaccurate information. It's like talking on a mobile phone when the connection is bad. You only catch certain words and you can't understand what the other person is trying to say. In the human body these disrupted communications act like a computer virus and this is what cancer is. Cells are constantly reproducing and all is well while they are copied accurately. For this to happen, the DNA/RNA communication to the cell needs to be accurate. Once an electromagnetic field or other source disrupts the quality of the information, the cell begins to reproduce flawed copies, often at inappropriate speeds and we call this cancer. It can spread like a computer virus affecting ever greater areas of the program until the computer can no longer function. I had a virus in a computer that began with a slight disruption and gathered pace until you could not even switch the thing on. And what do we say in those circumstances? The computer is dead. So it is with the body.

The potential for the malfunction we call illness is immense in the 'modern' world because of the way society is structured. We are told that stress is a great killer. Yes it is – but why? When emotions get out of balance they begin to affect the communication network. One of the first places to be troubled is the intestinal area with 'butterflies in the stomach', fear, nausea and 'the shits'. This is okay so long as it is within reason and not a constant burden to the system. But when the stress reaches seriously high levels, and especially if it's ongoing, a much wider area of the system begins to malfunction. We see skin rashes, stomach ulcers, cancer and that major expression of stress – heart disease.

There is also another aspect to emotional disease that I experienced in Hawaii. In the chiropractor's waiting room was a book by Dr John E. Sarno, Professor of Clinical Rehabilitation Medicine at the New York University School of Medicine and attending physician at the Howard A. Rusk Institute of Rehabilitation Medicine at New York University Medical Center. It was called *Healing Back Pain: The Mind-Body Connection* (Warner Books, 1991), and detailed his more than 20 years of research linking pain to the mind/brain. For sure, it is the brain that manifests pain by decoding the messages sent from the apparent source of discomfort. When you bang your toe you don't actually feel the pain until the brain has processed the message and decided it hurts. One way that severe pain is treated is by stopping the messages from, say an arthritic knee, from being communicated to the brain. Without the message there can be no pain. If you can use your consciousness to change the belief system of the brain you can walk through fire without being burned. Many people do firewalking across red hot coals without feeling any heat, let alone discomfort. They are walking through the fire only in their heads and whether it hurts or not is decided by the way their brain interprets reality. There are those, like some Yogis and Tibetan monks, who can slow their heart rate to almost nil, sit naked in freezing weather and consciously generate such internal heat that they can dry wet towels laid on their backs. They are using their consciousness to override the program and wrest control of their reality from the Matrix.

Dr John E. Sarno identified the connection between mind and body and how mental and emotional states can lead to physical consequences. Sarno's findings, backed up by two decades of successfully treating 'untreatable' cases, suggest that the major cause of pain in the back, neck, shoulders, bum and limbs is repressed emotion. The chiropractor told me how he had suffered from severe back pain that nothing would alleviate until he read Sarno's book. He followed the advice to identify the emotions that were being suppressed and he realised he had been in fear of something without even knowing. Once he made the connection the back pain disappeared. This is how Sarno has successfully treated many thousands of patients without surgery or drugs even though conventional medicine said they were incurable.

The act of observation and identification of the emotional cause unlocks the information stored in the hologram (hard drive) and allows it to be deleted. When the data recording the emotional response is removed, its 'physical' expression disappears just as quickly. The chiropractor's wife had been suffering from serious neck pain and he could do nothing to help her until they connected the problem to the death of her cat some weeks earlier. She'd had the cat since it was born and the loss caused severe emotional trauma, even more than she realised. When the link had been acknowledged her extreme neck pain was gone. It's funny how we say of people who cause us emotional upset or frustration: 'They are a pain in the neck'. I also saw the connection between my own neck and spine problems and serious emotional challenges I had been experiencing for weeks before. Again this is the interaction of the mind and emotional programs of the DNA and how they disrupt the balance and accuracy of the communications.

You can experience this interaction just by thinking of something sad, depressing or frightening. It doesn't have to be happening because your thoughts alone are enough to trigger the emotional response. Scientists have established that the same parts of the brain 'light up' whether a person is actually having an experience or just thinking about it. The Illuminati are constantly manipulating this system by delivering information to the collective mind designed to trigger the desired collective emotional reaction. Healer Mike Lambert also points out that the areas of the body that Dr. Sarno treats most effectively are directly connected in acupuncture to the gall bladder (a source of depression when imbalanced) and the liver (a source of anger when imbalanced). The interconnection between body and emotion through the DNA means that emotions can affect the body and the body can affect emotions. Toxins in the cells can cause depression and anger while this – and all emotion – stimulates the release of chemicals that are absorbed by the cells. Talk about a vicious cycle. But it can be broken by consciousness.

Interestingly, the study of the body's meridian system at the Necker Hospital in Paris using the radioactive tracers revealed that energy passed more slowly through the meridian of a diseased organ than it did through a healthy one. Mike Lambert also told me of experiments that showed how e-*motion*-al states caused the flow of information – *motion* – around the body to slow down. As this vibrant movement of information is curtailed, the body computer malfunctions and so e*motion*al stress causes illness. Heart attacks in particular are caused by static energy and this is how those with severe grief are said to have 'died of a broken heart' soon after they lose a loved one. The slower the energy moves the slower the vibrational state of the body and we get pulled further into density. When we are in a depressed or emotionally stressed state we actually talk about 'feeling heavy'. Rigid opinions and suppression of free thought and action also stem the flow and cause the hologram to vibrate slower. Valerie Hunt, Professor of Kinesiology at the University of California in Los Angeles, has developed the use of technology to measure the human energy field and this has confirmed that a person's state of being effects their vibrational speed or frequency. Those focused only on five-sense reality (mind and emotions) have energy fields that vibrate at a lower frequency than those who use their higher senses (consciousness). As humans became dominated by fear, so they fell further into density (the 'Fall of Man'??).

Chemicals in food and drink also emit frequencies that disrupt the information flow and the appalling 'food' produced by the Illuminati corporations is destroying human health. Everything in the Matrix is a frequency carrying a harmonious or disruptive resonance. With chemical food it's the latter and this can quickly undermine the input/output signals of the DNA/RNA. Morgan Spurlock's movie, *Super Size Me* (see **supersizeme.com**), revealed the devastating effects on the body of eating fast food. The New Yorker ate three meals at McDonalds every day for a month and his health was monitored by doctors. The outcome was devastating. Within days he went from being a fit, healthy 33-year-old, to vomiting, suffering headaches and depression, and losing his sex drive. His liver became overwhelmed by saturated fats and Dr Daryl Isaacs described Spurlock's liver test as shocking. 'It became very, very abnormal', he said. Spurlock put on a lot of weight in just one month and he said he became desperately ill. 'My face was splotchy and I had this huge gut, which I've never had in my life', he said. 'It was amazing – and really frightening.' Goodness knows what the health effects are going to be on today's fast-food chomping, cola-swigging, chemical-riddled generation. You might note, too, that Spurlock said that he became depressed while on his fast food diet. This was the chemicals affecting the DNA communications we call emotion.

The computer I am working on now is protected by software called Norton AntiVirus. It seeks out disruptive codes and information that would normally spread like cancer through the computer until it eventually 'died'. The body has its version of Norton, too. It is called the Immune System. This is the software that seeks out the body's version of the computer virus and removes it before it gets out of control. But, as with the liver, the immune system can become so deluged that it can't cope, and it also faces attacks that undermine its own strength and efficiency.

When this happens disease runs rampant, as we see with the immune destroyer known as Acquired Immune Deficiency Syndrome, or AIDS. People don't die from AIDS; they die from diseases that their shot immune systems can't deal with. Ironically, vaccinations are supposed to boost the immune system when, in truth, they undermine it. All the crap they put into vaccines is another attack that the immune defence has to cope with and this *reduces* its ability to meet other challenges effectively by making the DNA/RNA misfire.

Even the process of making the vaccine includes using monkeys, chick embryos and surgically aborted human foetuses, along with disinfectants and stabilizers that include streptomycin, sodium chloride, sodium hydroxide, aluminium, hydrochloride, sorbitol, hydrolyzed gelatin, formaldehyde and a mercury derivative called thimerosal. The Diphtheria, Pertussis (whooping cough) and Tetanus vaccine contains the following:

Sodium Hydroxide: among other things, this can burn internal organs, cause blindness, lung and tissue damage, and be fatal if swallowed. It is found in oven, bathroom and toilet cleaners.

Formaldehyde: a neurotoxin known to cause cancer. It may also cause insomnia, coughing, headaches, nausea, nosebleeds and skin rashes. It is, appropriately, used to embalm corpses.

Hydrochloric acid: this can destroy tissue on direct contact and is found in aluminium cleaners and rust removers.

Aluminium: toxic cancer causer.

Thimerosal: a mercury derivative and extremely dangerous preservative. It is made from a combination of ethylene glycol (antifreeze) and ethanol, thiosalicylic acid, sodium hydroxide and ethyl mercuric chloride. These chemicals are deadly and can cause cancer together with brain and liver damage.

Phosphates: these suffocate all forms of aquatic life and are found in laundry and dishwasher detergent and cleaners.

(For more details see **www.vaccinationnews.com/dailynews/may2001/ whatsinvax.htm**)

This poisonous trash is attacking the very immune system it is supposed to be supporting and yet in fascist-controlled America parents are being taken to court for not allowing such potential killers to be given to their children. The public is frightened into accepting this tyranny by being told of the potential effects on their children of coming into contact with non-immunised kids. But if they've been vaccinated, there shouldn't be a problem should there? It's the same with the drugs peddled by the Illuminati pharmaceutical cartel. The reason they 'treat' one problem and cause another is because the drugs disrupt the information passing through the DNA/RNA. You had this problem and now we've treated you and we've given you a few more. But never mind, we have drugs for them, too.

One of the biggest killers and causes of illness is pharmaceutical drugs. Dr Bruce H. Pomeranz, principal investigator and a neuroscience professor at the University of Toronto, headed one study that revealed how more than 100,000 Americans are killed by pharmaceutical drugs every year and some 2.1 *million* are seriously harmed. Other studies put the number much higher. The figures did not include prescribing errors or drug abuse, only those killed or adversely affected by what was supposed to be an accepted treatment and dose for their condition. This made doctors' prescriptions the sixth biggest cause of death in the United States behind heart disease, cancer, lung disease, strokes and accidents. These are the same doctors, within the same cartel-controlled medical industry, that condemn alternative therapies as dangerous quackery! Look at the way they treat cancer in the butchers' shops of conventional medicine. They use chemotherapy and that's just another way of saying they poison people. Chemotherapy kills cells. Er, that's it. I don't mean just *cancer* cells, but *all* cells. 'Modern medicine' simply hopes that this horrific poison will kill the cancer cells before it has killed enough healthy ones to kill the patient. Subtle, eh?

'Hey Ethel, I've got a cure for your headache.'

'Oh great, Chuck, what is it?'

'I got this shotgun and I'm going to blow your friggin' head off.'

'Gee, thanks, Chuck ... you'd make a wonderful doctor.'

But it gets even more ridiculous when you realise that chemotherapy also kills the cells that form the immune system. Even if your 'chemo' does manage to kill the cancer cells before it kills you, the immune system, your defence against cancer and disease, looks like a scene from the Battle of the Somme. This is the very environment in which cancer and other disease can flourish unchallenged. I saw a documentary once that showed the immune system's white blood cells destroying cancer cells. This is an everyday occurrence. When your immune system is working properly you don't die from cancer because the problem is nipped in the bud. It is when the system is undermined or overwhelmed by multiple attacks that the defences are breached, and our Illuminati-created societies are designed to do precisely that with all the shite food, drink, stress and electromagnetic pollution. The drug thalidomide rewrote the DNA/RNA program in unborn children to such an extent that they were born without limbs and, for the same reason, the radiation scattered across Iraq by American and British weapons containing spent uranium has led to the unspeakable birth defects in children that I highlighted in *Tales from the Time Loop*. Radiation short-circuits DNA communication.

What we call genetic diseases are flaws in the parents' DNA passed to the child when the two 'disks' are downloaded onto one in what we call procreation. Genetic disease is an inherited problem with the DNA's ability to communicate accurately and, depending on what form this takes, the child becomes more liable to manifest a particular disease. The current attacks on the DNA by the Illuminati are likely to lead to an increase in genetic flaws because of the changes being caused by our food, drink, electromagnetic pollution and other environmental factors. But, and it's a very big but, this doesn't have to be. We can use our consciousness to dictate the program and wrest control from food additives or any other disruptive influence. Consciousness is not more powerful than a Tetra mast or a chemical sweetener? *Please*.

Japanese scientist, Masaru Emoto, has found that low frequency water reacts extremely negatively when exposed to low frequencies; but high frequency water is not affected at all by low frequencies. This makes sense because they are not on the same wavelength and when we operate in high frequency states we are not affected by the low frequency bombardment in our food, drink and environment. As I said earlier, Valerie Hunt, professor of kinesiology at the University of California in Los Angeles, has found that people focused only on five-sense reality (mind and emotions) have energy fields that vibrate at a lower frequency than those who use their higher senses (consciousness). This whole Illuminati global society is designed to keep us in a low frequency state so we play by their rules in their vibratory realm.

I am all for the development of what is called alternative, or complementary, healing. These are the healing techniques that treat the body as a series of vibrational fields, which can be harmonised through hands-on healing (transmitting energy to the patient); acupuncture (rebalancing energy flows and DNA/RNA communication); reflexology (using a smaller version of the hologram to treat the whole); aromatherapy (accessing the hologram through the sense of smell); and the countless other methods that operate on the same principles. But these are not the end in themselves. They are stepping-stones to the realisation that we can use our consciousnesses to heal ourselves. DNA is a receiver/transmitter/amplifier and it can either be aligned to the transmissions of the Matrix and its inherited 'genetic' program, or to Infinite Consciousness. We can allow the Matrix to communicate to our DNA and dictate events, and flaws in the DNA to control our life; or we can impose our consciousness on the situation and change the outcome. It is not DNA that is the problem, but what is communicating with it and disrupting its balance. There is no need to cut out bits of the body to 'cure' people. We just have to restore vibrational harmony to replace the disharmony that causes dis-ease. And we do that through vibrational means, not the scalpel and the drug.

Consciousness has the power to communicate its will to DNA and override the dictates of the Matrix and the inherited software. We can rebalance the DNA and heal ourselves – and even stop the illusory ageing process – by sending different instructions and rewriting the program. We can be governor of our own experience even within the Matrix if we choose to wake up from our hypnotic state. A computer may be able to do some amazing things, but in the end *you* are in control of it. Type in the right codes and it works perfectly. Type in the wrong ones and it can go haywire. It is the same with the body hologram. The DNA is a transmitter/receiver and it does not have an exclusive contract with any single broadcaster. Are we going to allow the Matrix to dictate events through our DNA or are we, Infinite Consciousness, going to intervene and demand our right to decide our own experience? Are we going to ride the horse or go on letting the horse ride us?

Now, let's go to another level with this because what I have been describing are also illusions. When you deprogram still further you realise that there is no illness because there is no body. How can your body be ill when you haven't got one?

'Good morning, doctor; I have a pain in my belly.'

'Madam, you don't have a belly so it cannot hurt.'

'Thank you, doctor; I think that's cured it.'

Illness, like everything else except Infinite Love, is illusion. We only get ill because the program tells us to *believe* we can get ill. It is feeding us that reality and our DNA/RNA is decoding the messages into our apparent 3D experience. My DNA/RNA is manifesting the illusion that I have arthritis and until I can disconnect from that reality at a deep level my joints will remain swollen and painful. I have said that we see with our brain and not our eyes. But here's another little shocker. *There are no eyes.* If reality is constructed in our brain how can we have any eyes on the outside of the brain? Look in the mirror and you can see your eyes, but everything you are seeing is happening *inside* your brain – including the eyes staring back at you in the mirror. People who have 'near death' or 'out-of-body' experiences describe how they could still see while they were looking down at their bodies lying on the operating table or wherever. If we see with our eyes, or indeed even our brain, how come we can see without them? Because they are another level of the illusion. I am sitting here now wearing reading-glasses so that I can see the computer screen because 'my eyes are not what they were'. But how can my eyes not be what they were when they never were in the first place?

We are told that light comes in through the eyes and is turned into electrical signals that the brain decodes. On one level of the illusion that does appear to happen; but go higher and there are no eyes so how can they process 'light'? There is no 'light' as there is no 'dark'. They, too, are illusions. People go blind when they have a defect in the eyes for the same reason that I have arthritis. The belief that you need eyes to see is written into the program and the DNA/RNA decodes this as blindness when the illusory eyes appear to malfunction. Only consciousness can change that by overriding the software. Like I say, the brain is another level of the illusion sold to us by the Matrix. It is the body computer's central processing unit decoding the false reality broadcast by the Matrix into the 'world' we think we see. But the brain is also a hologram and therefore an illusion. There are many levels to the maze and when you peel them away you are left with only Infinite Consciousness – Infinite Love.

The world looks a lot less scary when you realise there is no world, eh? And the fear of death loses its power when you know that you have no body and so it cannot 'die'. What a hoot it all is, this 'life' we take so seriously. Go on, have a good laugh, mate; it's bloody hysterical.

———

Note:

When I had completed this book and it entered the production stage, I saw reviews on the Internet about a book called *Vernetzte Intelligenz*, which details the findings of Russian scientists and researchers with regard to DNA. Their discoveries support the theme of DNA as a 'biological Internet', and you will find a summary of their work in Appendix I.

It is worth reading Appendix I on page 199 before proceeding because it closely relates to much that you have read so far.

CHAPTER SIX

The God Program

It is well for his peace that the saint goes to his martyrdom. He is spared the sight of the horror of his harvest
Oscar Wilde

One of the major expressions of the Matrix program in this reality is what we call Religion, and that's not only Christianity, Judaism, Islam and the others we associate with that term. I also mean the religions we call money, politics, the pursuit of 'success', television, the cult of celebrity and what has been dubbed the 'New Age'. Anything, in fact, that dictates your sense of reality and entraps you in the illusion.

The Matrix loves religions. They are the diversions that hold consciousness in the headlights of an oncoming fairytale. *Which* fairytale you choose to believe doesn't much matter so long as you buy into one of them and, of course, your DNA is always there to guide you. The idea is to keep you focused on one obsession so you don't see the guy at the stove preparing the gravy. Horses have wide peripheral vision and some wear blinkers to ensure they can only see what's in front of them and not the panorama they would normally see. The blinkers are there to focus the horse on the desired activity – the race – and stop it being distracted by other horses or influences. The religions in all their forms are blinkers for humans. They are there to discourage consciousness from seeing beyond the program because they are focused on one predominant belief or goal. The *Silent Weapons for a Quiet War* document said: 'Keep them busy, busy, busy, back on the farm with the other animals'. The Matrix wants to keep the cell door bolted and religions have served the cause magnificently. They entrap people in laws, irrelevance, and fine detail to such an extent that the big picture is never seen (*Figure 62, overleaf*).

A great example of this is hair. I didn't realise that hair was so important until I began to check what different religions told their followers to believe about it. The things you learn. Did you know that the Torah (the five books of 'Moses' in the Old Testament) forbids a male Jew from removing hair from his sideburns? No, really, this must be very profound then, I guess. But why, dear God, is this considered so vital? Well the Torah, no, let's be specific, Leviticus 19:27, says: 'Do not shave around the sides of your head, nor harm the edges of your beard'. Is that it? Yep, seems like it. If you really study the detail, though, there are some get-out clauses.

Figure 62: *'We will now sing hymn 364 –*
The Lord is My Shepherd'

Phew. The sideburns merely have to be long enough that you can pull on the hair; and the beard can be shaved, but only if you use an instrument that isn't sharp. Mmmm. Is it me or do you see the same contradiction here? But this is God's law and there can be no contradictions, so it must be us, I suppose. The law says you must not use a straight razor, including safety-razors, on your temples or to shave your beard. Jewish men who don't want a beard have various options, I read. They can use 'depilatory powder' (hair removal products), or scissors with 'two relatively dull blades to pinch off the hair, rather than one very sharp blade slicing it off'. Ouch. There is some good news, though – electric shavers are okay! Yippee. But hold on. Aren't they sharp so they can cut the hair, isn't that the idea? God must have missed that one. Not all electric shavers are within the law and you are advised apparently to check with your local Orthodox rabbi for acceptable brands. He might have a stock in the back room. The Devil's in the detail so here's some more from faqs.org:

'Actually, the sideburns merely have to be long enough that one can pull on the hair, and the beard area can be shaved with something other than a sharp blade (many people accept the use of electric shavers). But, specifically within the Chassidic community, there is a custom not to shave (and frequently not even to trim) the beard, and to permit the sideburn area (all the way up to the top of the ear) to grow long as well (the long sideburns are called peyos). Some tuck the hair up under their kippa/skullcap, while others curl the hair. Many Orthodox say the payos (aka earlocks/sidelocks) begin right at the temple, to just behind the ear, and must grow no shorter than the top of the cheekbone. Then they are to be worn pushed forward of the ear so as to be visible … Many who grow long peyos do so for Kabbalistic reasons. One of the opinions in Kabbalah is that the peyos need to be worn long only until the beard grows in. Once the beard grows, the peyos of the side of the head should not be allowed to grow down beyond where the sides of the beard begin to appear.' [1]

Zzzzzzzzzzzzzz. Has he finished yet? All these laws about the hair on your face are only one example of the web of control, often fine-detailed control, provided through the *God Program* software and it's not only Jewish people who have their lives dictated in this way. Muslims wear beards, too, and the Koran tells them what to think, as the Torah and other blinker-books tell Jews and Christians. I typed the question, 'Why do Muslims wear beards?' into *Google* and saw that many don't seem to know. But one guy, Dr Muzaffar Iqbal, the founder-president of the Center for Islam and Science in Canada, did offer an explanation in his column in the *New Islamabad*. In summary, he says that Muslims should be inspired to be like the Prophet and, 'when applied to the outward aspects', this meant that such a person 'makes an effort to change one's habits, dress, appearance and routines of the day to a close resemblance to the life of the Prophet, upon whom be peace and blessings'. Beards for men were one such attribute, said the doctor, in line with the Prophet's command reported in *Bukhari, Book 72, no. 781*: 'Trim your moustaches and leave the beard [as it is]'.[2] Well, some guy in the seventh century is reported to have said don't trim your beard, so who are we to question it? No wonder the word 'Muslim' means 'One who surrenders'.

So now we have Jews being told by the Torah to wear beards and Muslims told by the Koran. The hair thing is just as important to Sikhs, too. At least Jews and Muslims can cut the hair on their heads, but not so with Sikhs. They are to barbers what vegans are to the meat industry. Sikhs don't cut their hair and instead gather it together under a turban. They also go for the *Long Beard Program*. One reason for this is that if hair wasn't pleasing to God, they ask, why did he cause it to grow? The Sikh gurus (see rabbis, priests and clerics) strongly advised Sikhs to accept God's will (common to all versions of the *God Program*) and not cutting the hair symbolises this, so I read. Sikhs believe that God didn't make any mistakes in how he created the human form (George W. Bush, I rest my case) and out of respect for that belief Sikhs choose to keep their bodies unchanged from the way God created them. This includes the fact that Sikh men remain uncircumcised, except for medical reasons (I thought God didn't make mistakes ...). But as with all belief when faced with practicality, they pepper in the contradictions to get themselves out of the dogma-created holes. For instance, they say that if God didn't want hair to grow why did he make it grow? But I have a question: why do Sikhs cut their nails then? Have no fear, they have considered the fine print and there is an answer to this contradiction that I have, once again, quite wrongly identified. A Sikh website exposed the error of my observation:

'Sikhism believes in having a truthful, honest living and progressing in life. Nails have been given to us so that we may work and walk. For example, if you lift any object up with your fingers you will see the pressure on your nails. Nails also help us to walk. If you decide not to cut your nails, when you work they will eventually snap off. So therefore Sikhism allows them to be cut.'

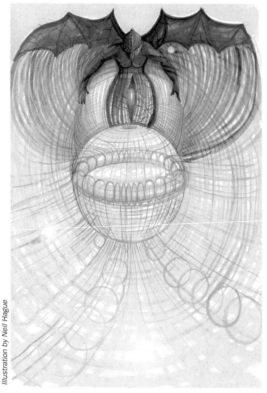

Illustration by Neil Hague

Figure 63: *The Matrix God Program ... Worship MEEEEE!*

I wonder how long the lawyers worked on that one. I also read how some believe the hair must not be cut because it is an antenna that connects us to God. So where does that leave bald people? What have *they* done for God to block their e-mails? But, not to worry, the hairless can make contact with another part of the *God Program* by being a Buddhist. They have no problem with baldies. Buddhists shave their heads to 'renounce all the mundane desires and longings to more readily achieve purity, be free from delusions, remove hindrances and enter the way of practice'. And once they shave their heads, they can easily be distinguished from others (if not from each other). Roman Catholic nuns also cut their hair as a symbol of their life of self-sacrifice to God and re*nun*ciation of worldly things. A woman's hair is considered her crowning glory and is often a source of vanity, the Roman Catholic thought-police say. In order to avoid this vanity the nun covers her head and cuts her hair short. Now what's the word I am looking for with all this? Oh yeah, *pathetic*.

The scale of religious imposition can be breathtaking and its underlying weapon is always the fear equation: fear = control = power for the Matrix (*Figure 63*). Firstly, the *God Program* puts its followers in a state of fear about upsetting God and missing out on the ticket to paradise. Then it gives them rules to follow to keep God sweet and save them from the place where the fires burn. Dean Hamer, an American molecular geneticist, concluded after comparing more than 2,000 DNA samples that a person's capacity to believe in God is linked to brain chemicals. He explained his theory in *The God Gene: How Faith is Hardwired into our Genes* (Doubleday, 2004). This certainly fits with what I am suggesting in this book. The *God Program* will be more powerful in some people than others because the realisation that religion is nonsense rewrites the DNA software and dilutes the influence of the men in frocks on others in the same genetic line. It also works the other way, too, of course. I am not surprised that Hamer connects belief in God to brain chemicals because this is a way the software interacts with the body hologram.

In September 2004, I saw a television documentary series called *Jewish Law*, on Britain's Channel 4. What it revealed was a fantastic example of what I mean by religions serving the Matrix. The series featured Jewish people trying to follow the strict Judaistic law in every area of their lives. And I mean *every*. It was so extreme it was almost funny, but by the end I found myself deeply sad for these people. They are imprisoned in a daily dictatorship of fear, based on laws decreed through ancient Biblical texts written thousands of years ago by unknown authors and administered by the Rabbinical Thought Police. Early in the first show we found Rabbi Kaye, a kosher-inspector for an organisation called Beth Din in Manchester in the North West of England. He was in his library where the shelves were packed with books detailing the shoulds and shouldn'ts, musts and mustn'ts, which an orthodox Jew has to observe. He said:

'This book here actually tells us what you do when you get up in the morning, how one gets dressed, how one acts – before praying in the morning we don't eat – how you can greet someone in the morning, what you can say before you pray, what you can't say, how you get to the synagogue, what you do in the synagogue, what happens if you turn up a little late for prayers, what bits you miss out, all these things are all there.'

You get the picture. The Beth Din organisation employs 30 'dietary inspectors' to police the establishments where kosher food and drink is produced. You probably know about the kosher meat laws which insist that animals are bled to death, like the halal meat of the Muslims – but kosher law goes much further than the technique of slaughter. It ensures that everything conforms to the astonishingly voluminous and complex dietary laws written down more than ten centuries ago. As Beth Din's Rabbi Furst said: 'We have a tradition given down to us from Mount Sinai. When God gave Moses the written Torah he also gave him an oral explanation of all of this in the tiniest, tiniest detail.' It must have been a long conversation from what I could see and Moses must have had a memory to die for. Rabbi Furst also explained that the law allowed them to eat part of an insect, but not a whole one. I'm not sure there is much good news there, really. Kosher food-inspector, Rabbi Klarberg, added the rider that this did not mean they could purposely cut up an insect to find a loophole in the law that says you can't eat a whole one. I breathed deeply wondering if I had morphed to another planet. Why anyone would want to circumvent a law that says you can't eat an insect was lost on me. But then I was in really strange territory.

Sholem Josephs, of the Swiss Cottage Bakery, said that if he had meat in one of his ovens he wouldn't dare bake anything else in there until he had called the rabbi and agreed a way to make the oven kosher again. He also pointed out that kosher food costs more, not least because, like all such businesses, he is billed every month by Beth Din for policing his kitchens and giving the crucial stamp of approval. Maintaining the kosher eating laws is very profitable as well as being spectacularly over the top. But how can you question Moses or whoever invented him? That would be blasphemy. In another scene, a guy was visiting a rabbi with a new electric kettle. Rabbi Brodie explained to him that Jewish pots, pans and kettles were immersed in a body of water because it was considered a sign of purity. I think it's what the rest of us call cleaning new pans before you use them. But no, this was a spiritual and religious ritual. 'I hope you have many, many good cups of tea from it', the rabbi said. 'Having sanctified it, I'm sure the tea will taste better.'

Soon we were back with kosher-inspector, Rabbi Kaye, and the drama heightened. He faced a serious problem. A rabbi in London who was flying up to join him the next morning for an inspection in Aberdeen, Scotland, was worried that his flight time would stop him from praying when the law said he must. He would have to leave home before it was time to pray and would be in the air at the critical moment. I didn't understand why he couldn't just pray on the plane, something I have done many times myself while flying with local airlines in South America. From what I gathered – and it did get a bit garbled at this stage – the rabbi had to pray in the first four hours after dawn. God demanded this, apparently. Rabbi Kaye went to work to solve his friend's crisis. He opened the Hebrew calendar on his laptop and there was great relief. There was a way around it. Somehow you always knew there would be.

In his hotel room, as he waited for the London guy, Rabbi Kaye covered his head and performed the first of the obligatory three prayers of the day – as opposed to the five of the Muslims (I wonder who wins on penalties?). The rabbi's prayer involved rocking back and forth in the way I have seen them do at the Wailing Wall in Jerusalem. At one point, he also wore a sort of little black chimney or box thing which are collectively known as tefillin. It was a square, and far smaller, version of the top hat worn by the Fat Controller in *Thomas the Tank Engine*. In another programme we were told more about why Jewish men 'strap on boxes', as the narrator put it. This immediately took my mind to cricket, baseball and other sports in which the manhood has to be protected from injury by a hard 'box' or cup. But these tefillin do not protect the balls, they perpetuate it. They contain little compartments each filled with a parchment inscribed with religious texts and they are worn to remind Jews that God rescued them from bondage in Egypt. He was obviously on vacation when the Babylon captivity deal went down.

The legitimacy of the tefillin has to be checked regularly. Rabbi Dansky told us that this must be done because if you don't follow the will of God you earn 'no brownie points'. Hold on a second while I come to terms with how stupid this God must be, what a total wally-brain, to be concerned about whether anyone wears this thing on their head or what is in it. Nope, that level of ludicrousness is beyond my imagination. Anyway, Rabbi Dansky is nothing if not thorough. We saw him with his measuring gauge to ensure the tefillin were square to within one millimetre. He said they don't really understand why they have to be square, it was a mitzvah (law) decreed some three thousand years ago that 'we just have to accept and do without [knowing]'. You suspect there are a lot of those. Each scroll had to be in the right order or the tefillin would be invalid, the same with even a small scuff on the leather chin strap, the rabbi said. When they wear out they have to be buried, even the little stitches that become detached. Rabbi Dansky told us that he made sure this happened by hoovering his office and burying the dustbag. He seemed to bury quite a lot. He said that all old prayer books, even newspaper articles about the Torah, had to be buried, too. The previous year he had buried seven tons of the stuff.

Rabbi Kaye and his London friend headed for the fish market in Aberdeen. The voice-over told us that in order to be kosher the fish had to have fins and scales. I thought what a relief it must have been to find that they had, not least for the fish. This statement was given no elaboration and I take it this meant the fish had to have fins and scales when on the dinner plate, but I can't be sure. Every additive to the fish and every other kosher food has to be checked. Kosher certificates must be going out thick and fast – matched, of course, by the cheques coming the other way. As he drove home with what appeared to be a music tape playing in the car, Rabbi Kaye told us that they were not allowed to listen to music, except at weddings. I guess anything by Meatloaf would definitely be out anyway, unless he had been inspected. So was the rabbi breaking the law as the music played in his car? Oh no, all sorted. See get-out-clause No 766, 859, 494. His tape was not music, it was purely vocal, he said. You got the impression that even he didn't buy that one.

Animals are only kosher if they have split hooves and chew the cud. One documentary took us to a farm where they were making kosher and non-kosher milk. A farmworker said there wasn't much difference in the process, really, but I guess the farm still had to put the cheque in the post. Listening to the farm's kosher-inspector from Beth Din, it seemed like easy money to me. I quote him word for word in case you think I am making this up:

'I would be here quite a lot during the milking to ensure that there are no other animals in the herd other than cows.'

Other animals such as?

'A buffalo.'

After a slight pause for reflection on how daft his answer was, he went on:

'… We do know there are no other animals in the herd, it's very unusual to have a mixed herd anyhow, but all the same the requirements are that we are here. That is what makes the milk kosher, the very fact we are here checking, although there is no real difference in the milk.'

Could you file that one with the insect loophole, please? Thanks so much, the file's marked 'Bewildered'. Rabbi Furst stood beside a pile of dough, the bread kind. He said it contained a piece of every dough made at the bakery in the last 36 hours and he was going to perform a special blessing to separate something from the dough in line with the Commandments. I never did understand exactly what he was separating and even after playing back the video I couldn't work it out. Perhaps that was a good thing. He said some Hebrew words as he piled bits of dough on top of each other and announced that he had designated this as 'Halla' or

Sabbath bread. The term Halla, a Jewish website told me, is 'a name used in ancient times to designate the priest's share of the dough'. I know, I thought the same. Rabbi Furst said that his words had made all the difference. 'Now it has a special level of holiness and I have to dispose of it in a respectable way.' Dispose of it? If it was that holy why bin it, respectfully or otherwise? The rabbi had the answer. If they had a temple this dough would go to the priests, he said, but as they hadn't it would be thrown in the trash. Well, not directly because it would be disrespectful and against the law to do that. Instead, he explained, he put it in a plastic bag and then put that in *another* one. Wow, deep respect. 'The fact that we have doubled-bagged it is considered to be a respectful way of disposing of it', he said. The rabbi told us that he had no choice but to dump the dough because no one except the priests was allowed to eat it. All other Jews were 'not in a state of spiritual purity'. Who said so? The priests, I suppose. Once the rabbi had said his words to make the leftovers holy, he said that all the rest of the dough, from which the holy pile came, was considered not holy and ordinary Jews could eat it. Are you still there, you've gone quiet?

Rabbi Furst was filmed cracking what seemed to be an endless line of eggs to see if they had any blood spots in them. The reporter asked him to explain what he was doing and the rabbi said the law on this was complicated. I instinctively trembled at what might be to come after my experience with the severed insect, buffalo man, and the holy dough deal. He said the Torah ordered implicitly that a Jewish person shouldn't eat blood from an animal. Simple enough, but not for long. There was the question of what *kind* of blood was in an egg and if it was blood they needed to worry about or not. Orthodox Jews, like the obsessive advocates of all the major religions, seem to do a lot of worrying, but then that's the idea. He concluded, for reasons that escaped me, that blood in eggs was not the type that was so important to avoid but, nevertheless, he would still check every egg to get rid of it. Rabbi Furst said that they spent a lot of time saying, 'what if'? What if this happened, what if that happened? By now you had no trouble believing him. I'll let him speak for himself about the theological minefield that is a Cheese Danish:

'Now they make a little Danish and they put a dollop of cheese in the middle. Sometimes the cheese will overflow the edges. If that Danish happened to be at the end of the sheet and the cheese spread out and over the edge of the tray it would fall onto the floor of the oven; and it would give it a dairy quality; and if they then put a loaf of bread in there right away that bread would have a dairy quality.

'So, I have gone to great lengths to convince the bakers to bake their Cheese Danish in trays that have edges on all four sides so they won't have this possibility of "what if the cheese goes over the edge?"'

By now I wondered if it was me or the rabbi who would be joining the cheese first. I am sure that thousands of years ago, sometimes even today, there were health reasons for some of these dietary habits, but the obsession with them and the life-controlling strictness of them is off the wall, Wailing and ever other. There are also the hypocritical expressions of the Jewish laws like the one that bans the drinking of wine that is not made by Jews. **AskMoses.com** says that wine is only kosher if it has not been 'handled by a non-Jew before the bottle is sealed …'. I wonder why that isn't considered racist when it would be if anyone else did the same? Personally, I don't care what anyone freely chooses to eat and drink, it's none of my business, but I am sick of this we-can-do-it-but-you-can't arrogance that pervades such matters. The *God Program* is full of this hypocrisy. Rabbi Dayan Berger (there seemed to be a lot of them) explained that the wine law was there to 'put obstacles and difficulties in the way' to discourage the misuse of wine. How it made any difference to get pissed on wine made by Jews or wine made by non-Jews was never made clear and I wondered if they weren't making up much of this as they went along. It is a common trait with the 'interpreters' of religious law – 'I think what God *meant* to say …'. The rabbi said the Jews-only wine thing went back a long time to when idol worshipping was prevalent (what ten minutes ago?) and 'people came across a bit of wine, they somehow tried to turn it into an act of worship …'. I do know the feeling. Rabbi Furst said the ovens in kosher bakeries can only be turned on by a Jew and only brought up to temperature by a Jew. 'That makes the bread a more spiritual product', he said. If a Christian Caucasian said that he would be called a 'White Supremacist'. What's the difference?

Another programme in the *Jewish Law* series focused on the laws of the Sabbath every Saturday, and the Passover, the biggest Jewish festival of the year, that commemorates the exodus of the Israelites from Egypt. During the eight days of Passover they are not allowed to eat anything that rises (okay, okay, enough) like leavened bread or anything that has been fermented. Rabbi Dovid Jaffe told us that this was because the Jews left Egypt in such a hurry that the bread they had made didn't have time to rise. During Passover they eat flat bread instead. Not only is leavened bread forbidden, all traces of it have to be purged from the house. Rifka Domnitz said from her kitchen: 'The whole house is cleaned out because we're looking for leaven, anything that might be bread, cakes, any sort of crumbs; also we don't have whisky, vinegar, anything that's fermented, [like] beer. So the whole house has to be scrubbed.' I'm not sure about the 'has to'. There is no 'has to' unless the will is conceded to insane religious 'law'.

In another house a 'special Passover cooker' was hauled from the back shed and it replaces the other one for eight days a year. I must say the two looked remarkably similar. Even a microwave was covered in tin foil to thwart any lingering bread crumbs that might be poised to condemn the occupants to the fires of Hell. The lady of the house told us that no matter how clean she may get the microwave there might still be something there. 'If I put a hot pot of chicken soup under [the microwave] the steam might dislodge crumbs or leaven into the pot.' That was a close one then. They were 'very, very stringent about everything', the lady said, and you needed no convincing. By way of confirmation we cut to a woman using a paint-stripper flame-thrower to make sure there was absolutely no leaven on the sink and draining board. If only people were equally obsessed with making sure no one went without food, warmth, shelter and the opportunity to live their dreams. But I suppose God is too busy panicking over the deadly perils of a Cheese Danish to concern himself with such irrelevance. It was pointed out that the women do all the work while the men 'set the religious tone'. As one woman said of her husband: 'He sets the spiritual tone and I do it the way he wants. Left to my own devices, I don't know what I'd do. I have no idea.' Sadly most people have no idea what they would do either if left to their own devices because they've never tried it.

The best bit was when Rabbi Avraham Jaffe told us that all rabbis had sent forms to their congregation asking that they appoint their rabbi to sell all their forbidden products to a non-Jew for the duration of Passover. The non-Jew pays his money and all the stuff belongs to him. There is, however, a clause in his contract that says that if he wants to sell it all back after Passover because he can't make a profit on it, then that will be okay. They will 'kindly' let him off and the deal will be null and void. Nothing moves; it's just a paper transaction. The non-Jew is the official owner of all that Passover forbids throughout his local Jewish community, but he sells it back for the same price when the festival is over. The buyer in the film, Colin Day, said he had been doing this for 30 years. He said of Passover: 'Virtually in that time, I'm a millionaire'. But, although he bought all the booty for a few pounds, he sells it back after eight days because he 'can't make a profit'. How ridiculous it all is, and what a sham. Does God not know He is being conned here? Do they think 'He' is that stupid?

At least Passover is only once a year; the Sabbath, or Shabbat, is every week. We saw a family rushing around and panicking as the Sabbath loomed at sunset on the Friday evening (although there is argument over whether this is what 'God' meant). Rochel Jaffe said she had to have the oven going the whole time because you can't cook on the Sabbath. Who says? Whoever wrote the texts of the Old Testament thousands of years ago and no one knows that. 'Once it starts getting close to the Sabbath it's music off, video off, computer off, everybody gets dressed and gets out and they know they have to move quick, you know', said Mrs Jaffe. She consulted the 'when it's the Sabbath' chart behind a cupboard door. '3.53, Sabbath is 4.31 … 31 and 7 is 38 minutes, 38 minutes, it should be okay.' Let's hope so or goodness knows what God will do. Still cooking when the sun goes down on a Friday? Condemn her! As soon as Sabbath starts the father and boys must head for the synagogue while the wife and girls say prayers at home. Rabbi Brodie said that turning on a light, answering a phone or turning on a kettle is banned once Sabbath has begun. Rabbi Kaye returned at this stage. I'd missed him. He told us there are 'so many dos and so many don'ts … can't put a light on [during] the Sabbath, mustn't make a fire … Sabbath we are not allowed to burn a fire … [so we] … can't drive a car because you are burning combustion'. As you'd expect with Rabbi Kaye, we were soon into serious detail:

'You should not burn a fire, but if a fire's burning … I can let it continue burning. If you came to my house on a Saturday and saw me sitting in the dark and thought, "Ah, the lights are off here, okay, I don't like you sitting in the dark," put the light on and walk out, I would have to leave the room because I am benefiting from something done for me on the Sabbath.

'But if I say, "John, let's have a drink, only problem is the room's a bit dark," and you say "Oh, I'll put the light on," and you sit down, the light's been put on for you. And when you leave the room, I say, "John, do me a favour don't turn it off", that's fine.'

Whenever I need a way around the system, Rabbi Kaye is my man. As he pointed out: 'Turning off something is slightly different to turning something on'. You get the feeling that if the word 'no' did not exist in the orthodox Jewish vocabulary they would all be permanently speechless. Mind, it's the same with all religions in the *God Program* and don't start me off about the Southern Baptists. One of the most bizarre of the Judaistic rituals is during the compulsory eight days of mourning that orthodox Jewish people must go through when a relative dies. They have to sit on a special low chair (reason never explained) and all mirrors must be covered (ditto). One poor guy was visited by Rabbi Jaffe after the death of his sister to have his cardigan hacked at with a knife. This comes from the story of how Jacob reacted to the death of Joseph by tearing at his clothes. So, thousands of years later, Rabbi Jaffe pulled out his blade and cut a hole in this man's jumper while exchanging 'holy words'. This is supposed to happen whenever a relative dies, much to the delight of clothing manufacturers. I must say also that whenever these guys said their 'holy prayers' there seemed to be a surprising lack of feeling and the words 'parrot' and 'fashion' came to mind. It was like hearing someone recite their two-times-table. The only ritual that looked like fun was called Purim, or Pour-in as it seemed to be. This is when Jews are told to relax and it is a mitzvah from God that the men must get pissed. It is what you might call a *bar* mitzvah. It was the only time in the series when the participants did not seem rushed and breathless, panicking to fulfil the next law in the daily timetable. After all that had gone before it was nice to see them relaxed and happy, albeit not for long.

An important part of the *God Program* software is to force or pressure children to follow the parents' beliefs. An orthodox Jewish mother said she had friends who were worried sick that she had a daughter of 20 who wasn't yet married or betrothed. She said she wasn't worried herself (you got the feeling she was) because God would find her daughter the right man. But even so she would make a few inquiries within the Jewish community. 'We'll find someone', she said. *We'll* find someone? For me, it is nothing sort of abuse to manipulate or even, in many cases, *insist* that your son or daughter marry someone who meets the approval of yourself and/or the laws of your religion. This happens in a number of cultures and it's a bloody disgrace. The same mother told us that God doesn't like anyone who is full of themselves and the ego must be purged. They had to 'get rid of arrogance and haughtiness', she said. How this squared with pressurising children to get married and forcing them to follow your religion was never explained.

Behind all this apparent nonsense I have been describing in this chapter is *control* – control by fear. Rabbi 'Cheese Danish' Furst summed it up as he continued with his 'What if?' theme:

'We apply this kind of thinking to everything we do – what if this can happen, what if that can happen because we are **afraid**. We are afraid of the spiritual damage that may come to us.' (My emphasis)

He said food could affect a person's soul. If they ate food that had been made in the kosher way it had a positive spiritual affect on the soul – 'and God forbid if he should eat things that have been made in a way that violate strict kosher laws, it can have a negative effect on the soul'. One of the kosher slaughterers who bleeds animals to death made the same claims: 'If a person eats non-kosher food it reduces his spirituality; if he sticks with kosher food it leaves his spirituality intact and in fact it grows because of the discipline behind having only kosher products. We believe this whole package of laws, as far as eating is concerned, elevates … the soul to a higher spiritual level.' Utter bilge water. It certainly seems to do nothing for their health. Not one of these guys looked healthy. All this imposed behaviour is about the *cosh* not the kosher. It is to maintain a state of daily fear and servitude about the consequences of not doing as you are told. It is the *God Program*. As Rabbi Furst said:

'We have got to understand that in the world to come we are going to have to deal with this score card that we have developed over our life and … the mistakes that we made we get punishment for them. However … if we fix up the mistakes we made in this world then we don't have to deal with it in the world to come.'

What will the punishment be for mixing cheese with meat, one wonders? The eternal damnation of eating at *McDonald's* maybe. The game is simple. Get yourself a long list of laws you say were given by God, appoint a mafia priesthood to 'interpret' what God meant, and frighten the followers shitless by telling them what will happen if they break God's law. It's a cinch. I felt so sad for these guys in the *Jewish Law* series and those whom they themselves control through fear. Rabbi Furst seemed a nice, jolly man to me, but there he was living every day in fear of the consequences of breaching laws written by who knows who thousands of years ago. The Matrix has him by the Cheese Danish.

Where is consciousness in all this? Where is Infinite Possibility? The Do Not Ask (DNA) religions, which you are told to follow without question, are software programs and what I have just described is one of the more blatant examples. But there are many others. Christians are similarly told, or pressured, what to think, do and say. Through the imposition of monumental tosh, the Roman Church has held billions in the grip of terror – control – throughout its sorry existence. What a disgrace it is, this 'church' of hate and fear that claims merchandising rights to a 'loving God'. Then there are the sick minds at the lunatic extreme of the Muslim faith in countries like Iran where, as Amnesty International has reported, even mentally ill teenaged girls face being flogged, stoned to death or hanged for adultery, having sex before marriage and 'acts contrary to chastity'. This applies, it seems, even if these kids are forced into prostitution by their parents. The coldness and viciousness of these fanatics comes from the fact that they are software programs devoid of consciousness under this book's definition. There are also the Mormons, Jehovah's Witnesses, Muslims, and the grotesque caste system of the Hindus that selects a child's life opportunities by the family it is born into. These are different names for the same basic mindset and the very fact they can give a name for what they believe means they have divided Oneness in their reality. If you can put a name to what you are or believe, the Matrix has you because names measure division not wholeness.

These religions and so many more have one key thing in common: they are *all* bollocks. For readers from outside the United Kingdom, the British slang word 'bollocks' means both testicles and utter nonsense, as in 'a load of bollocks'. In the context of religions I use the word in both definitions. Like I say, *which* religion you choose is not important to the Matrix, so long as you fall in line with one of them because then the blinkers are on and the Matrix has you. What makes me smile is that they all think they are following a unique faith when they all come from the same blueprint, and they all have a need to wear uniforms. If you saw an orthodox Jew wouldn't you know immediately with the beard, black hat and long black coat? Would you not know a Muslim immediately, or Sikh, or Buddhist, or Christian priest? It's the herd mentality made manifest. Another hook in the *God Program* is obedience to the founders of the faith. To Christians it's Jesus; to Jews it's Abraham or Moses; to Muslims it's Mohammed; to Sikhs it's Guru Nanak; to Buddhists it's Buddha; and to Hindus it's Krishna. I wonder if he was a Hairy Krishna? No, that would make him a Sikh. I can't keep up with all this.

I think I will start a new religion called Bollockism. I shall be the guru known as the Bollock (unlike with human males there cannot be two Bollocks) and my followers shall be known as Bollockists. We shall be distinct from all other religions in that we will shave the hair from our testicles, and keep it in a plastic bag stuck to our chins. I shall create a women's version in which vaginal hair shall be considered sacred and must be worn under a turban. As you can imagine, it will be a celibate faith.

The greatest movie about religion yet made was Monty Python's *Life of Brian*. It exposed it all for the bollocks that it is and I recall the scene where Brian (symbol of Jesus) was running away from his followers and lost a sandal. One of the followers picked it up and shouted, 'It's a sign, it's a sign'. They then all took off a shoe in reverence to their master. What made the movie so funny was that it was true. Religion is one of those flytraps of the spirit in which, as with the Matrix itself, you can often only see the nonsense of it when you are looking from the outside. I have met many former Christians over the years who have wondered why they couldn't see how crazy it all was when it later became so obvious to them. But then indoctrination and repetition are very powerful when your consciousness is on vacation and letting the DNA program mind the shop. In the United States, Christian believers also dominate the conspiracy research field and this is why they only go so far in what they say, but no more. They are fine while their research supports their religious beliefs, but they won't cross the line, or even consider information, that would take them into levels of understanding that undermine the validity of their faith. They think they are free from the manipulation because they know about the five-sense conspiracy, but the Matrix still has them through their religion and their belief in 'God Bless America'.

One of the reasons that religions survive despite their nonsense is a major manipulator of human reality that I call *assumptions*. I watched a documentary in which Christian academics had to admit that they had little idea who was responsible for writing the Bible. They conceded that the contradictory Gospels were certainly not written by eyewitnesses to the events they claim to describe and even the earlier Biblical texts were rewritten by the Church to fit the political agenda of the time. But despite this demolition of what Christians are led to believe is the 'word of God', the academics said this had not dented their faith. One said the 'holy spirit' must have been working through those who wrote and rewrote the Bible, even though they made contradictory statements (maybe 'God' was confused). The reason for this self-delusion was the *assumption* that Jesus must have existed and that the foundations of the story must be true. This assumption holds the belief together no matter what revelations may expose the religious deceit. Despite all the provable lies and contradictions in the official version of 9/11, most people assume that the basic story must be correct and, therefore, they will never grasp what really happened. Assumptions edit reality because they are *beliefs*. As the Nazis used to say, the bigger the lie the more it will be believed – *assumed* to be true. Albert Einstein made some belief-shattering scientific discoveries, but he was, himself, imprisoned by belief. He was one who proposed the quantum theory but, once he realised the implications of this breakthrough for his assumptions about God, he spent the rest of his life trying (in vain) to disprove the findings of quantum physics. The perception of me among those programmed by media reports is constantly edited by preconceived assumption. The media has portrayed me as crazy and those who believe such 'reports' filter whatever I say through that belief without hearing what is actually being said. Wiping the hard drive clean of all programmed assumptions is essential because 99.9 per cent (at least) turn out to be flawed.

The Bible, when portrayed as the actual word of God, is the most destructive book on earth. The literal rather than symbolic interpretation, no matter how contradictory, leaves no room for independent thought or reappraisal in the light of new understanding. It is a sheep pen for the mind. There is no question, no discussion, no debate. The religion dictates what is and what isn't and that's all you need to know. The sight of soldiers praying to God and asking Jesus for support before battles of mass murder in Iraq reveals a level of contradiction, self-delusion and childlike naivety that beggars belief. I also cringe when I see sports people crossing their chests and asking Jesus to help them win. What has he got against their opposition then? An England rugby captain said when appointed that he had always believed this was what the Lord had planned for him. I am sure Jesus thought of nothing else. 'Say, Dad, we need a new England rugby captain, but leave it to me, I've got just the bloke.' And God saw that it was good.

The depth of programming is such that even when faced with the illusory nature of reality the *God Program* can still prevail. I read an article on the Internet by a guy described as an 'intelligent Christian'. I beg to differ if it's all the same with you. He had experienced reality-altering drugs and saw that the 'solid' world is illusion. Ah, but there's a catch. God *wants* us to believe the illusion is real, he said. I quote: '… the "perception" is exactly what God wants us to see and any attempt to get beyond this perception is sorcery'. This art was explicitly forbidden in the Bible again and again, he tells us. Quantum physics is sorcery, it seems, and part of Satan's plan to enslave us. *Plan?* You mean that what we have now is freedom? The spirit world was just as real as the physical and was accessible through various methods, this Christian chap continued, but to do so was unethical. 'The problem is, as usual, fallen man is pursuing knowledge on his own terms and, while gaining accurate data, is not subjecting the findings to God's law word.' He said the Bible confirmed that God did not want us to know the world is an illusion because it never mentions the fact. By this time I would have given anything for a conversation with Rabbi Furst about the dangers of molten cheese. Let me cut to this guy's chase:

'Everyone DOES know that God exists and that He is in charge. All unsaved humanity does seek to be free of what they see as his "tyranny". We are at a threshold in history. Never before have the techniques of "breaking free" – the techniques of sorcery, been so close to being presented to the general public. And the presentation is such that it bypasses all "religious" terminology.'

Only to a victim of the *God Program* could breaking free be condemned as the work of the Devil. It is sobering to realise that no matter how much knowledge is put in front of people some are so utterly caught that they will go to any lengths to make it fit their religious belief.

The Matrix created the 'gods' of the religions and in fact there is only one Matrix 'God' worshipped in different ways by the different versions of the program (*Figure 64, overleaf*). The Red Dress bloodlines were once again used to found the religions and fast asleep consciousness has been trapped in the web. The Illuminati families have played a predominant role in the creation of the major theological and fiscal religions, everything from Christianity and Judaism to the New Age and the worship of money.

I outlined earlier, and have detailed at length in other books, how the Illuminati were heavily centred in ancient Babylon and then relocated to Rome. This is why the Roman Church, which became the foundation of Christianity in all its later forms, is the Church of *Babylon* under another name. You will find that 'Christian' holy days are the holy days of Babylon and the 'Christian' trinity is the Babylonian trinity in disguise. Nimrod (the fish), his son, Tammuz (who died to save

Figure 64: *Religions worship the same Matrix 'God' through different versions of the program*

Figures 65 and 66: *The fish god Oannes (Nimrod) as symbolised in Babylon; and the mitre-headed Pope of the Roman Church. Do you think by any chance they could be connected??*

humanity), and his 'mother', Queen Semiramis (the dove), were transformed into Christianity's Father, Son and Holy Ghost. The Babylonian symbolism has been continued both in the religions they founded and the symbols and architecture of our cities. Nimrod was also symbolised in Babylon as the Fish God, Oannes, and in *Figures 65* and *66* you can see the ancient depiction of Oannes/Nimrod alongside the Pope with the mitre on his head. Notice any similarities?? Roman Catholicism venerates Mary, the virgin 'Mother of Jesus' and 'Queen of Heaven', in the same way that the Babylonians did with Semiramis, the virgin 'Mother of Tammuz', and 'Queen of Heaven', and the Egyptians did with Isis, the virgin 'Mother of Horus' and 'Queen of Heaven'(*Figures 67, 68* and *69, overleaf*). Semiramis was said to have been 'immaculately conceived' by 'God' – the rays of the Sun God, Nimrod, also known as Baal.

The 'virgin-born sons', Jesus and Horus, were both connected to the symbol of the fish, as was Nimrod. The Gospel stories, on which 'Jesus' and Christianity were founded, are a mass of Egyptian/Sumerian/Babylonian mystery school symbolism relating to sun worship, secret rituals and other esoteric concepts, as I detail in *The Biggest Secret* and *Children of the Matrix*. The same basic story of 'born on December 25th, died to save humanity, etc., was widely told thousands of years before Christianity about the exploits of the sun gods in many and various cultures, including Rome (Mithra) and Babylon (Tammuz – the 'son of the Sun God'). The halos used in pictures of the Gospel heroes are inspired by the way the ancients portrayed their sun gods with halos to symbolise what they represented – the sun.

The myth of Jesus has been a constant source of conflict, death and destruction, and we have seen this yet again with the Mel Gibson movie, *The Passion of Christ,*

Figures: 67, 68, and 69: *Three of a kind: the Christian Mother Mary and Jesus; the Egyptian Isis and Horus; and the Babylonian Queen Semiramis and Tammuz. It's the same myth under (barely) different guises*

the horrific violence of which must have had sadomasochists having orgasms in their seats. First the Illuminati Anti-Defamation League (which spends it's time defaming people) said the movie was 'anti-Semitic', but from what I see there is very little in the ADL's juvenile mind that is not considered so. Next we had the New Black Panther Party in America condemning the film for portraying Jesus as white when they said he must have been black. The ADL said the movie was racist for blaming Jews for the death of Jesus and the New Black Panthers said it was racist for misrepresenting the way he must have looked. Over here a second guys, get this: there *was no Jesus* – black, white or pink with blue stripes! You are all arguing over someone who didn't exist. The Jesus myth was sold to the black slaves by their captors as a means of control and now we have the pathetic sight of the so-called most powerful country in the world dominated by a belief in a religion based on the worship of a non-existent man. Unless a would-be president professes a deep belief in this myth he has no chance of being elected to office. I can hear the Matrix laughing from here.

In Babylon, Queen Semiramis proclaimed that Nimrod/Baal would be present on earth in the form of a flame, and that is the origin of the Illuminati symbol of the flame or lighted torch held by the Statue of Liberty – a portrayal of Queen Semiramis given to New York by French Freemasons in Paris, where they have a mirror version on an island in the River Seine (*Figures 70, 71* and *72*). Queen Semiramis also became the British goddess deity, Britannia (*Figure 73*). When Tammuz died, Semiramis said that he had 'ascended to his father', the sun or Baal, and would also be worshipped as a flame. The 'Christian' festival of Easter comes from the same source. Easter originates from the Babylonian goddess, Ishtar, (Semiramis again) and it celebrated her son, Tammuz, who was the 'only begotten son of the Moon Goddess and Sun God' – Nimrod and Semiramis. The 'Easter'

Figures 70, 71, 72 and 73: Queen Semiramis as depicted on an ancient coin and the Statues of Liberty in New York and Paris. They are the same deity, as is the British Britannia. Note also how the Babylonian Semiramis is holding the 'Christian' cross thousands of years before Christianity

(Ishtar) eggs and the 'Easter bunny' also come from Babylon. Queen Semiramis said she came from the moon in a giant egg and this became known as the Ishtar egg. Tammuz was said to be very fond of rabbits and so we have the Easter bunny. They also ate 'sacred cakes' with a 'T' on the top – the origin of our hot cross buns. The 'T' is a major symbol of Freemasonry partly because of its associations with Babylon and Tammuz. The Christian wafer used in Catholic ceremonies comes from the Egyptian ta-en-aah, the sacrificial bread of the moon. Christians think the bread symbolises the 'body of Jesus' when they are really involved in a ritual about an Egyptian moon deity!

Judaism in its Biblical form was also fundamentally influenced by Babylon. In 587BC, the Babylonian army of King Nebuchadnezzar overran Judea and took most, though not all, of the people into captivity in Babylon. This was a melting pot of peoples and bloodlines, and a centre for what we would call satanic ritual and black magic. The Judeans were captive in the sense that they couldn't leave, but they were allowed to go about their business and came into contact with the religious stories and myths from Babylon and the earlier Sumer in the land also known as Chaldea, Mesopotamia and today, Iraq. It was after the 70-year captivity that the Levite priesthood and others mixed ancient writings with the Babylonian influences to produce the Torah (the law) – the first five books of the Old Testament also known as the Pentateuch, which are officially attributed to 'Moses'. This was hundreds of years after the events were supposed to have taken place. Babylon was also the inspiration for the rabbinic teachings known as the Babylonian Talmud, a massive influence on Jewish belief and deeply racist. Whenever they wanted the people to do something they wrote that 'God' had commanded it and thousands of years later orthodox Jewish people are still agonising over their Cheese Danish and hacking at their beards with blunt scissors to make sure they conform.

The Levites and company took Sumerian and Babylonian stories and transferred them to their own, often made-up, characters. One was the tale of how the Mesopotamian King Sargon was found as a baby floating in bulrushes on the River Euphrates by 'Akki the irrigator' and he was brought up to serve as gardener in the palace of Kish. The story went that the goddess Ishtar favoured Sargon and he eventually became king and emperor. The Levites and their cohorts changed Sargon to Moses in their version of the same basic story. They also introduced the character of St Michael, the Sumerian Tas Mi-ki-gal, the dragon-slayer and Lord of Agriculture. He was later called Lord of the Air and given wings to fly. There were no angels in Israelite belief until the Babylon captivity. The Great Flood of 'Noah' was also a steal from the far older Sumerian/Babylonian account of Gilgamesh. As with Christianity, Babylonian holy days were turned into 'Jewish' holy days. The Levites relocated Sumerian, Babylonian and Egyptian stories and themes to the land they called Israel. The high initiates have always understood the coded meanings, but the mass of the people have been sold a lie, a cover story, to imprison their minds and make them slaves to their hierarchy. Even circumcision, so fundamentally associated with the Jewish faith, came from Egypt. You can see the common Babylonian origin for the Jewish and Christian religions in the beliefs and methods of Judaism and the Roman Catholic Church. Both terrify their victims into conforming to 'God's law' by the fear of what will happen in the next world if they don't obey the priests and the Bible in this one.

I also see that some Sikh writers highlight the Old Testament story of Samson to support the belief that cutting your hair weakens you. But the myth of Samson is a symbolic story relating to sun worship, not follicle power. The ancients symbolised the earth's journey around the sun as the life cycle of a man. He would be born or reborn on what is our December 25th, three days after the winter solstice when they said the sun had 'died' or reached the lowest point of its power in the northern hemisphere. The 'man' would reach the peak of his strength at the summer solstice when he would be depicted with long golden hair, symbolising the powerful rays of the sun at that time of year. When he began to grow older and lose his strength as he entered the autumn, or fall (the astrological house of Virgo the Virgin, the 'House of Delilah'), he would be portrayed with shorter hair reflecting the failing power of the rays. Samson is Sam-*sun*, just as every syllable of Sol-om-on is a word meaning the sun. Jesus was also a symbol of the sun and not the literal man of the Gospels. I expand on this at length in other books and it is no coincidence that, according to the Bible, it was three days after Jesus died that he was 'resurrected' – just as they said about the sun between the winter solstice and what became our December 25th.

Islam also includes many elements of the Babylonian-inspired Christianity and Judaism in its belief system and accepts the literal existence of Jesus and the 'father of the Jews', Abraham, whom it calls Ibrahim. Muslims believe that

Abraham/Ibrahim was a prophet carrying the same message from God as the later Muhammad. Abraham is claimed to have erected the Ka'ba, the most holy place in the Islamic world at Mecca. Most of the stories about Abraham in the Islamic tradition come from sources other than the Koran and there are many parallels to the life of Moses. Muslims also believe that Abraham circumcised himself at the age of 120 and that he died at the age of 175. On the day of resurrection they say that Abraham will sit to the left of God and lead believers into Paradise. What we have here, and they are not alone, are religions created and designed to imprison consciousness in the Matrix by selling the same basic belief package: those that believe in the religion and do as it demands will have a one-way ticket to Paradise as the chosen ones of 'God'. Jews claim to be the chosen people; Christians say that only by believing in Jesus will we go to heaven; and Muslims say that only those who follow the Allah version of 'God' will you book a seat on the cloud. It is the *God Program* – Matrix software for the imprisonment of human consciousness.

Only the details appear different to give the illusion of religious choice and create the fault lines through which the desired conflict between beliefs can be orchestrated. What strikes me about religions is not their differences, most of which are irrelevant detail, but their similarities. They are the same in the way they coerce and bully their followers; they overwhelmingly have the same origin; and even the uniforms are often similar. Jews, Muslims and the Roman Catholic Pope all wear the skullcap. If the Pope had a beard he would have the set. The priests of Babylon shaved their heads in a circle at the crown, known as a tonsure, to signify their allegiance to the sun god and this was continued by the Roman Catholic clergy because it was the Church of Babylon relocated. Some tribes in Africa and some South American Indians shave their heads in the same way. The skullcap (called the kippa or kippah by Jews) is symbolic of the commitment to the sun god – the religion of Babylon and Chaldea. Alexander Hislop writes in *The Two Babylons* (Chick Publications, reprint edition, 1998):

'Over all the world, where the traces of the Chaldean system are found, this tonsure or shaving of the head, is always found along with it. The priests of Osiris, the Egyptian Bacchus, were always distinguished by the shaving of their heads. In Pagan Rome, in India, and even in China, the distinguishing mark of the Babylonian priesthood was the shaven head. Thus Gautama Buddha, who lived at least 540 years before Christ, when setting up the sect of Buddhism in India which spread to the remotest regions of the East, first shaved his own head, in obedience, as he pretended, to a Divine command, and then set to work to get others to imitate his example.'

The Sikh and Hindu turban can be found in ancient Babylon and the western traditions that came from there. Ezekiel 23:15 in the Old Testament says that '... with belts around their waists and flowing turbans on their heads; all of them looked like Babylonian chariot officers, natives of Chaldea'. Ezekiel 44:18 orders that 'they are to wear linen turbans on their heads and linen undergarments around their waists'. I didn't realise how many times the turban gets a mention in the Bible, the book quoted by far more religions than Judaism and Christianity to support their beliefs and impositions. Major world religions are the offspring of Babylon. The gods of religious extremism are a Matrix program designed to be the blinkers that block peripheral vision. What the Matrix needs for its vibratory illusions are polarities, the two points between which a frequency can resonate; so Left is as important as Right to the Matrix because one cannot exist without the other and Christianity is as important as Judaism, Islam, Hinduism, Buddhism – any of them. You will also notice how the original religion is divided into a mass of competing, often warring, factions. We have Protestant Christians and Roman Catholic Christians and the Protestant faith is itself a mass of competing subgroups. Jewish beliefs present the impression of being united when there are many different groupings in competition. Islam has its Sunni and Shiite factions divided by conflict over the so-called caliphs, the alleged successors to the Prophet Mohammed. Here is an explanation of this conflict. Please read slowly and concentrate:

> 'There are a number of differences in the Shi`ah (Shiite) and the Sunni Juristic opinions. However, not all these differences can be termed as the "basic differences" in these two major sects of Islam. The basic difference in the two sects is that of the Shiite faith of the system of "Imamah". The Shiite faith of "Imamah" implies that after the Prophet (pbuh), there shall be no other prophet but, the only true leader of the Muslims, at any given time, is an "Imam" who, like the prophets of God, is directly appointed by God. The appointment of the first "imam" was made by God through the last Prophet (pbuh), while every subsequent "imam" is appointed through the "imam," who precedes him. Another qualification of the "imam," according to the Shiite belief is that he shall belong to the family of the last Prophet (pbuh). The Shiite belief holds that the "Imams," like the prophets of God, are "ma`soom" (sinless, innocent) and, therefore, should be obeyed in all matters and under all circumstances. The "Imams," according to the Shiite faith, are thus not just the political leaders of the Muslims but also their religious leaders and clergy. The Sunni school, on the other hand, does not ascribe to any such belief.' [3]

Okay, have you got that or do you need a bit longer? So that's why they have spent so long fighting and killing each other. If children acted like the religious fanatics you would tell them to grow up. What insanity it all is. We are *Infinite Consciousness* so why do we need some priest, caliph or rabbi to tell us what to think and how to live our lives? It is spellbindingly ridiculous and everyone suffers the consequences of these schoolboy squabbles with the global disharmony they create. But conflict and division is what the Matrix desires and religions always deliver because so many of their advocates have lost the power of independent thought and discernment if, indeed, they ever had it.

   If you are awake enough to reject conventional religion, the Matrix has other options. You can worship the gods of money, 'status', and power over others. These obsessions are religions under other names and also dictate what you must do, think and say to achieve your goal. 'I must be what the boss wants me to be so I can get the foreman's job'; 'I must do what the Prime Minister wants me to do so he will make me a lord'; 'I must trample over people and ignore the consequences of my actions for others so I can make as much money as possible'. These religions also have a uniform – the shirt and tie. What is it with that? They say people have to go to work 'properly dressed' in shirt and tie and even schoolchildren often get the same treatment. Who decided that shirt and tie = properly dressed? It wasn't me, was it you? No? Then *who* and *why*? I was watching the television news when Tony Blair was making a speech about Iraq dressed in a shirt, tie and suit. He handed over to the interim Prime Minister of Iraq, the CIA and British intelligence asset, Ayad Allawi, a 'Muslim' who was also wearing a shirt, tie and suit. They then cut to the political correspondent (shirt, tie and suit) who handed back to the newsreader (shirt, tie and suit). How was the communication of that 'news' made any more effective because everyone was wearing the same uniform? Were the horrors inflicted on Iraq by Bush and Blair mitigated and made less abhorrent because they made the order to invade while wearing a shirt, tie and suit? Once again, it's all nonsense.

The shirt and tie has the same origin as all other religions and their uniforms, the ancient secret mystery schools in Babylon and elsewhere. It comes from a ceremony still performed today by the Scottish Rite of Freemasonry (another Babylon religion) in which the initiate has a noose, known as the cable tow, placed around his neck while blindfolded or 'hoodwinked', as it is called, and he is pulled along by the rope in the ritual. The tie, as in shirt and tie, is a *noose*. The initiates of the shirt and tie religions have a noose around their necks while being blindfolded by the Matrix, and how appropriate that the 'proper attire' for the 'professional classes', and Christian men attending church, is a shirt and tie. Even music comes with a uniform while claiming to be different. If you saw a rap singer (back-to-front baseball cap) or punk rocker (designer-dishevelled) wouldn't you know what they were before they played a chord? The official religions and those that worship money, power and celebrity are essentially the same. Only the name of the god is different. For Christians He's the Almighty; for Jews He's Yahweh; for Muslims He's Allah; for the shirt and tie religions He's status, title or bank balance; and for the celebrity religions He is the latest hyped flavour of the moment. All are expressions of the *God Program* and all have the same aim: human control.

There is one other point to make about religions in all their forms. They encourage or impose rigid beliefs and these stem the flow of energy through the DNA network and suppress (make correspondingly dense and rigid) the resonance of the human hologram. This locks people deeper into the low frequencies of the Matrix program. American psychiatrist, David Shainberg, from the William Alanson White Institute of Psychiatry in New York, believes that thoughts are vortices that can become fixed and rigid. He suggests that these manifest themselves as fixed opinions, unchanging views and a rigid sense of reality that is resistant to change. He is correct and this is reflected in the brain where fixed neuron connections caused by rigid belief close down the central processing unit to higher perception.

When you fall for the *God Program*, the Matrix has you – big time.

Sources

1   http://www.faqs.org/faqs/judaism/FAQ/05-Worship/section-42.html

2   http://www.ecademy.com/node.php?id=26320)

3   http://www.understanding-islam.com/related/text.asp?type=question&qid=417

CHAPTER SEVEN

Old Age, New Age – Same Story

To disagree with three-fourths of the British public is one of the first requisites of sanity
Oscar Wilde

If you can see through the conventional religions and the pursuit of materialism, the Matrix still has its backstop, the goalkeeper when every other defence has been breached. It is called the 'New Age'.

Ironically, the New Age, in all its forms, is significantly more enlightened than conventional religion and humanist thought. It understands that this world is only one of infinite dimensions of existence and all is but a different vibration within an infinite whole. It speaks of Oneness and knows that it is possible to communicate between vibratory realms. I agree with the basic theme and there are many genuine and intelligent people who accept and articulate its beliefs. But what makes the New Age such an effective last line of defence for the Matrix is the very fact that it is more aware than atheism and conventional religion. Those who expand their consciousness to see through the absurdity of current human existence and the mainstream explanations for 'life', are in danger of sussing the virtual-reality game they are caught in. The Matrix needs a trap to ensnare them before the final pennies drop and the New Age is it. Put another way, it is the last cul-de-sac before the gold mine.

A key control system is the way the New Age and Spiritualism portray the divisions between this 'physical' realm and what they call the 'spirit world'. Even most of those who accept the existence of the Matrix would perceive it to be the reality we are now experiencing with the spirit world beyond it. Therefore, much of what is communicated through spiritualist mediums and New Age 'channels' is considered more enlightened than our reality and thus to be encompassed, believed or acted upon. We might hear lines like 'test the spirits', but the conscious and subconscious themes are that the 'other side' must know best. On one level this can have validity because they know by the very fact they are communicating with this realm from another one that there are many 'worlds' of existence. But while they may have that knowledge, the overwhelming majority of these communicators are also caught in the Matrix. It is a multi-dimensional system with different software programs for different levels of awareness. The Matrix is empowered by the energy generated by imprisoned consciousness, not only here, but in other dimensions of itself.

I wrote earlier about the interspaces where the Reptilians, the manipulating ones, anyway, appear to reside and the New Age talks about the realms of deep malevolence that it calls the lower astral. These realms are Matrix energy generators, too, under the control of other software. The game may be a little different, but the aim is the same. 'Death' in this world and the transition to another level of the Matrix is like swapping Super Mario for the Sims on the same computer or moving between strands in the same web. This is one fundamental reason why we 'forget' where we've come from when we are born into the Time Loop. We enter a different program and unplug from the last one. Only through our Infinite Consciousness can we remember who we really are.

Any realm in our current experience that takes form, vibrates or has rules, is a program of the Matrix. New Age thought describes the different bodies that we have in different dimensions. We have a 'physical' body in this world, but in the astral realms we have an astral body that resonates to the frequency of that dimension and so on. I agree with this, but these different holographic bodies relate to different software programs within the Matrix and they are illusions. The program is delivered to us through the DNA receiver/transmitters and these other 'bodies' within the Matrix have their version of DNA which, when you go beyond the hologram, is a frequency field or waveform. Only when we become pure consciousness in awareness of itself can we ditch the bodies and with them the Matrix. Communicators from these other realms of the virtual-reality game speak of living in a place that vibrates quicker than this world and so we cannot see it from our density. Again, I have no problem with that. But the crucial word there is *vibrates*. As the voice in Brazil said: 'If it vibrates, it's illusion'. What I experienced in what I was told was a state of Oneness beyond the Matrix did not vibrate. It was still or, at most, a slow-motion wave here and there. Everything just was and there were no rules. This is a critical point. If there are *rules*, it's the Matrix.

The voice said, for example, that there were no laws of physics, only scientists using illusory 'laws' to measure an illusory universe. They were merely 'laws' that we believed in. There were no laws of any kind because everything just was. 'Do you think the Infinite needs "laws" through which to express itself?' the voice asked. The 'law' of gravity, like all the others, is just part of the software that can be overcome by consciousness that can disconnect itself from the program. This is what so-called miracles are – the ability to override the program and so override the illusory laws and limitations of the program. Rules are the illusion of DNA mind, not the creation of Infinite Consciousness. This world is drowning under rules because it is the densest part of the Matrix, but rules operate throughout the multi-dimensional system. Some scientists say that the different parallel universes they've identified have different laws of physics. But how can this be? Surely if the laws are real the same ones should apply everywhere? The reason they don't is because the different 'universes' are different software programs that operate with different manufactured rules. Communicators from other dimensions also tell of rules, like they can't help anyone in this world unless the person asks them. That's a Matrix program. Outside the Matrix there are no rules. This point is well made by

Morpheus in this conversation with Neo ('the One') in the first *Matrix* movie:

'I've seen an agent [software program] punch through a concrete wall. Men have emptied entire clips at them and hit nothing but air. Yet their strength and their speed are still based in a world that is built on rules. Because of that, they will never be as strong or as fast as you can be.'

'What are you trying to tell me, that I can dodge bullets?'

'No, Neo. I'm trying to tell you that when you're ready, you won't have to.'

The Matrix controls us because we play by its rules and the biggest mistake is to believe that there are any. It has been shown that the beliefs of the scientists performing an experiment will affect the outcome because belief creates reality and laws are only what we believe them to be. Remember, the 'world' the scientists are exploring only exists in their heads, too. They are seeking to dissect and label an illusion while thinking it's real! The DNA programming is selling us the reality of 'laws', but our consciousness is more than powerful enough to overcome that. The New Age, as a Matrix phenomenon, is full of rules, as are the Eastern philosophies on which it is based. You have to do this ritual or that ritual, speak to the spirits in a certain way, or protect yourself with a mantra. I have seen New Age advocates speak to the earth by looking in turn to north, south, east and west. They have their sacred trees, swords, rods or staffs and their awe of these symbols matches anything you will find in conventional religions. Yet all this is just more *illusion*. The earth has consciousness, but its physical form is a software program; so is north, south, east and west, and the other planets and stars. Why are we in awe of a cosmic Game Boy? It's just a trap.

I am not saying that everything the New Age proclaims is mistaken, not at all. But what it perceives to be *outside* of the system of control is not. Take astrology, a major New Age tool. In the right hands, it can be extremely accurate and sometimes very useful in a 'this world' sense. The movement of the planets and stars is a Matrix program, a holographic version of the one projected on the ceiling of a planetarium. These planetary movements trigger vibrational changes that affect humans and other life on earth because it affects the DNA and the input/output system. The point at which we enter the Time Loop also impacts the DNA. Astrology is the interaction between the vibrational fields created by the celestial cycles and our DNA program is affected by where in the cycle we are 'born'. But I stress that this interaction is not between our *consciousness* and the planetary movements; it is between the planets and our DNA, which includes the *mind* and *emotions*. At this level, astrology in its deeper and detailed form is certainly relevant, but when we move our awareness beyond mind to the consciousness of the 'One', we cease to be affected by the astrological 'laws'.

What is referred to as 'Fate' is not the inevitable experience of consciousness; it is the inevitable outcome of the DNA computer program unless consciousness intervenes. Fate is Matrix software. Oneness doesn't do fate. There is no such thing as a done deal within All Possibility. The voice in Brazil said that astrology was another Matrix tool to enforce the illusion about the progression of time and to encourage people to identify with their illusory 'personality' – I am a Taurus, Leo, Capricorn or whatever. It emphasised the division of parts, not the whole. 'Do you think the Infinite has its astrology read?' asked the voice. 'Do you think it consults a psychic about its "future" or visits a tarot card reader?' As I was hearing these words, I was shown a symbolic scene of the Infinite sitting at a table when someone brought the morning paper. The Infinite turned to the list of birth signs on the astrology page and said: 'Oh, my goodness, this will take me all morning because I am all of them'. This doesn't mean that gifted psychics and tarot card readers do not have a role to play, only that we need to understand that, with rare exceptions, they are communicating with entities and energies within the Matrix that are also caught in illusory reality.

The most profound delusion of New Age thought in my view is the idea that we are 'evolving' though our experience. I can see how it looks that way, but this is the spiritual version of the theory of evolution attributed quite wrongly to Charles Darwin (see *And The Truth Shall Set You Free*). While the 'Darwin' theory speaks of the survival of the fittest and genetic change triggered by necessity over aeons, so the New Age believes in a cycle of repeating experience in this world called reincarnation, through which we spiritually evolve over the vastness of time. The idea is that we move between the physical earth and the 'spiritual' realms experiencing every life possibility. In doing so, it is said, we learn and evolve spiritually to reach higher vibrations and eventually merge with the One. But we are *already* Infinite Oneness and All Possibility. Why do we need to evolve into something we already are? This belief is a crucial means through which the Matrix maintains its grip on our reality, not only in the Time Loop, but in its non-'physical' levels too.

We don't have to evolve to enlightenment, we *are* enlightened; we have simply forgotten because we are caught in the illusion. 'Do you think the Infinite has to reincarnate?' the voice said to me. 'Consciousness in the Matrix is also the Infinite, so why does that have to reincarnate?' I hear people say they have learned from experience and I understand that. But I would put it another way. The experience has not taught them anything, merely removed a layer of the veil so they can remember more easily what they already know. I have no problem with the idea of reincarnation, although I think there is a lot more to understand about it. I'm sure it's correct that consciousness is caught in a cycle of moving between the other levels of the Matrix and different parts of the software program or Time Loop DVD. It is not this that I challenge, but the belief that it is necessary to find enlightenment.

I would say the opposite is the case because reincarnation reinforces the 'we must evolve' reality the Matrix seeks to pedal. This keeps consciousness enslaved through the belief that it is getting somewhere. As the voice spoke in Brazil, I was shown a picture of people symbolically dropping from the sky onto a footpath across a field. The voice said that because consciousness in the Matrix was caught in a cycle of moving in and out of the Time Loop through reincarnation, people were not only conditioned by the beliefs of one 'physical' lifetime – they were conditioned by endless experiences in the Time Loop (different parts of the DVD). Between these 'physical' excursions they were in another form of illusory state. They were already conditioned even as they entered the Time Loop reality for still more conditioning. This was why humans dropped into the conditioned, servile mentality so easily; they had been there many times before. When these words were being spoken, I saw the footpath being worn away by the trampling feet going over the same ground until the path looked like a sort of record groove. It got deeper and deeper and the figures walking the path went further and further down until they disappeared. 'Is it any wonder that humans look up for their God?' the voice said. 'It is the only place where they can see any light!' Advocates of the reincarnation/karma cycle might also ponder on how much 'past-life' memory is actually the program carried in the DNA and not the recall of incarnate consciousness.

The point about continuing in an illusory state even after what we call death is extremely important, not least because these other levels provide the sources for most (though not all) of the psychic and channelled information of the New Age and Spiritualism. That is not to say that some of this is not worthwhile and valid, but we need to understand that the communicators are in the Matrix too. These other realms could be even more open to illusion because they operate on a higher vibration with far less density. Compared with the treacle-like density of the Time Loop, it must indeed seem like Heaven. The voice in Brazil, and at other times since, described how other levels of the Matrix include a Christian 'heaven', Islamic 'heaven', Hindu 'heaven' and Jewish 'heaven', etc. These weren't 'real'; they were the manifestation of belief in the same way that we create our reality in this world. They are software programs of the mind which sell us that reality, but we don't have to buy them.

If Christians believe deeply that they will see Jesus when they 'die', then they will. They will edit reality in line with the belief in that reality. What's more they will see the version of Jesus that European artists invented because that has become their belief of what he looked like. I have met many psychics over the years who have told of their experiences with Christians who have died, especially Roman Catholics, who are stuck in some in-between realm, maybe an interspace, waiting to be judged by God because that is what they believed would happen. The illusion doesn't end at 'death' because the Matrix is multi-levelled. I love the line 'death is no cure for ignorance', because it's so spot on. At what we call death, 'incarnate' consciousness is drawn by the principle of sympathetic resonance to realms that vibrationally mirror its own state. Put simply: what you believe when you 'leave' decides where you 'go'. But wherever you 'go' within the Matrix, it's still illusion.

We need to break the cycle of programmed belief and open ourselves to Infinite Consciousness. If people like Rabbi Furst believe in punishment in the next world for actions in this one, that is what their consciousness will create. It ain't true, unless you believe it is. Psychics and channellers are constantly connecting with 'dead people' who talk of being in Heaven or of continuing their spiritual evolution by having instruction at 'Halls of Learning' in their new dimension or world. I am not saying this isn't true in their reality, only that it is another Matrix program. It had them by the Cheese Danish and now it has them by the Halls of Learning. It is another version of the 'we must evolve through experience' scam. We are the *One*, all enlightened, all consciousness, all knowing, no schools necessary. New Age thought also believes that the earth is a spiritual 'university' where people learn tough lessons and work out their 'karma'. This was illusion, the voice in Brazil said. 'Do you think the Infinite has to go to school to learn anything when it knows everything there is to know?' As for karma, the idea that you experience what you have made others experience, the voice asked: 'Why should the Infinite have to experience what it has made itself experience?' The idea of karma is a Matrix myth to confirm a belief in evolution over 'time' and encourage a state of guilt and self-loathing. 'Infinite Love does not judge itself or loathe itself – these are illusions of disconnection', the voice said. While I was pondering all this I had a picture in my mind of the Matrix as a snakes and ladders game. Consciousness thought it was progressing up the vibratory levels towards 'God', when at some point it would stand on a snake and come sliding down to begin all over again (*Figure 74*). The Matrix is a system that wants to entrap more consciousness, not free that which is already caught in the net.

When you observe the New Age you see constant parallels with the conventional religions that it claims to reject. It talks a good story about the need to express your own power and not give it away to others, but it is, in blatant contradiction, awash with hierarchy. There are endless 'spiritual masters' in this world and others. As mainstream religions hand their minds to gods and priests, so the New Age bows its head to masters, gurus and other-dimensional communicators. There is the so-called 'Great White Brotherhood' and the fleets of alleged UFOs headed by 'Ashtar Command' who communicate 'enlightenment' to their advocates. This is just more tosh to fuck with our heads. The Great White Brotherhood (also known as The White Lodge/The Brotherhood/The Brotherhood of Light) is claimed to be a spiritual organisation composed of those 'Ascended Masters' who have 'arisen from our earth into Immortality'. They could have gone to the 'Cosmic Heights, leaving our brothers and sisters on earth behind', but instead they said they would 'stay and assist'.[1] It is said that they have 'transcended the cycles of karma and rebirth and ascended into that Higher Reality which is the eternal abode of the soul'.

This Brotherhood, I learn, has been 'sponsoring the release of the spoken word through conclaves, seminars, writings, books, and through personal discipleship and training'. They are also releasing the 'full teachings that the Dispensations of Cosmic Law allow at the dawning of the Great Golden Age of Saint Germain [a member of the Brotherhood]'. Here yer go. We must have our 'Cosmic Law' because this is the Matrix. And why does this Saint Germain guy have to copyright and trademark this golden period? Isn't it supposed to be for everyone? Isn't the New Age about not conceding your power to others? But when you are caught in the

Figure 74: *The New Age Matrix: consciousness caught in the illusion of evolving through reincarnated experience is playing a sort of snakes and ladders game. It believes it is progressing 'up the dimensions', but the Matrix is designed to make sure it doesn't escape*

Figures 75 and 76: *The Christian depiction of Jesus and his New Age alias, Sananda. Even though this classic image of Jesus derives only from western artists, both Christianity and the New Age manage to portray him the same way*

Matrix you must have the obligatory hierarchy and pedestalled heroes. If there is a hierarchy, it's the Matrix because such structures do not exist in Oneness. How can you have a hierarchy when there is only One?

The Great White Brotherhood is claimed to be a 'Spiritual Order of Hierarchy', an organisation of Ascended Masters united for the highest purposes of God in man as set forth by … wait for it … 'Jesus the Christ, Gautama Buddha and other World Teachers'. The boy Jesus turns up everywhere. To the New Age he is known as Sananda, an 'Ascended Master with the Great White Brotherhood'. Funny how 'Sananda' is depicted in the same way as the Christian Jesus (*Figures 75 and 76*) and yet this classic facial image comes only from the works of western artists. There is nothing in the Bible to suggest what Jesus looked like, not least because the writers had no idea either! But, even so, the Christian and New Age images of 'Jesus' somehow come out the same. The Great White Brotherhood also includes 'Members of the Heavenly Host, the Spiritual Hierarchy directly concerned with the evolution of our world, Beneficent Members from other planets that are interested in our welfare, as well as certain unascended chelas'. What? How did those *unascended* chelas get in there? Did they get a wild card or did they pearly gatecrash? What is a bloody chela anyway? Hold on, I'll find out, won't be long. Thank goodness for *Google*. It seems that a chela is a sort of disciple to a mahatma. I never would have thought. They apparently take part in something called 'chelaship' and the Sanskrit word 'chela' is used, I see, because it has a more specific significance than the words 'pupil' or 'disciple' as understood today. To be a chela 'implies a peculiar degree of loyalty to one's chosen teacher and to the principles underlying his teachings'.[2] Well, on that basis, this world is overrun by chelas, billions of them, all with a peculiar degree of loyalty to their chosen teacher and to the principles underlying the shite they are told to believe (see religion, politics, economics, medicine, law, military, ad infinitum).

It would appear from what I read that Ashtar Command is the 'airborne division' of the Great White Brotherhood. Why do the Ascended Masters, 'who have transcended the cycles of karma and rebirth and ascended into that Higher Reality', need a flippin' air force? This whole UFO/extraterrestrial belief system is another part of the Matrix program, just like the 'human' version. I am not saying for a moment that there are not other body-types operating elsewhere in the Time Loop and its associated realms that we call ETs. But they are caught in the illusion, too, and they are just another subplot in the holographic movie. I saw an advertisement for 'UFO invasion' screensaver software – 'a multi-functional screensaver incorporated with classic arcade computer games, images include UFOs, aliens, military aircrafts, and many more characters'. All this extraterrestrial/UFO stuff is a holographic version of that. I have seen it suggested that the 'goblins', 'pixies', 'fairies', and 'little people' of folklore manifest today as what we call ETs. This could well be true because the Matrix will provide the software that compliments the part of the 'DVD' that is being experienced. At the point in the movie we call say 1306, the 'ETs' might take a form that fits with that era, while in the computerised, so-called hi-tech world of the 21st century they take the appearance of sci-fi space beings. Or, in the case of Ashtar Command, they are only a fairytale that their followers believe.

I put Ashtar Command into Internet search and found more than 17,000 pages including pictures of 'him' (*Figures 77 and 78, overleaf*). The belief is that this extraterrestrial cavalry is coming to save the day. It is the same program that stars Jesus in the Christian version and the Messiah in the Jewish edition. We even have the same theme of the 'chosen ones' in that Ashtar followers have told me how they are going to be taken from the planet, 'turned into fifth dimensional beings', and brought back to teach humanity. One website provided a message from 'Commander Starene of the 7th Fleet in the Ashtar Command'. Apparently her ship, the Rainbow Light, has been 'called into our solar system to aid in the balancing of the Harmonics for our Planet Earth!' Hey, let's party. She was doing this from the Venusian system by sending love on pulsar waves and working with the other ships in the command to 'send the Harmonic Rays directly to the affected areas that are causing the disharmony!' Sounds like a cosmic haemorrhoid cream. All anal retentives should apply Harmonic Rays to the affected areas. The 'message' was peppered with exclamation marks, a symbol of the naive overexcitement that you find in many areas of the New Age. Commander Starene was working with the geometrics and all ships were planning strategies to work with the leaders and countries to find solutions! I hope this includes a solution to the problem of people believing this trash. The ships were on standby as always, the message continued, and were ready for any mishaps if there were 'going to be any ascended beings

Figures 77 and 78: *Two of many New Age depictions of 'Ashtar'*

leaving this planet!' (See chosen ones whipped off to the fifth dimension and all that stuff.) Commander Starene said that all was being looked after and watched over. 'All members of the command are very busy doing their jobs as we are in spirit and in our spirit bodies or lightbodies!!!' The message concluded:

Dear Beloved Ones, I, Starene, send you the Most Golden Rose LOVE vibrations to each and every one of YOU! We are so glad that you are listening and connecting with us! Be at PEACE within as without … Be at LOVE …!!! We ALL LOVE YOU!!!!!!

Adonai! Kadoish, Kadoish, Kadoish, Adonai, Tsebayoth!!!!

Loves & Lights!

ShaLaeLa!
i.e. Cdr. Starene, 7th Fleet Ashtar Command

It is the saviour–messiah theme in another guise, a different version of the *God Program* and, as with all of them, whenever it is predicted the saviour will come, in this case Ashtar Command, there is always a reason why it has to be delayed. I find it interesting that the major Illuminati goddess in Babylon, Queen 'Statue of Liberty' Semiramis, was also known as Ishtar or … *Ashtar*. I think we have another coincidence going here. They are taking the piss. You'd expect Jesus to be involved somewhere and, of course, he is. Ashtar Command is an 'etheric group of extraterrestrials, angels and lightbeings and millions of "starships" working as coordinators of the activities of the spacefleet over the western hemisphere', all under the 'spiritual guidance of Sananda (the Most Radiant One), the ascended master who walked the earth incarnated as Jesus the Christ'. You know the guy, also called Tammuz, Mithra and Dionysus, among endless other aliases. One Ashtar website carried Christmas greetings from Mother Mary, another of the New Age–Christian crossovers in the *God Program*. Ashtar himself, the commander of the galactic fleet and representative for the Universal Council of the Confederation of Planets is, I understand, currently engaged in earth's ascension-process. I am most relieved. This is the deal:

> 'There are 144,000 light workers called Eagles connected to the Command and that is the minimum of souls required for the ascension process. These Eagles are a group of souls who don't identify with a special planet. They know they are one with all, and that they are Christ (fundamental to any discussion of New Age Christology is the recognition that New Agers distinguish between Jesus, a mere human vessel, and the Christ consciousness variously defined, but always divine, and often a cosmic, impersonal entity). They serve like cosmic midwives in the ascension process; the birthing of humanity from dense–physical into physical–etheric bodies of Light, capable of ascending with the earth into the fifth dimension. Light work is incorporating Jesus's message of Love and Light into our daily lives, ultimately connecting with our Higher Self.' [3]

A lady once told me that she was one of the 144,000 and I asked her how she knew. She said she had attended a workshop in Glastonbury (a British version of Sedona, Arizona) and the host had told her the good news. The host had also had a vision of her as a goddess walking down stone steps in Atlantis. A few months later another woman mentioned that she was one of the 144,000. I asked her if she had been to a workshop in Glastonbury where the lady had a vision of her walking down steps as a goddess in Atlantis. 'How did you know?' came the reply. I also read that Jesus (as Sananda) and Lady Nada (never did work out who she was) both work with the 'sixth ray' to heal fanaticism and to raise the focus of devotional worship. And that's the point, really. All these Matrix programs advocate forms of 'devotional worship'. But we are *Oneness*, so on whom are we projecting such worship? The Matrix wants us to find something or someone to look up to because it creates a mindset of me down here and 'them' up there. That's not Oneness, it is division and hierarchy.

The New Age talks of Oneness, but uses the language of polarity – the very system through which the world of vibration can manifest. Like the mainstream religions, the New Age believes in the existence of 'light' and 'dark', but these polarities create each other. If you believe in the light you must believe in the dark or you would not have to distinguish between the two. Belief in one creates the other. There is no light or dark, this is one of the greatest illusions that pervade the Matrix. Light and dark are programs, the same with good and bad, male and female. Everything is *One*. There are no divisions, merely the illusions of them. 'Demons only manifest in minds that believe in them', the voice in Brazil said. If Infinite Love is the only truth and everything else is illusion, how can demons be anything but illusions? I have said before that what you fight you become and it is also true that what we fight we create and give power to. This is not a fight for the light or a fight against the dark or anything else. Fighting is a Matrix program. It doesn't care why we fight or who we fight, so long as we do.

I have been seeking to show how all the religions, be they worshipped in a church, stone circle or stock market, are the same *God Program* in different guises. They are fundamental to the reality maze that is the Matrix and it is always trying to guide you, through the DNA, onto a road to nowhere. If it doesn't get you one way, it will try another. This is not a condemnation of those who pursue a religion, only an effort to expose the traps that lie within. There are many wonderful people with big open hearts who advocate Christianity, Judaism, Islam, the New Age, Sikhism and all the others I mention. They have a right to believe what they do, as they have every right to say that I am talking through my anal muscles. One radio caller in America even called me 'Satan' because I said Jesus did not exist. Fine, it doesn't matter to me because people have a right to express their opinion and I say Jesus and Satan are different expressions of the same *God Program* anyway.

I have been attacked and condemned by many Christians, Jews, Muslims, New Agers, all shades of political opinion, and even many of those researching the global conspiracy. Normally these people would appear to have little or nothing in common, but in fact they are profoundly connected. They all have a dogma to defend and I am challenging dogma and its imposition. This is why I seem to unite sections of these apparently disparate groups in mutual condemnation. The religions are different versions of the same program spawned by the Matrix, and in exposing this virtual-reality game I will inevitably upset those who allow it to think for them. If that is as it must be, no problem. They have a right to believe in their religion and I have a right to say what I do. It's called Freedom.

Funny how religions, and people in general, want the freedom to promote their own beliefs, yet seek to silence those who present another view. But, then, that's the Matrix for you. Fairness and justice were never its strongest points.

Sources

1   http://www.ascension-research.org/gwb.html

2   http://www.theosociety.org/pasadena/gdpmanu/mahat_ch/m_c-5.htm

3   http://ashtar.galactic.to/

CHAPTER EIGHT

Another Look at 'Society'

Education is a wonderful thing, provided you always remember that nothing worth knowing can ever be taught
Oscar Wilde

If you believe the world is 'real', or that some benevolent god is in control, you can drown in the apparent contradictions we constantly experience. 'Why are things done this way when it would be much better for people if ...' WHOA, hold it right there.

Societies are not structured to be 'better for people' or any other life form. That's not the idea. They are designed to serve the *Matrix*, full stop, end. When you observe what we call society from the perspective of the virtual-reality game, and understand its agenda, you can see the method in the apparent madness we call 'life'. The Matrix is a multi-dimensional, self-powered, free energy machine. The definition of free energy is something that produces more energy than it needs for itself. It is like your computer taking electricity from the plug for its own needs while somehow using that to produce energy for the whole house. The Matrix is a system which manipulates consciousness trapped within its vibratory illusions to generate the energy that fuels the system. That energy is *fear* and its related emotions. To achieve this, the Matrix must:

1   Entrap consciousness in an illusory reality and cause it to 'forget' what it really is – the Infinite One. This is done through the system of broadcasting information in waveform that the DNA/RNA decodes into holograms that appear to be a 'solid' world.

2   Manipulate consciousness to believe its thoughts and emotions are its own and not the programmed reactions of the body software through the DNA. This is not difficult when we are constantly hearing thoughts and feeling emotions. Why would we think they were not ours unless we understand the game? Most people have no problem with the idea that mind control can implant thoughts (just watch a stage hypnotist at work) and what the Matrix does is just an infinitely more advanced version of this principle.

3   Instil a belief in the passage of time by using the *Ageing Program* and the *Solar System Program* that includes a night and a day. As Oneness is a state of 'no time', any consciousness caught in the illusion of time will disconnect from awareness of the One. Vibration (time illusion) and stillness (no time) are not easy to connect when you are caught in the dreamworld.

4   Convince consciousness that it is not in control of its own destiny and instead is at the mercy of random events or some version of God (same program, different uniforms). The use of the *God Program* software ensures that religious advocates spend their lives on their literal and symbolic knees while hoping this will bring them reward from their God in the next world. This is also part of the *Carrot and Donkey Program* – put them in a state of perpetually living for 'tomorrow' so they will follow your orders today. But 'tomorrow' never comes and the carrot is always in the 'future'. The crucial word in this program is 'hope', which always locates your focus on some distant point that never arrives because hope, by its very nature, exists only as an illusory forward projection. This is also a version of the *Carousel Program* – no matter how fast you go you never get closer to the one in front. Never mind, you can always hope you will.

5   Convince consciousness that it is not in control of its own destiny and instead is at the mercy of random events because life is an accident of evolution, a series of chemical reactions, and death is a ticket to oblivion, no returns available. This I'm a *Cosmic Accident Program* is for those who don't go for the God scam. Prominent victims are most mainstream scientists and academics, and groups like the Humanists. They also include those, like my father, who equate religion with life after death and so, when they rightly reject religion, the baby and the bathwater both end up in the street.

6   Structure society with different races (DNA software) and beliefs (DNA software) through which you can manipulate conflict and therefore … *fear*. Ah, nectar. The more wars you manipulate, the more fear you generate, and you supplement this diet with the *Fear I Won't Survive Program* and its trademarked offshoots, the *Fear My Loved Ones Won't Survive Program* and the *Fear My Country Won't Survive Program*. All these are available in a boxed set called *Scare Them Shitless – The Greatest Hits*.

7   Plant your own software programs, the Red Dresses, throughout society to Pied Piper-conscious beings in the direction you want them to go. You install these software 'bloodlines' to control the religions, including the worship of the Money God, and to create dependency on these 'families' by the conscious population, not least by making money the major focus of both success and survival. There are different versions of this throughout what we call history (*Figure 79*).

Illustration by Neil Hague

Figure 79: *Behind the scenes Illuminati operatives and puppets, who often appear to be on opposite 'sides', work together to impose the global centralised state. Some do this knowingly while some have their actions manipulated without understanding the full implications of what they do*

From these seven points the entire control of the Matrix is possible if consciousness buys the sales pitch, and the manipulation I described in chapter one can now be seen in much sharper focus. We can understand at a far deeper level why the Illuminati – the Matrix Red Dresses – are so obsessed with controlling the flow of information through ownership of the media. They want to prevent conscious beings from communicating thoughts and facts that challenge the implanted reality of the software broadcast through DNA. Also, by presenting the 'news' in a form that stimulates fear, conflict and division, they are constantly activating the emotional responses in the DNA that slumbering consciousness misguidedly believes are its own. In falling for these DNA emotional triggers, and allowing them to dictate its state of being, consciousness generates the fear that powers the Matrix. It is like watching a horror film with the theatre feeding off the fear it produces from you. This is how the system produces more energy than it needs for itself. It takes energy to run the communication networks of the Matrix, but deluded consciousness in a state of fear, stress, guilt, anger, hatred and frustration, generates far more. The Matrix also absorbs enormous amounts of fear from the daily killing rituals of the 'natural world'. Consciousness experiencing animal DNA software is similarly in a perpetual state of fear caused by predators and the battle to survive. The *Fear I Won't Survive Program* applies to animals as to humans, of course, and so does, at least in most cases, the *Fear My Offspring Won't Survive Program*, as with the example of the Grey Whale, among millions of others.

Controlling the information that people absorb is crucial to the Matrix because consciousness must be held in the illusion by every means possible. I have used the analogy before of the ball floating on top of a tank of water. That is its natural state, floating on the surface, and to hold it on the bottom demands constant effort. The moment you let go, whoosh, it is back at the top again because that is its prime reality. It is the same with consciousness. If you don't bombard it with hypnotic messages to implant an illusion it is going to revert or, in the language of computers, 'default', to its prime state – Oneness in awareness of itself. The education system or *Sausage Machine Program* is a vital part of this hypnotism. The 'education' program is encoded with three main aims:

1 **To implant a belief in reality in line with the Matrix illusion.**
   This is simple enough. You just give students the official version of science, history, religion, mathematics and the world in general. You do this by programming the teachers through school, university and teacher training college and you send them out to program the next generation with the same crap they have been told to teach and believe. As Oscar Wilde said: 'Most people are *other* people. Their thoughts are someone else's opinions, their lives a mimicry, their passions a quotation.' Most teachers, like doctors, scientists, media people and so on, are what my friend, Mike Lambert, calls 'repeaters'. They just repeat what someone else has told them instead of accessing, through consciousness, their own truth. It is second-hand reality. The process is similar to downloading information onto a disk (teacher) and then making lots of copies (children and students). Little or nothing is allowed to be discussed in the schools and colleges outside of this mainstream version of life and there are few, if any, points of alternative reference from which to observe this indoctrinated reality from another perspective. Children go through this mind machine while living with adults (more repeaters) who have absorbed the same programming and while watching a media (still more repeaters) parrot the same official story. No wonder they believe the illusion is real when every source of 'information' is telling them it is.

2 **To turn children into robots who follow the orders of the 'teacher' (system).**
   This requires the *Carrot and Stick Program*. You make it much easier for students to accept the will of the teachers (the system personified) than to question their authority and what they tell them to believe. You reward one and punish the other. 'Do as I say and believe what I tell you' is instilled from the earliest of ages in the daily indoctrination we call school, college and university. Exams are the system demanding to be told what it has told you to think. They are proof or otherwise of downloading. When you download something onto a computer a little box comes up that says: 'Do you want to open this file now?' You open it to make sure the information has downloaded correctly. This is what exams are. Maverick children who refuse to download are considered a disruptive influence. Have you noticed that while there may be disagreements on *how* children are taught, there is rarely discussion about *what* they are taught? This is because the Matrix has such a grasp on human reality that *what* is taught is pretty much universally accepted. Indeed, if schools introduced courses on spirituality relating to the Oneness of all and the illusion of form, parents controlled by the *God Program* would furiously protest that this was an offence to

their Christian, Jewish, Islamic etc., etc., beliefs. Children are not only fed poison through their mouths, but through their minds, too.

3 To squeeze out of the target population (children) any idea that they can be unique and spontaneous.
Schools are mostly no-go areas for spontaneity and free thought because they are consumed by rules. This is perfect preparation for the adult world which is structured in the same way. The only difference is that the teachers for adults are called police officers, government officials, tax inspectors and all the other, mostly unknowing, clones that serve the Matrix. I was reading how a senior school in England has banned pupils from holding hands or cuddling with their boyfriends and girlfriends on the premises. The headmaster justified this by saying that such behaviour by adults would not be allowed 'in the workplace'. This sad man was actually revealing a simple truth. Schools are primarily there to prepare young people to be adult cogs in a machine called 'the workplace'. Children are moulded to become a collective 'hive' mind (a trait of the reptilian brain) rather than expressions of uniqueness. Do the same, behave the same and believe the same. Another thing: why shouldn't adults be allowed to kiss and cuddle 'in the workplace'? Jeeez, only in the Matrix could affection be legislated.

Control doesn't only involve the suppression of information. It also targets the DNA/RNA and its central processing unit, the brain, to further scramble the circuitry and the ability of consciousness to see beyond the veil. This is the real reason behind the chemical additives in what we eat and drink, and all the electromagnetic pollution. When consciousness dictates the reality of the DNA instead of the program, none of this will matter; but while we are slaves of the DNA/Matrix reality we can be seriously affected. It is important to stress that we are in control if we open to consciousness because to say that this chemical or that technology will cause this or that illness can program the computer to manifest the outcome by believing in it. I wonder how many health scares trigger the very problems they warn about? So I emphasise that the following can and does happen, but it doesn't *have* to. We have the power to override it.

Genetically modified food is produced by manipulating DNA and the idea is to use this to manipulate *our* DNA. A vital point in relation to GM food is that DNA is interchangeable between species. As that article in the *San Francisco Chronicle* said: '... DNA is a universal software code. From bacteria to humans, the basic instructions for life are written with the same language'. A brain cell in one species, for example, will work in all the others (remember how the rat cells flew the jet simulator). It is quite possible, therefore, to target and change human DNA through the DNA in what we consume – and that's precisely what they're doing. They're rewriting the software to suit their agenda of control.

In North America, GM food is in ever wider circulation and the Illuminati biotech companies are seeking to exploit hunger in places like Africa to dump their foul products and rewire the people in that continent. When these corporations say they are doing this because they want to help the hungry and downtrodden, it's like the Nazis saying they built the concentration camps because they wanted to help Jews, gypsies and communists. Michael Meacher, the Minister of State for the Environment, sacked by Prime Minister Tony Blair in 2003, has highlighted the lack of research and the serious risk posed by GM food. He also said that Blair appeared uninterested in the science and was determined that GM be given the go-ahead. This is because Blair is an Illuminati pawn following their agenda. Pressure on the UK government has delayed the official permission for GM crops to be grown in the UK, but those behind the plan know that the contamination of non-GM crops is like a cancer. The GM 'trials' in Britain will have already contaminated a much wider area than the government admits and once a new location has been affected it, in turn, contaminates even further. Plus the fact the UK is now controlled by the Illuminati European Union and this fascist power bloc will make the ultimate decision. The EU, no matter how it presents its myth of 'tough safety measures', will eventually give the biotech companies (Illuminati) what they want unless there is a *mass* public campaign to stop it.

The overseas experience has confirmed the dangers of contamination and the creation of genetically modified 'superweeds'. In Canada, contamination has been a disaster for non-GM farmers and a 2003 report in Mexico revealed that it was much worse than believed possible. Analysis showed the presence in apparently non-GM crops of two, three and four GM varieties, all patented by transnational biotechnology companies. Once contaminated, even if it is your worst nightmare, the corporations can, and do, demand royalties for growing their patented crops! The arrogance of the biotech companies knows no bounds. In one media report, Simon Barber, a spokesman for the EU biotech industry association, EuropaBio, said organic farmers were being unreasonable to demand absolutely no cross-pollination. 'Cross-pollination is normal and natural – it happens', he said. What a prat. GM food is about control of the food supply, control of farming through GM 'royalties', even from those who don't want it and, crucially, the manipulation of our DNA and it's ability to communicate accurately. This is part of a coordinated chemical, electromagnetic and vibrational onslaught against the human body, mind and emotions.

The loudest voice behind GM is Monsanto of St Louis, Missouri, one of the most important Illuminati companies on the planet. These were the guys behind Agent Orange, used to grotesque effect in the Vietnam War and this is also the corporation marketing the brain-scrambler known as *aspartame*. This was manipulated through the Food and Drug Administration (FDA) 'safety checks' by Donald Rumsfeld, the US Defense Secretary under Boy George Bush, and CEO of Seale Pharmaceuticals when he used his buddies in the Reagan–Father Bush administration to have fundamental doubts about the safety of aspartame ignored. Searle later sold out to Monsanto and now aspartame is in an ever-growing number of drinks and foodstuffs, a trend only stemmed by the fear of class action lawsuits over its effect on human health.

You will find aspartame in instant breakfasts, breath mints, cereals, sugar-free chewing gum, cocoa mixes, frozen desserts, gelatine desserts, juices, laxatives, multivitamins, milk drinks, pharmaceutical drugs and supplements, shake mixes, soft drinks, tabletop sweeteners, teas, instant coffees, topping mixes, wine coolers and yoghurt. And these are only some examples. Aspartame is 200 times sweeter than sugar and marketed under its own name and trademarked brands like NutraSweet, Equal, Spoonful, and Equal-Measure. Some of the 90 different documented symptoms reported to be caused by aspartame include: headaches/migraines, dizziness, seizures, nausea, numbness, muscle spasms, weight gain, rashes, depression, fatigue, irritability, tachycardia (abnormally rapid heart rate), insomnia, vision problems, hearing loss, heart palpitations, breathing difficulties, anxiety attacks, slurred speech, loss of taste, tinnitus, vertigo, memory loss and joint pain. The reason for this appalling catalogue of disease is that aspartame disrupts the DNA communication system.

The US Air Force formally warned all its pilots not to consume diet drinks in their official flying safety bulletin in May and August 1992 because of the effects of aspartame on their ability to fly a plane. Many other non-military pilots have complained of the same symptoms, including seizures. A 1990 edition of *Plane and Pilot* magazine told the story of an Air Force pilot who traced the patterns of tremors and seizures he suffered for two years directly to his consumption of NutraSweet. When he stopped drinking diet sodas his symptoms stopped, but when he resumed so did the tremors. His problems worsened until a grand mal seizure ended his career. But, once again, his symptoms disappeared when he ditched the NutraSweet. *Plane and Pilot* also reported this case:

'After only two cups of artificially sweetened hot chocolate, a pilot experienced blurred vision so severe he was unable, in flight, to read the instruments and very narrowly avoided a tragic landing. Safely on the ground, he related his symptoms to the secretaries in his office. [He told] of experiencing similar symptoms after ingesting aspartame products.'

Aspartame contains methanol (wood alcohol), a poison that causes blindness and death. Two teaspoons are considered lethal. Smaller doses destroy the brain (DNA central processing unit) little by little, because the effects are cumulative. Depending on the tolerance level of the person, the effects can be severe like epileptic seizures, including grand mal, blindness, chest palpitations, blurred vision, bright flashes, tunnel vision, ringing or buzzing in ears, migraine headaches, dizziness and loss of equilibrium. Other psychological problems are caused by the phenylalanine in aspartame depleting levels of serotonin, a brain chemical and *neurotransmitter* that regulates, among other things, behaviour and sleep patterns. Laboratory tests have also shown that aspartame can *change the DNA*. Here we go again, and this is the prime reason behind the daily chemical bombardment through food, drink and environmental sources. Imagine what the effect on children is going to be of all the aspartame-poisoned shite they are consuming by the bucketful today, especially in soft drinks.

Damage to the brain and the DNA is a constant theme when you research the poisons that infest what we consume, breathe, and absorb through technologies. Aspartame is what is called an excitotoxin, or neurotoxin, and so is the 'flavour enhancer', *monosodium glutamate*, or MSG. You'll find this in almost every mass-produced foodstuff and it tricks the brain to taste more flavour than is actually there. It is often disguised in the list of ingredients as 'natural flavour/flavourings' when it is nothing of the kind in the form it is used. MSG also hides behind terms like 'hydrolyzed', 'autolyzed', and yeast extract or nutrient, among many other pseudonyms. Americans alone are apparently consuming 160 million pounds of this stuff every year and yet it is a *brain poison*. Dr George Schwartz, a toxicologist and author, says that two tablespoons of MSG will kill a dog in minutes. Some of the health effects linked to MSG include heart problems, Alzeimer's, Parkinson's, asthma, cancer, birth defects, obesity and ... brain damage. MSG attacks what is called the brain–blood barrier, a defence system that normally prevents toxins entering the brain. Even tiny amounts of toxic substances like MSG and aspartame can cause the brain cell to so overreact that it becomes exhausted and dies. Hence they are called excitotoxins. MSG, a *crystalline* substance like DNA, damages parts of the brain like the hypothalamus that govern many systems in the body.

As with aspartame, MSG also causes food cravings and can make people fat. The epidemic of obesity exploding across the world is largely caused by these additives, the use of which has mirrored the rise in overweight people. This epidemic is caused to a large extent by the effect on the hypothalamus that regulates hunger and weight. Rats fed MSG became massively obese and their hypothalamus was found to be in a shocking state. Another similarity with aspartame is the way MSG was allowed onto the market without adequate safety checks and most of the later studies into its health effects have been conducted – as usual – by 'researchers' linked to the food giants. The food corporations that profit massively from MSG say that it's safe. Phew, that's okay, then, you had me worried for a second.

I mentioned in an earlier chapter how vaccines contain *mercury*. Even in small amounts this, yet again, is known to damage DNA and impair its ability to repair itself. It also destabilises the neurotubules that are fundamental to normal brain cell function. Mercury activates microglial cells and this, as with aspartame and MSG, increases excitotoxicity that adversely affects brain function. The potential neurological consequences include autism. Studies by the University of Calgary Faculty of Medicine discovered rapid damage to brain cells from minute amounts of mercury. They concluded that it causes neurological damage consistent with Alzheimer's. An indication of the potential for mercury to devastate the DNA body–mind–emotion network is the story of an English woman called Mary Stephenson. At the age of 21, she had 19 teeth filled with amalgam (52 per cent of which is mercury) and she began to suffer from crippling suicidal depression that no therapist or antidepressant could treat. It was only *40 years* of hell later that a friend suggested that her condition might be caused by her mercury fillings. She had them replaced, went on a mercury detoxification course to clear the residue, and her depression disappeared. 'Every morning when I woke I thought, "Oh no, another day, how am I going to get through this?" Now I can't wait to jump out of bed in the morning to get on with life.' The only difference was the mercury in her mouth that, as with all amalgam fillings, was seeping into her bloodstream and short-circuiting her brain. The cell receptors that 'catch' the peptide chemicals secreted by emotional states are the same ones that absorb mercury and other chemicals in drugs, food and drink. As I said earlier, emotional chemicals affect the body and chemicals absorbed by the body affect emotions.

The Illuminati want *fluoride* to be added to drinking water because it, too, is a brain and DNA scrambler. For many years it has been established that fluoride inhibits the enzyme, acetylcholinesterase. This is involved in *transmitting signals* along nerves. Russian studies, both clinical and physiological, established that patients with dental fluorosis also suffered from disturbed nervous activity and *brain dysfunction*. Chinese scientists reported in 1995 that fluoride lowered the IQ. They compared children aged eight to 13 who had no fluorosis with those who had slight, medium and serious levels of it. Their findings revealed a five to 19 point *decrease* in IQ score for the children with severe fluorosis compared with those who had none. A second study of children aged seven to 14 consuming different levels of fluoride confirmed the findings. Fluoride attacks the immune system, our Norton AntiVirus, by diminishing its ability to recognise threats and causing what is called Autoimmune Disease. Cancer, rheumatoid arthritis and sclerosis are just some of the conditions that result from such malfunction. The effect of fluoride on the thyroid, which regulates the metabolism, can cause endless problems throughout the body and a 1955 report in the *New England Journal of Medicine* showed a 400 per cent increase in cancer of the thyroid in San Francisco during the period its water was fluoridated.

Most people have no idea what is in this stuff and where it comes from. They just accept without question that it is good for teeth because this is what they are told to believe. Fluoride is a waste product of the aluminium industry and has been used in rat poison. Now it is in many drinking-water supplies (with plans for continuing expansion) and almost every brand of toothpaste! The claim that fluoride protects teeth from decay is nonsense and this lie is demolished in *And The Truth Shall Set You Free* and in endless other publications and studies. Dr Hardy Limeback, head of the Department of Preventive Dentistry for the University of Toronto and president of the Canadian Association for Dental Research, was his country's leading advocate of fluoride. Then he woke up to the fact he had been given false data and that 'the vast majority of all fluoride additives come from Tampa Bay, Florida, smokestack scrubbers'. He said that unsuspecting people were being exposed to deadly elements of lead, arsenic and radium, all of them cancer-causing. 'Because of the cumulative properties of toxins, the detrimental effects on human health are catastrophic', he said. A study at the University of Toronto discovered that fluoride was 'altering the basic architecture of human bones'. Limeback also said that Canada was spending more money treating dental fluorosis than treating cavities. He said that fluoride had been in Toronto's drinking water for some 40 years while Vancouver was fluoride free, but that Toronto had more cavities per head than Vancouver. This scam is nothing to do with teeth. It is about its effect on the brain.

The Nazis put fluoride in the water supplies of the concentration camps to mind-suppress the inmates, and destabilising brain function is the motivation behind its wider introduction. Dr Limeback said that he had unintentionally misled people for 15 years because he had refused to study toxicology information readily available to anyone. 'Poisoning our children was the furthest thing from my mind', he said. I admire his honesty, and his words encapsulate why we have a medical profession claiming to know what is safe and good for us when all they are doing is repeating what the system tells them to say and believe. They are just sitting on their lucrative perches saying, 'Who's a pretty boy, then?'

Mobile phones are another attempt to short-circuit the central processing unit. Dr Gerald Hyland, a British physicist, said that if mobile phones were a type of food they 'simply would not be licensed'. If Donald Rumsfeld was behind them they probably would, but the point is taken. Dr Hyland's findings were published in the medical journal, *The Lancet*, and reflect a gathering concern about the effects on the brain of mobile-phone frequencies. One of his concerns is that cellphone use can be linked with aggressive behaviour in children, but it goes much further. A study by the Spanish Neuro Diagnostic Research Institute showed that a two minute call can open the 'blood–brain barrier', allowing toxins in the bloodstream to kill brain cells. This is what MSG and aspartame do. Even such a short call also disrupts electrical activity in a child's brain for up to an hour. 'This has potential for psychiatric and behavioural problems and impaired learning', the Spanish study said. Sweden's Lund University Hospital supported these findings and claimed that radiation emitted by mobile handsets and relay towers can destroy cells in areas of the brain responsible for memory, movement and learning.

Japanese scientist Masaru Emoto exposed water to the electromagnetic waves of a mobile phone and you can see the impact by comparing *Figures 80* and *81*. The water crystal was slaughtered by the effect and that is what these phones and masts are doing to us! Cellphone relay towers seem to be everywhere now and a common location is near *schools*! In November 2004, a report by the BBC, also detailed in *The Mail on Sunday*, revealed how Britain had 40,000 mobile-phone masts and one in ten schools had a mast located within 200 metres of the classrooms. A Central London school had *27 masts* within this distance, many of them hidden from public view inside road and petrol station signs.

When three mobile phone giants: T-Mobile, Orange and Hutchison 3G, were allowed to erect a 25-metre mast near three schools in Harrogate, North Yorkshire, a group of parents took the case to court. They wanted to protect their children from this blatant danger to their health, but the outcome was inevitable because the courts represent the system not the people. The local council had refused permission for the mast and the phone companies went to the High Court to have the decision overturned. The parents didn't want it, the local council didn't want it, but it was forced upon them by judges hundreds of miles away in London who will never go near the place. The parents challenged the decision at the Court of Appeal,

 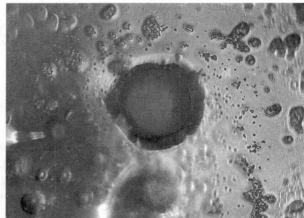

Figures 80 and 81: *The effect of a mobile phone on water crystals - and the human body in this reality is mostly water! On the left the water was exposed to words of love and gratitude; on the right, what happened when it was subjected to cellphone frequencies*

(For more examples see the books, Messages from Water, volumes one and two, *by Masaru Emoto)*

but Lord Justice Laws decreed that 'perceived health concerns' would only be considered (by system-appointed judges) in 'exceptional circumstances' (when the system didn't mind). Even the National Radiological Protection Board advises a 'precautionary approach' to locating masts near schools, but Lord 'Justice' System knew best. 'It remains central government's responsibility to decide what measures are necessary to protect public health', he said. Oh, please.

As this book was going into production in 2005, Professor Sir William Stewart, chairman of the National Radiological Protection Board, published a study warning parents not to allow children under eight to use mobile phones and highlighting the potential dangers for all users. The report, 'Mobile Phones and Health', said that four investigations had caused concern about the effect on the brain of cellphone frequencies, including a German study that suggested an increase in cancer around masts. Professor Stewart said that 'evidence of potentially harmful effects had become more persuasive over the past five years'. Translated, this means that governments have been quite happy to use the population, including children, as guinea pigs for the transnational corporations, when anyone who had the most basic understanding of the workings of the brain would know from the start how lethal they could be. There are 4,700 new cases of brain tumours every year in Britain – an increase of 45% in 30 years, according to the UK Brain Tumour Society. I wonder why? Duh?

Neil Cherry, a biophysicist at Lincoln University in Christchurch, New Zealand, considers the proliferation of cellphones, microwave towers and microwave pollution to be a serious contributor to cancer, brain tumours and increasing neurological problems. Leif Salford, head of the Lund University research team, said the exposure of the brain to microwaves from mobile phones is the largest human biological experiment ever. As use of the technology continues to expand,

156 Infinite Love is the Only Truth, Everything Else is Illusion

he said, people may 'drown in a sea of microwaves'. He warned that neurons, which would normally not become senile until people reached their 60s, could now do so 30 years earlier. 'We can see reduced brain reserve capacity', he said. This could lead to an increase in Alzheimer's, or dementia and, at best, people would have 'a significantly diminished number of non-dysfunctional brain cells and brain subsystems throughout their lives'. George W. Bush must have never been off the phone. The point that even these researchers miss, however, is that mobile phones and their towers are not a biological 'experiment' at all. They are part of a coldly calculated attack by the Illuminati on brain function.

It's not so much the power of electromagnetic emissions that poses the greatest danger, but the frequency they resonate. The frequencies once again disrupt the messages passing between the DNA/RNA and this inaccurate and confused information leads the cells and other systems to malfunction, just as a computer would in such circumstances. The pulses of digital mobiles mimic the signals of the body's cells and the DNA becomes an antenna for the frequencies emitting from the handset. How appropriate that they are called *cellphones*. The *Journal of Cellular Biochemistry* reported that heavy cellphone use could cause brain cancer and other diseases by interfering with DNA repair of wayward cells. Dr George Carlo, an epidemiologist, conducted a six year study and found that wireless phone radiation caused DNA damage. The common theme of all this crap they are feeding us through food, drink and technology is ... *DNA damage and disruption, especially to the brain*. They are seeking to short-circuit the DNA/RNA communications to stop consciousness imposing itself in the Matrix. People with what used to be called *mental handicap* do not have a problem with their consciousness, but with its ability to be expressed through a damaged central processing unit. It is the same with mental illness. Outside of this vibrational reality they are not handicapped or mentally ill, it happens on the level of DNA – the target of the Illuminati for humans in general.

Yet despite all of this, the social programming is such that mobile phones are now considered an essential part of childhood culture. A study reported in the UK *Daily Telegraph* found that mobile phones are 'indispensable' to teenagers and text messaging is 'an integral part of how they express and define themselves'. More than three-quarters of those surveyed agreed with the statement: 'I could not bear to be without my phone'. The Matrix has them.

I keep hearing how misbehaved children are today and how it is more difficult to control them, and so on. But are you surprised? Children more than anyone are being deluged with attacks on their DNA and brain circuitry through the horrendous chemicals in their soft drinks, fast food and vaccines, even without the mobile phones and transmitter towers. A *Time* magazine article in April 1994 highlighted the rise in child behavioural disorders. Attention deficit hyperactivity disorders that had been unheard of 15 years earlier were affecting 3.3 million American children when the article was published. Goodness knows what the figures must be today. Now let us do the maths: 1994 minus 15 = 1979. So the enormous rise in child behavioural problems began in the 1980s. MSG and aspartame (the duel attack is particularly damaging) had flooded the food industry by the mid-1980s and this is no coincidence.

The system's reaction to children affected by the poisons the system feeds to them is to prescribe brain-damaging drugs like Ritalin and Prozac from the system's pharmaceutical cartel to poison them even more. These drugs are also used to suppress children who refuse to download the system's reality. Peter R. Breggin, Director of the International Center for the Study of Psychiatry and Psychology at Johns Hopkins University, says that Ritalin decreases blood flow to the brain and routinely causes other gross malfunctions to what I call the DNA's central processing unit. As he put it: 'Ritalin does not correct biochemical imbalances – it causes them'. Other Ritalin effects include possible shrinkage or other permanent physical abnormalities of the brain, disruption of growth hormone causing suppression of growth in the body and brain, psychosis (mania), depression, insomnia, agitation, addiction, daily withdrawal reactions, impaired ability to learn, and the worsening of hyperactivity and inattention – the very symptoms the drug is supposed to improve! I found a website where you can order Prozac, produced by the Bush family-connected Eli Lilly, without prescription. The section about side effects said you should consult your doctor if you experience any of the following:

Fever; seizures; suicidal tendencies; heart pounding; anxiety; weakness; weight loss; loss of appetite; nausea; dry mouth; upset stomach; sleeplessness; nervousness; drowsiness; tremor; sweating; flu syndrome; headache; diarrhoea; dizziness; sore throat; sinus inflammation; sweating; gas; changes in vision; rash; yawning; decreased sex drive; abnormal dreams; impotence; abnormal ejaculation; chills; bleeding; increased appetite; vomiting; weight gain; agitation; amnesia; confusion; changes in behaviour; sleep disorder; ear pain; changes in taste; ringing in the ears; frequent urination; increase in blood pressure.

Prozac is a *brain reprogrammer* like all the others, and it is handed out like candy to children and adults under the guise of controlling bad behaviour. But far from doing that, Prozac has been linked to many of the children and young people involved in infamous acts of inexplicable violence. One of the effects of these drugs is that people lose their capacity for empathy. Eric Harris was on Prozac when he walked around Columbine High School laughing as he killed his schoolmates, even those he liked. So were others who have exhibited similar behaviour. What is happening to children is nothing less than legalised child abuse. The Illuminati are at war with the kids, especially with their minds, and so are the parents who won't wake up to what is happening. Even when they do they face the gathering power of the fascist state that seeks to control their children. The Bush Administration launched the Orwellian 'New Freedom Initiative' that plans to introduce the *compulsory* screening of *every* American for mental illness and they are starting with the kids. A 'commission' was recruited from the Illuminati pharmaceutical cartel in 2001 to study mental illness in the population and it reported that 'despite their prevalence, mental disorders often go undiagnosed'. As a solution to this problem it recommended comprehensive mental health screening for 'consumers of all ages', including preschool children, because the emotional disorders of childhood were often 'undiagnosed and untreated'. Who will decide who needs treatment? The government and the pharmaceutical cartel will – in other words, the Illuminati.

All these attacks on brain cell communication will also be having consequences for the role of the corpus callosum that connects both hemispheres of the brain and transmits information between them. It is in the interests of the Illuminati to stop us integrating these 'two minds' into a unified whole because it keeps us in a state of imbalance and separation. They particularly want us to be dominated by left brain reality, which is mirrored in the materialistic, bottom-line, 'western society' that has colonised the world. The more they can suppress information passing from the intuitive right hemisphere into the left, the more they will imprison perception in the world of 'matter', words and holographic form – the Time Loop. I'm sure the corpus callosum is a major target of the chemical and electromagnetic onslaught on the human brain.

I describe the *microchip* as the jewel in the crown of the Illuminati (Matrix) agenda because it is their most effective potential weapon in the control of our DNA/RNA. Microchips are about surveillance on one level, but that's not the main motive. They want people to be microchipped to give them a direct connection to the DNA circuitry that regulates our 'physical' health and our mental and emotional states and responses. The mind and emotions are phenomena of the DNA and can be manipulated by reprogramming the DNA and the way the RNA reads the program. This is why the CIA scientist told me in 1997 that messages sent from the computer to a human microchip could kill people, cause severe pain or illness, and manipulate them mentally and emotionally. He said this included making them docile or aggressive, sexually high or suppressed, and affecting their thought processes to the extent that they couldn't think straight or were influenced in their actions by what the chip was receiving. How appropriate that the central processing unit in a personal computer is housed in a single *microchip* called a microprocessor. The Illuminati microchipping agenda is about inserting a mini brain which they control.

Once you realise the nature of the game, and what the world really is, you can see from a much wider perspective why the Illuminati do what they do. As I will come to later, an awakening is gathering pace, and consciousness is beginning to impose itself on the DNA program in increasing numbers of people. Suppressing this by making the DNA misfire through attacks from microchips, GM food, aspartame, and all the other assaults on brain communications and activity, is what all this is really about. This war on the human body/mind/emotions includes government policies to ban the use of health food supplements and vitamins, or to make the dose so small that it makes no difference.

Illuminati societies are founded on dependency because this allows the few to dictate to the dependent many and limit, again, through fear, what people will or will not say and do. Even most of those conscious beings that have begun to see through levels of the game will not act or speak about their realisations because they fear the consequences. These invariably involve fear of losing job, money or status, often all three. As I said in chapter one, society is structured as a pyramid of dependency with almost everyone having a boss to answer to. Through this dependency, and divide and rule, the system itself becomes the governor. A factory worker may have to answer to the supervisor, the supervisor to the manager, the manager to the CEO, the CEO to the chairman and the chairman to the shareholders. But in the end they *all* answer to, and depend upon, the *system – It That Must Be Obeyed*. The system is a Matrix program.

No matter how powerful you may appear to be, even a president or prime minister, the system is God. World leaders come and go, as do top bankers and business tycoons, but the system rolls on. It is designed to think for us and most people concede their reality to its threats and seductions. Ask even genuine politicians why some humanitarian policy cannot be implemented and they'll say the way the system is structured won't allow it. Why can't we just give our surplus food to people in poor countries who are starving? No, that would destroy local farmers and disrupt our own agricultural policy. Well, why don't we have the transnationals give those people back their food-growing land so they can feed themselves then? No, that would harm our big companies and affect food supplies, jobs and the economy at home. Here are hungry people and here are two ways of feeding them, but neither is believed possible because of the system. It is designed to block changes that don't serve its desire for the suffering, stress and conflict that generate its life force – fear.

Every year the BBC has a telethon, called *Children in Need*, to raise money from viewers for kids and their families who are often desperate for help and support. The projects the money is spent on should be 'gimmes' in any decent, consciousness-led society. But children who are handicapped, in poor health, poverty or emotional distress, have to depend on a night of charity to enjoy what should be a right. It is blatant confirmation that the system, and those who serve it, are deeply sick. In 2004, *Children in Need* raised £17 million during the evening from donations and fund-raising events across the country. In 2003, more than *£90 million* worth of missiles, bombs and ammunition was fired by British forces in the first *11 days* of the Iraq war. America is another country plagued by poverty and basic need and yet estimates by the National Priorities Project using official records said that by the start of 2005 the cost of the war had exceeded $152 *billion* (see costofwar.com for details). All this in a world in which, as the UN reported in 2004, a child dies of hunger every *five seconds*.

To think that all those people voted for Bush because they said he stood for moral values. There is never enough money to help people, but always enough to kill them. Tony Blair, who committed billions to the Iraq invasion and occupation, had the nerve to say how much he supported *Children in Need* (good PR, see). 'There's this huge sense of coming together', he said, 'And the whole country comes together and says this is a cause worth supporting'. If Mr Blair was not a system-serving software program the cause would not require support because there would be no children – or anyone else – in need. But the system wants the wars and it wants the suffering. There are no contradictions between money spent on need and money spent on war once you realise why the system is structured as it is.

The priorities of the Matrix, and the Red Dress programs I call the Illuminati/ Reptilians, are not the same as incarnate consciousness. One wants to generate fear and the other desires happiness and joy. This simple understanding reveals so much about why the world is how it is. We may cringe at the daily slaughter in the killing fields of Iraq, Israel and endless other locations around the world where horror is a way of life. We may survey the tens of millions killed and maimed in the two world wars and reflect on how appalling it all was. But to the Matrix, wars are orgasmic orgies of fear that provide its power and means of existence. A war, especially a world war, is like having billions of power stations feeding energy into the grid. Not only do the troops and civilians immediately involved generate terror and stress, so do all their relatives and entire populations worried about what the outcome will be. It is not only wars that do this. Society in general is designed to keep the energy flowing.

The study I mentioned about anxiety and depression in teenagers increasing by 70 per cent in less than 20 years is terrible news for anyone seeking a happy, joyous and harmonious planet. But to the Matrix it is a magnificent five-course dinner. The fear of those Jewish people terrified of breaking 'God's Law', and all the other religious followers controlled by the same software, are also terrific generators of energy for the Matrix; so is fear of the future and guilt from the past; fear for the kids and regret about the kids; fear of losing your job and anxiety that you won't get a new one; fear of what people will think and the frustration of not being yourself. Look at your own life and the world in general and it is a global power station generating fear, frustration and anxiety. If you observe what we call history, you see that every generation has been in fear and under stress for different reasons. Humans (and animals caught in the *Laws of Nature Program*) are manipulated to fear and vampired by the Matrix for the energy it produces. The Red Dress programs of the Illuminati are encoded to create the division, conflict, war and anxiety that serve this end.

The complexity of the system is structured to act like little flying mites biting you and getting you ever more frustrated as you symbolically wave your arms around in search of peace. It wants to keep you in a constant state of anxiety and worry. I am talking about all the forms to fill in, tax laws to observe, speed cameras to watch, licences to keep valid, and this is now intensified by the 'war on terror' and political correctness which pressures you to pre-scan everything you say. Even the ludicrous, incomprehensible road systems and one-way mazes in many towns and cities are squeezing more frustration from us as we go round and round looking for a way out (see Los Angeles). The same goes for traffic jams, lawyers and the endless red tape designed to suffocate and frustrate us. I am sure you can name a long list of things that frustrate you in the way the system operates. And here's the point. At the level of control from which society is manipulated, it is *meant* to be frustrating. It might appear to be bureaucratic incompetence and stupidity, and there are serious numbers of incompetent and stupid bureaucrats, but to the Red Dresses it is calculated design to keep us anxious, frustrated and boxed in. Actually, when I wrote that last sentence I mistyped 'incompetent' as 'impotent'; it was an appropriate slip. Bureaucrats may seem to have power, but they are really only impotent cogs in the machine and they are as controlled by the Matrix as anyone, often more so because of their rule-obsessed, law-obsessed, do-it-in-triplicate mentality.

The Matrix wants incarnate consciousness to be a mirror of the DNA software. In other words, to react to stimuli/input like a computer does. This is one reason why society is so robotic with, for most people, every day pretty much the same as another and ruled by illusory time measured by hands on a clock face. The structure of society is a barrier to spontaneity and increases the speed at which we concede our uniqueness to robotic responses. I mentioned this earlier with reference to education, but the same applies everywhere. Spontaneity is the music of the soul, the inspiration of the One – and maverick spontaneity is the worst nightmare of the Matrix. It opens your DNA to the realms beyond the illusion and it sings to a different resonance, beats to a different drum. The spontaneous is constantly targeted with an endless array of laws that say do, don't and can't, or insist you have the right form, licence or permission before anything can be done. The insane multi-million lawsuits issued when people have the smallest of accidents are now seeing the most innocuous games and pastimes banned that were part of everyday life when I was a kid. Most of the idiots behind this political correctness have no idea that forces they cannot begin to comprehend (remembering to breathe is a challenge) are behind this nonsense to further erode what we are allowed to do without the sanction of authority. It is the Matrix program operating through its imbecilic zombies that *think* they control the bureaucracy.

The car park at the apartment block where I live has been patrolled by a private 'security' firm contracted by the management company to stop people parking in spaces designated for residents. I had nothing to do with this decision, but I was given a card to put on my windscreen to stop me being issued with a fine for parking in my own space. When one day the card had fallen from the screen a parking ticket was stuck to the car by this security firm demanding £60 – well in access of $100 for, yes, parking in the designated space I had been using for some four years. When I invited the firm not to be so ridiculous they said it was a 'legitimate ticket', even though they accepted that I had every right to park there! Only when I made it clear that they would go to their maker still waiting for the money was the demand dropped. This is the level to which we have now descended in terms of policing each other and, in doing so, serving the system of control. The system is structured to make one person's loss another one's gain and this provides the incentive for the divide and rule on which it depends.

Another expression of the robotic agenda is the way diversity of culture is being consumed by a universal, vacuous, wasteland known as the 'modern way of life'. It is a land of fast food and fast 'news', instant coffee and instant opinions, the worship of celebrity and irrelevant banality, the soulless kingdom of the five senses. The cities in this one-track world look ever the same, their distinctive diversity lost to sky-scraping concrete and corporate identity. It is the perfect backdrop for the robotic mind and is, indeed, its creation. The whole rationale of the planned global dictatorship is to complete this cycle of robotic uniformity through a world government, central bank, currency and army – underpinned by a microchipped populous. What we call globalisation is designed to stop whole countries from being spontaneous and making decisions that fit their particular wants and needs. You can't do this or you'll face a fine from the European Union and you can't do that or you will face a fine from the World Trade Organisation; this decision can't be made without permission from the IMF and that decision can't be acted upon without sanction from the World Bank. Ah, yes, banks.

The entire banking system, controlled by the Illuminati Red Dress families, has one aim in its programmed mind: to suppress choice (spontaneity) by making almost every choice dependent upon the 'money' it controls. Choice is linked to money and money is controlled by the banks, so the banks control choice. Or we are led to believe they do. The idea is to shackle the population with a constant need to earn money to survive another day, week or month. Hate your job, unhappy and frustrated every day? Well, that's just too bad. You have that mortgage to pay, debts to service, and a family to feed. What do you think you are, Infinite Consciousness? Keep their heads down, concentrating on survival or pursuing some system-defined 'success', and they will be prisoners of the five senses – the DNA. Gotchaaaaaaa!

Here you have the main reason why society is obsessed with the five senses of sight, touch, sound, taste and smell. Virtually everything, certainly everything produced by Illuminati manipulation, is aimed at this. Watch any group of television advertisements and the five senses will be the target. These senses are the access codes to the DNA and its central processing unit because they are decoded and defined by the brain and the DNA/RNA network of crystalline transmitter/receivers. What you taste and how it tastes to you is decided by the brain/DNA, as is what you see, feel, hear and smell (or believe you do). The five senses are illusions and they are fundamental to holding us in the bigger Illusion, the Matrix. What you eat, with few exceptions, is produced with chemicals and poisons from Illuminati biotech and pharmaceutical companies that manipulate your brain and tell you what to taste. What you think you see is defined by what the Illuminati, through control of media and education, have told you to see. What you hear, like music, is produced by Illuminati corporations who decide what artists to support and sounds (frequencies) to market. Hook the five senses and the fish will swim in the Matrix unaware of what lies beyond the surface. If we look again at the words of writer Michael Ellner, we can appreciate with an even greater awareness why the world is as he describes. He said:

'Just look at us. Everything is backwards; everything is upside down. Doctors destroy health, lawyers destroy justice, universities destroy knowledge, governments destroy freedom, the major media destroy information and religions destroy spirituality.'

The *why* is now obvious:

- Doctors destroy health because they are pill dispensers for a pharmaceutical cartel that seeks to control people – not heal them.

- Lawyers destroy justice because the 'law', together with banking, is one of the major means of control and suppression.

- Universities destroy knowledge because the Illuminati want an ignorant population programmed to believe the illusion is real.

- Governments destroy freedom because they are Illuminati corporations designed to dictate to the people – not serve them.

- Major media destroys information because its role is to captivate the five senses and peddle the illusion.

- Religions destroy spirituality because they were not created to free the spirit, but to trap it in a web of fear, limitation and ignorance.

This world of illusion is founded on the need to survive and the fear of not doing so. Pick any point on the Time Loop DVD and you will find the same scenario: control through dependency and the perceived need to survive. The Matrix itself is in fear of survival, the loss of the energy source on which it depends, and it has structured the illusion to mirror its own state of being. How could it do anything else? Its 'laws of nature' are the very epitome of the survival mentality that generates its food source. Crucial to the fear of not surviving is the *Fear of Death Program*. It is this that motivates the constant pursuit of survival to postpone our inevitable fate. Fear of death is the spectre that haunts our society and inspires the desperation to survive at all costs. Chinese philosopher Chang-Tzu said of this:

'The birth of a man is the birth of his sorrow. The longer he lives, the more stupid he becomes, because his anxiety to avoid unavoidable death becomes more and more acute. What bitterness! He lives for what is always out of reach! His thirst for survival in the future makes him incapable of living in the present.'

It is the fear of oblivion, Judgement Day or the fires of Hell, depending on which version of claptrap you choose to believe in. When Rabbi Furst prepares to depart for that great Cheese Danish in the sky can you imagine his terror of what may await? It's so sad when our only punishment is that we which inflict on ourselves. We followers of Bollockism do not fear death, nor punishment, for they do not exist. There is only *Love* – the rest is illusion. To know this at a deep level is to be free from the fear that concedes control to the Matrix and without which it cannot prevail.

While chemicals in the food and mobile-phone frequencies do affect us in our Matrix state, they don't have to. They are illusions too, more subplots in the movie. We can connect with realms of consciousness in which the laws of the Matrix do not apply because they are seen for what they are – figments of delusion. When we access that level of awareness we can rewrite the program in the DNA and cease to be at the mercy of fear and dis-ease.

*Free*dom is the absence of *fear*dom and this is the revelation that will bring this silly game to its rightful conclusion.

CHAPTER NINE

It's *all* Bollocks

The play was a great success, but the audience was a disaster
Oscar Wilde

The most effective way to disconnect from the manipulations of the Matrix is to laugh in its face. Once we take it seriously we become attached to the game through mind, emotion and fear. The Matrix only exists because we believe its illusions are real, but we don't have to.

The mind-game has such a grip on reality that people get angry, obsessive or outraged about the most irrelevant bollocks and this myopia cements their arses to the web. In fact, it's *all* bollocks. There is nothing, except Infinite Love, that *isn't* bollocks. But oh, my – *how* we get caught. For example, I made the point in *I am me, I am free*, about the word *fuck*. Oh my God, did he really say that? 'Ethel, he's just said that rude word, it's outrageous.' I love it how newspapers, moral guardians that they are, always write the word as f***. What the fuck is that all about? When you see f*** what goes through your mind? *Fuck*, exactly. So it is morally OK to *think* fuck, but not to say it. What bollocks!

Nothing encapsulates how deeply the Matrix has control of the human psyche than our attitudes to the word *fuck*. It may not be the most beautiful of sounds, but if you hit your thumb with a hammer I challenge you to find a better one to sum up your feelings. Like all words it can be said with venom, matter-of-factly, or in humour and it is the *energy* and *intent* behind a word that has the effect, not the word itself. *Fuck* is just a *sound* that can produce a disruptive or harmonious resonance depending on the intent. So what's the big deal about this word when the same is true of all the others? Once again it's programming. We are told from childhood that the word is taboo and this imprint dictates the lifetime reaction in most people when they hear the dreaded four letters. To say sexual intercourse is fine, though not encouraged because even that's embarrassing to many, but its one syllable stablemate is *definitely* persona non grata. Yet imagine if *fuck* meant something else, say *sandwich*.

Two pieces of bread with something in the middle is believed to be named after the fourth Earl of Sandwich because, it is said, in about 1762 he asked for meat to be served between slices of bread to avoid interrupting a gambling game. He had originally intended to take the title of Earl of Portsmouth and, if he had, we

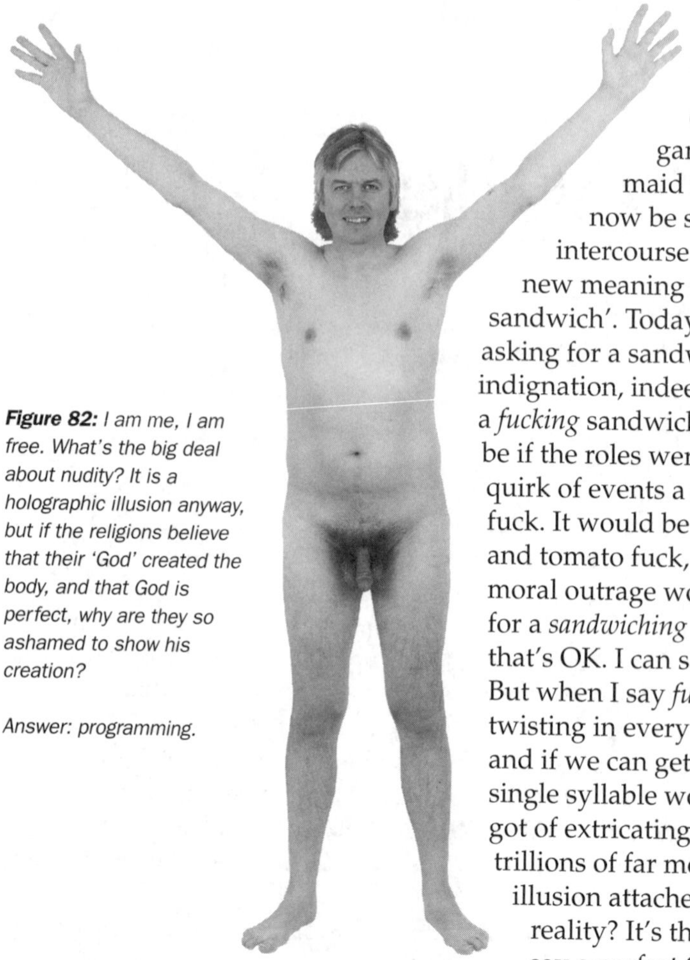

Figure 82: *I am me, I am free. What's the big deal about nudity? It is a holographic illusion anyway, but if the religions believe that their 'God' created the body, and that God is perfect, why are they so ashamed to show his creation?*

Answer: programming.

would now be eating *portsmouths*. It is also quite possible that if the earl had left his gambling game to have sex with a maid the word sandwich might now be slang for sexual intercourse. It would certainly give new meaning to 'I'm going for a sandwich'. Today we have no problem asking for a sandwich, but there would be indignation, indeed horror, if you asked for a *fucking* sandwich. How different it would be if the roles were reversed and by some quirk of events a sandwich was called a fuck. It would be fine to ask for a cheese and tomato fuck, heavy on the mayo, but moral outrage would ensue if you asked for a *sandwiching* fuck. I can say *buck* and that's OK. I can say *duck* and that's OK. But when I say *fuck*, there are knickers twisting in every direction. It's so pathetic and if we can get this uptight about a single syllable word, what chance have we got of extricating ourselves from the trillions of far more powerful ways the illusion attaches itself to our sense of reality? It's the same with nudity. They say a perfect God created the human body and then condemn you for showing it. For goodness sake, they are just illusory willies and illusory breasts. If the taboo programming was not there in the first place no one would give a toss about nudity (*Figure 82*).

People talk about wanting to be free and yet they can't get past first base by not being outraged by a bare bum or a single word. Deep breath … Fuuuuuuuuuck. There, see, did anyone die? No one's been hit by a lighting strike or a cruise missile? It's just a fucking word and we are *Infinite Consciousness – All Possibility*. Jeeeez. I saw a notice outside the studios at a Los Angeles radio station listing all the words a government agency decreed could not be used on air. It said the fine for doing so was $500,000. One of these words was … *shit*. You can say excrement and pay nothing, but use the word shit for the same substance and you are threatened with a fine of half a million dollars. Give me a shove will you? I'm ready to wake up now. We are so focused on the twigs, like *fuck* and *shit*, that we can't see the trees, let alone the forest. I am not saying everyone should go round swearing if that's not their choice, but if someone else does, so what?

Sex is another of the moral stickies that keeps people attached to the illusion. I saw an American right-wing Christian say that he was worried about gay marriage and wanted Bush elected to stop it. He was *worried* about *gay marriage*? Well, I think I see a way out of this: don't marry a gay, then. There, simple, what shall we do now? I am tempted to start an Internet advice column and call it noneofyourbloodybusiness.com. What right has anyone to decide if a gay marries a gay? It's *their* business and what the hell are we doing moralising about relationships never mind legislating for them? Whether you are gay or what they call 'straight' it is only a software program transmitted from and through the DNA/RNA. Infinite Consciousness is All Possibility, the balance of everything, and it doesn't have our version of 'sex' in its non-Matrix form. The super-hologram is where 'physical' sex takes place and gay or straight it doesn't matter. They are both expressions of duality, as is all that male–female stuff. It only happens in the realms of illusion and division. From the perspective we are discussing here, the sexual act, whether between 'straights' or 'gays', involves inserting a holographic illusion into a holographic illusion and our central processing unit telling us if we are enjoying it or not.

'Willy to brain, are you receiving me?'
'Loud and clear, Willy, just worried about premature ejacula … oh, there you go.'

I know I should be taking this more seriously because I heard a sex therapist on the TV talking at length about this 'serious problem'. What baloney. Premature ejaculation is caused by fear of premature ejaculation and the fear of not giving a 'good performance'. Someone asked me if I was good in bed and I said I didn't know because I am asleep at the time. Maybe I should fix up a camera to find out. This 'being good' business means getting your partner's body computer to agree that you are good. If you can do that you are macho and, in the tabloid jargon, a 'great lover'. This is don't-scare-the-children speak for being great at sex, by the way, and should not be confused with being a great expresser of love. Sex that involves consciousness can be an awakening experience and infuse non-Matrix energy into the DNA, but an obsession with sex of merely the body-to-body kind can lock you deeper in the Matrix because it is only a meeting of DNA and central processing units. It's like linking a PC to a laptop so they can exchange information. I say, what a pair of portals on that one. There's nothing wrong with connecting computers and it can be entertaining, just like body-sex can be. It is not a matter of right and wrong, but of understanding what is happening so we dictate events and not the software.

When the Matrix wants us to focus on something it must be important for control and this is true of the obsession with sex. Without sex many tabloids would be leaflets. I am waiting for *Who's Who* to publish a new edition called *Who's Having Who* because from what I can see they would sell out. There is an obsession with 'celebrity' sex that appears to be far more important than what the 'celebs' actually do.

'I think that woman's a great actress.'

'Really? What movies has she made?'

'I can't remember, but I know she's had it off with Ryan O'Neal.'

Sex sells newspapers along with the explosion of 'celebrity' magazines and, most importantly, it sells the Matrix. The sex drive comes from the reptilian brain, as does the interest in celebrity gossip. Robert F. Kennedy Jr, author of *Crimes Against Nature* (HarperCollins, New York, 2004), said of the media: 'They're airing stories that appeal to the prurient interests that all of us have in the reptilian core of our brain for sex and celebrity gossip, and now for terror'. Once again, this is no coincidence. There are calculated motives behind the selling and, perversely enough, the suppression of sex. Anything that holds focus in the five senses is of fundamental service to the Matrix and nothing does this more effectively than sex because it is an extremely powerful five-sense experience exchanging messages between the cells and brain. The desire for sex, which occupies people for far longer than the act itself, operates in the same way. Sexual fantasy makes you aroused simply by *thinking* of the experience. If you think of something that turns you on, your body will begin to react as if you were in a sexual situation. They talk about drugs and alcohol as addictions, but for many so is sex. In these cases they don't have sex – sex has them. It can grip them every bit as much as other addictions and hold them in five-sense reality. None of this is a problem so long as you know that the 'physical' is illusion because then you can enjoy it without getting caught in the trap of believing it to be real.

The *Worship Your Willy Program* is not only there to entice people to have endless sex; the game is more subtle than that. Newspapers and magazines are obsessed with the sex lives of the rich and famous few but, at the same time, they moralise about sex and make people feel guilty about it. 'We are exposing how this celebrity had group sex with three women. Isn't it disgusting?' Well, actually, as long as they were all in agreement, no it's not. This stuff is invariably written by moralising hypocrites who would love to have made it a foursome. The media is like the moral crusader who condemns pornographic videos while watching one after the other to confirm how terrible they are. They put sex in your face to sell papers while condemning 'immoral behaviour' and making you feel bad for doing the same, or even thinking about it. Another theme is that the celebrities have money, fame and sex with the beautiful people and, well, er, you don't. You are just an onlooker in life and we have launched this celebrity magazine so you can pay us to peek at what you will never have and never be, OK, HELLO? See how inadequate you are? Success is fame, fortune and being a sexual icon. Doncha' just wish you didn't work down the laundry?

This stimulation of envy and unfulfilled desire, especially the desire for sex, creates an ongoing frustration that can suppress the whole energy system of the body-mind-emotion network processed through the DNA/RNA. Frustration of any kind, not least sexual, can scupper the flow and manifest as disease, depression and sexual obsession. The Roman Catholic Church insists that its priests don't have sex and the same church has a global problem of priests using children for sex. One creates the other because whatever you suppress becomes an obsession. Energy flows where attention goes. To waft something in front of you and then say you can't have it, or should feel bad about it, is bound to stimulate an obsession with whatever's being denied and this happens with sex all the time in the media. Writer Oscar Wilde said: 'The only way to get rid of a temptation is to yield to it. Resist it, and your soul grows sick with longing for the things it has forbidden to itself'. Precisely, so long as you are not imposing your will on someone else.

Celebrity is the new religion with every genuinely talented or cynically manufactured 'star' sold as a Jesus Christ, albeit a fleeting one, to the pack of manipulated followers. Your old hero may have faded, but here's another from the Jesus factory; production never ends. Your software programmers have now decided that Rock is out and Rap is in and so that's what you'll get; and when we decide that Rap is now crap, we'll give you your Rock back, or Hip Hop, or Disco, or whatever we decide while making you think the decision is yours. It's a brilliant form of mind control called *marketing*, or 'hype' for short. People queue for hours in the rain for a brief glimpse of some film star or singer in their one-night designer frocks that cost more than the drenched congregation in the pews behind the security fence will earn in months. Performing someone else's script in a credible way, or singing a good song well, can put you on the 'A' list of iconic celebrity. They are the new pantheon used, like the old one, to sell an illusion within an illusion. John Wayne was a military hero without ever fighting a battle and, as we saw in California, a bodybuilder with the vocabulary of a three-year-old can be elected to political office simply because he grunted his way through some movies. The fact that he grunts his way through his political speeches, as well, is irrelevant in the ashram of celebrity when 'We love Arnie' is the only mantra in town.

We are told what to look like, what to say, what to think, how to act, who to worship, what to strive for. Norms are our guiding shite. But we are *Infinite Consciousness – All That Is.* What are we doing playing Little Me–Big Arnie when there is only one Infinite *I*? The Matrix seeks to divide this infinite unity by every means possible. Observe the 'world' and you will see a billion fault lines designed to divide and rule. We have religions, races, nations, classes, income brackets, men and women, politics, ad infinitum. The list is endless because new ones are being added all the time. This is essential to the Matrix because it depends on duality to manifest its vibratory illusion and it must keep entrapped consciousness in a state of perceived division to stop it connecting in awareness with the One.

Politics divides people all over the world, and billions take it seriously when political office is the almost exclusive bastion of the corrupt, stupid or myopic. It's not a matter of *who* we should vote for, but *why* we should even bother when the system is so blatantly rigged. You wouldn't let Boy Bush run a market stall without parental supervision and yet he's a two-term president who sends young men and women to kill and be killed while others of his mental age are at home playing with their Lego (*Figure 83, overleaf*). But people get so caught in this irrelevant tripe, as if their vote will change anything. 'Who do you think we should vote for? What do you think about Bush on the economy and Kerry on defence? What about their

Figure 83: *George W. Bush ... the prophecy of his coming:*

'As democracy is perfected, the office of president represents, more and more closely, the inner soul of the people.

'On some great and glorious day, the plain folks of the land will reach their heart's desire at last and the White House will be adorned by a downright moron.'

H.L. Mencken (1880–1956)

wives, which one would be a better first lady? Do you think Kerry would be better on Iraq? And what about his record in Vietnam, do you think he was telling the truth, and what about Bush avoiding the draft ...'
Will you shut-the-fuck-up?! It's all bollocks.

I give you *Political Elections for Dummies,* which, as you will gather from the title, is particularly aimed at anyone who voted for George W. Bush. Both candidates in US 'elections' (and other significant ones around the world, including Britain) are funded by the major Illuminati corporations and controlled by the same force. Global politics is just a game to fool the people (*Figure 84*). The money is handed over – well in excess of a billion dollars to Bush and Kerry in 2004 – and, in return, the piper asks the payer what music he likes. Those who funded the Bush campaign in 2000 have made incredible profits from the decision to invade Iraq by providing the weapons to destroy the country and the 'expertise' to 'rebuild' what their bombs had devastated. This includes that infamous duo: the Carlyle Group, fundamentally connected to father Bush, and Halliburton, the oil services giant headed by Dick Cheney until he left to become US vice-president and minder to the juvenile delinquent.

The 'party' system of politics was designed by the Illuminati to make it easier to control. Instead of having to manipulate hundreds of individuals making free decisions according to their own conscience, they only have to control the party hierarchies. In the UK, we have the 'Whip' system in which the party leadership tells it's Members of Parliament how they will vote every day. If the MPs don't follow these orders their political careers go no further, and yet they are supposed to be representing the people who voted them into office, not the party dictatorship. In fact, most bills that pass through Capitol Hill and the parliaments of the world are not even read by the Congressmen, Senators and MPs before they vote them into law! American 'Anti-terrorist' legislation that has destroyed fundamental freedoms since 9/11 had not been read by the voting fodder when they supported its introduction, as US Congressman, Ron Paul, has pointed out. This party structure is perfect for the manipulators because all they have to do is control the leaders to dictate what policies the party will support. The Illuminati make sure

Illustration by Neil Hague

Figure 84: Neil Hague's depiction of the 'Lucifer' – Matrix – card game in which the people are constantly dealt from a marked deck

they have their placemen in control of all the major political parties (and many others) and this allows them to daily manipulate the 'democratic process'. What we staggeringly call 'democracy' is another word for dictatorship.

In 2004, Bush and Kerry were both initiates of the Skull and Bones Society, an elite secret grouping for chosen ones from the Illuminati bloodline families. There are a few hundred initiates of the Skull and Bones Society alive at any one time and some 295 million Americans; but somehow this secret society managed to supply *both* candidates at a 'free' election. The Illuminati couldn't lose. Whatever the result they would have had their guy in the White House, and Bush and Kerry would have simply pursued the same course using different rhetoric to kid the people that they did have a choice. Both candidates were asked about their Skull and Bones membership in an interview on the Public Broadcasting Service (PBS) and both refused to talk about it. Bush said it was 'too secret'. The interviewer let them get away with this evasion when he should have asked them why two potential Presidents of the United States would not tell the people about their secret society background because it was 'too secret'. What the hell did they mean it was secret and what were the implications for open government of this secrecy? But you can spot most American journalists and television 'news' presenters quite easily; they are the ones on their knees with their tongues sticking out preparing to lick.

Terms like *Republican* and *Democrat*, *Labour* and *Conservative*, are masks on the same face. But, as in 2000, the man the Illuminati really wanted was George W. Bush because his so-called 'neocon' (fascist) controllers, who orchestrated the war on terror, had their networks in place throughout the government and they were to be left there to complete the task of setting the world ablaze and destroying America.

So, for the second time, the vote was rigged for Bush, not least through electronic voting machines with no paper trail to prove the desired choice had been recorded. Just trust us, okay? The machines were provided by Bush-supporting corporations that also counted the votes! Among them was Diebold Inc. of North Canton, Ohio. Its chief executive, Walden O'Dell, was a top fundraiser for the Bush campaign who wrote a year earlier that he was 'committed to helping Ohio deliver its electoral   . votes to the president ... ' It must have been entirely a coincidence that somehow Ohio managed to record 90,000 more votes than it has registered voters! There were also other vote scams detailed since the 'election' on the headlines page of my website: **davidicke.com**. To be a stooge in this corrupt farce, millions stood in line for up to seven hours for the 'democratic right' of making an irrelevant 'choice'. We also had the insane situation in the so-called 'beacon of democracy' of having the crucial election in Ohio run by Ken Blackwell, the secretary of state, a co-chairman of Ohio's committee to elect George Bush! The same was the case in Florida with secretary of state Katherine Harris when a vote scam there gave Bush the presidency in 2000. The governor of Florida was Jeb Bush, the idiot's brother. America is not even a democratic country, let alone a free one, but still most of the electorate continue to take politics seriously.

The power of manipulating the reptilian brain is such that staggering numbers also legitimately voted for Bush in 2004 and they sure seemed to have figured it all out before heading for the polling booths. Bush had made decisions that slaughtered tens of thousands of Iraqi civilians and more than 1,000 troops, but Christians voted for him because he was 'pro-life'. He triggered chaos and violence around the world and removed basic American freedoms, but half the electorate voted for him as the best man to protect them and their freedom. He is a womanising, coke-snorting liar responsible for the death and suffering of millions and yet people voted for him to protect marriage and American morality. He is an idiot with the intellect of a pea, but people voted for him as a 'wise leader'. He used his father's contacts to avoid the draft to Vietnam and, like his blueprint, John Wayne, has never seen a bullet, let alone a missile, fired in anger. But tens of millions voted for him because he showed courage in sending others to die on their behalf. The greatest irony is that a vote for Bush was seen as a vote for American patriotism, when the Illuminati are using Bush to destroy America. World government and superpowers do not go together because the superpower has the financial and military might to tell the global dictators where to shove it. What we are seeing is Bush being used to front a plan to exploit American troops and resources to advance the agenda for global conquest while, in doing so, destroying the United States as a financial and military superpower. They want to engineer an eventual conflict with China in pursuit of this goal.

'Yeah, but why do you think the people wanted Bush more than Kerry? Was it because Kerry's a liberal and soft on terror, or ...?'

Aaaaaaaaaaaaaaaaaaaaaaaaaaaaaaaahhhh!!

Race is also a big player in the game of divide and rule. What we call 'races' are different software programs. They are compatible because most of the DNA is the same, but the minute differences lead to varying skin colours, facial shapes and body size. Racism is like saying '*Google*' is better than '*Yahoo*'. I say there is no place in this world for *Google* supremacists, the *Yahoo* caste system or anti-Spamitism. The divisions of race are illusions, but powerful ones for the billions caught by the DNA.

The appalling murder of Ken Bigley, the British hostage beheaded in Iraq in 2004, provided a telling example of what a sense of race and nation can do to incarnate Oneness. There were religious services of respect and remembrance, government announcements of deep regret, Tony Blair reading from the Bible, and even a minute's silence before a World Cup soccer match between England and Wales. I understand this because what Ken suffered was unimaginable. But where is the outpouring of grief, the government statements of deep regret, religious services and a minute's silence for the now tens of thousands of Iraqis who have been killed and maimed as a result of the American and British invasion of that country? Are the children who have been blown apart or seen their parents, brothers and sisters scattered in pieces, not worthy of the same respect and response that followed the horrific killing of Ken Bigley? Why such a response for one Englishman, but not for all those dead Iraqi men, women and children, perhaps even 100,000 according to one study? A sense of race and nationhood, that's why. Ken was 'one of our own'. And that's it, you see. When the understanding is lost that we are all One and division is illusion, we forget that everyone and everything that exists is 'one of our own'.

Instead, we are trapped in the *Proud to be British Program* and *Proud to be American Program* (available in all languages like the *Proud to be German* and *Proud to be Iraqi Programs*). Even these have subdivisions such as the *Proud to be Texan* or *Proud to be a Londoner Programs*. This software insists that people have to be born on the same illusory piece of land as we were if they are going to be considered 'one of us'. When you watch English professional football games you will see the home crowd hurling abuse at a player on the opposing side. But when that same player represents the national team the same people cheer him! These are different levels of the *One of Us Program*. Such software has been responsible for endless wars with the populations programmed with the 'us and them' mentality fuelled by fear and ignorance. It leads to all sides killing people they don't know, have never met and would probably get along fine with if they did.

American and British troops have killed all those civilians in Iraq while Arab 'freedom fighters' have responded by beheading American and British civilians, along with others from countries not even involved in the invasion. The troops and the retaliators are the same software and so the same mentality, but they think they are different and on opposite 'sides'. The software sells the ludicrous idea that you can judge people by the colour of their skin or the shape of their body when all is the same one consciousness entrapped by illusion. If people like where they live or were born that's great so long as they know it's not real. By the '*Proud to be British/American Programs* etc'., I mean to believe that people born or living in 'your country' are somehow better or more important than others, worthy of more respect and attention;

and to put the interests of 'your country' before the interests of justice for all.

Many of the best-known conspiracy researchers and writers are wired to the *Proud to be American Program* as well as the *God Program*. I once went to a farm near Tucson where I'd been told a group was meeting to discuss the conspiracy. There was a massive Christian cross next to the farmhouse and a guy was sitting alone nearby taking a break from a lecture. As we chatted, the extent of his bigotry became clear. From what I now know, I would say he was definitely something out of Windows 95, maybe even an early prototype. I asked him how he squared the idea of some long-lost American freedom with the treatment of the native peoples when the settlers arrived. He said that God had designated this land for white people and the 'Indians' were only keeping it for them till they arrived. He, and his like, hanker for some mythical time when the United States was really free. Reality check: it never has been. Was it freedom when the Europeans arrived to slaughter the native population in a genocidal mass murder? Was it freedom to force them into poverty and starvation on reservations that were often little more than concentration camps? Was it freedom to coldly kill the buffalo simply to destroy the way of life of the native peoples and make them dependent on you? Was it freedom to purposely give them smallpox to kill as many as you could? Was it freedom to impose the Christian religion on them, and European settlers, through inquisition, violence and psychological fascism?

There never has been a free United States and there never will be until the population frees itself from the illusion of God Bless America, Land of the Free. 'How can you say that when it's the greatest country in the woooorld?' *Bollocks*. There *are no* countries. They are software programs that only exist as signals decoded in the brain. They are illusions written into the program to divide, rule and delude us. You are not American, British, South African, Mexican – any of them. You are Infinite Consciousness experiencing a holographic illusion designed to make you *believe* you are American, British, South African or Mexican.

By the way, some people think that when you expose the centralisation of global power you must be a nationalistic flag-flier. Well, some are, but the only good thing about flags for me is to tell you the wind direction. I watched an American cowboy show in which a John Wayne sound-a-like said: 'Look after your flag and your flag will look after you'. Given the dishevelled state of him I think his flag was in breach of contract. My challenge to global centralisation is about people having control over decisions that affect them, not pulling up the ladder and repelling all boarders. Nationalism and global centralisation are two expressions of the same bollocks.

There is a smaller version of these polarities known as parents and family. The parents invariably provide the centralisation of power and families, in general, operate on nationalistic lines – 'We're family, we look after our own'. Again, I can understand this, but it's still illusion. The only difference between a parent and child is the point where they entered the DVD/movie. The ones that entered at point A become the parents of those who enter a few scenes down the disk. They are parents only because they combined their DNA software to provide the holograms for others to experience the Time Loop. This 'blood is thicker than water' stuff is still more illusion. You can feel an empathy and connection to someone you have known for ten minutes that you will often never experience in a lifetime of trying with parents and siblings. This connection can happen within families, but it doesn't have to, as we see in so many cases. Even then, it is not the illusory holographic 'family' that is behind the connection, but the consciousness directing the software we *call* the family. It can also be that the DNA (body-mind-emotions) is programmed to be attracted to another program for a mutual experience in the Reincarnation–Karma illusion, but this is a different level of connection, often more a marriage of convenience than Infinite Oneness. I love being with my family and seeing them develop and I'm not for a moment saying that people shouldn't operate as a family unit if that is what they choose. We simply need to understand what a family really is and then we can enjoy the experience (or walk away) without the illusion controlling us. If we don't have this understanding, families can be a nightmare that haunts us for a lifetime.

Many parents seem to believe that they have the right to tell their children how to think, what to believe and how they should live their illusory lives. The arrogance of it never ceases to stagger me. I saw in that *Jewish Law* television series how children are brought up from birth to follow the strict and extreme beliefs of their parents. A boy's hair is not cut until he is three because Jews are commanded not to touch the fruit of the tree until the third year. At that point comes the ceremonial cutting of the hair, leaving the 'sacred side locks', and from this time he has to wear the Jewish cap. He is *three* and has no say in what religion, if any, he wants to follow. It is the same with Jewish babies circumcised only because religious law demands it, and Christian babies baptised into the church without any choice in the matter. The day after the hair-cutting ceremony (the Sikhs must be aghast) the Jewish toddler is taken to school to be taught the Hebrew alphabet. The shorn lad in the documentary looked totally bewildered at what was going on, but he had seen nothing yet. A lifetime of following the letter of the Torah awaited him.

Even the way children get out of bed is governed by the dictates of Jewish law. They have to dress from the top down with the right side clothed before the left. The kids are programmed with robotic behaviour from the earliest of ages. They have to put on the skullcap the moment they wake, and a bowl of water is brought for them to wash their hands. Rabbi Dovid Jaffe explained that the hands have to be washed immediately because 'they might have touched areas in the night which are spiritually unclean'. This is what is known to others as 'scratching the bollocks'. If God made bollocks, how can they be spiritually unclean? Girls and boys officially become adults in orthodox Jewish law at 12 and 13 respectively, when they become responsible for all their deeds, not their parents. From this moment they are not allowed to touch a member of the opposite sex until they get married, not even their brothers or sisters. One mother told us how difficult it could be to avoid contact when receiving change in a shop. The trick was, she said, to hold your hand lower so the change could be dropped in. Why are they doing dumping this nonsense on kids of 12 and 13? Happy Bar Mitzvah, my boy, welcome to a lifetime of fear and suppression.

Other faiths also impose their will on children through parental and religious dictatorship. Who are these people to tell their children what they will believe without giving them any choice or access to other possibilities? Can you imagine advocates of the Jewish faith encouraging their children to look at Christianity, Buddhism or this book before deciding if they want to follow the endless laws of Judaism that will dictate every aspect of their lives? Not a chance. Neither would Christian parents in relation to Judaism and other beliefs. No, your parents are Christian or Jewish and so you children will go to church or the synagogue and wear this cross or that hat. There has to be parental *guidance* for children to protect them from harm, but that is not the same as telling them what to believe and forcing your program on their reality. None of my children have followed a religion, but if that was their choice good luck to them. It's their life, not mine.

If young people want to be free they need to be strong enough to decide for themselves what to believe; they need to reject the download and not allow their parents or peer pressure to batter them into submission. Parents can be expert in playing the guilt card and making you feel bad because you don't do what they say or desire. If you want to be free, don't fall for that old mind game. If parents can't respect their children's right to freedom of belief then sod 'em, I say. They concede their right to be taken seriously. There are many fantastic parents who allow their children to develop without pressure and imposition, and many others who go the other way and couldn't care less about what happens to their kids, never mind offer guidance and support. Whichever type we have it is up to us to follow *our* hearts and not any parental blueprint downloaded into our reality. I can understand why people go through their entire lives feeling guilty about not living up to their parents' expectations, or are resentful at the way their parents treated them. But, hey, I bring you glad tidings of great joy here. It's all bollocks. In fact, there *are* no parents, only holographic illusions we call 'family'. It is consciousness, not family, that connects us.

Let us not forget, either, that the pendulum swings both ways. Children can also impose their will on their parents and use their own pack of guilt trips. 'Oh mother, you shouldn't be doing that at your age, it's embarrassing.' Well, piss off then and spare your embarrassment, the door is over there. Parents agonise over not being around for their children because circumstances prevent it. But we are Infinite Oneness; we are the 'parents' and the 'children', and the division and 'space' in between us are more illusion. I know how hard it can be to live that awareness, but only when we express love without irrelevant attachment can the freedom-bell ring.

Parental pressure is often connected to a major piece of software called the *You Must Make Something of Your Life Program*. This means 'succeeding' in ways that the system – and people programmed by the system – say constitutes success. This relates overwhelmingly to one of two things, usually both: status and money. We see the status software in what we call celebrity, but it extends to all the jobs and titles that make us a 'success' in the system's terms. This includes the status of being a president or prime minister, lawyer, judge, chief of police, military leader, doctor, top businessman, stockbroker or television newsreader. These are illusions perpetuating the bigger illusion and that's why the system stamps 'success' on their CVs. Why wouldn't the system – the Matrix – want people to aspire to the roles that most serve it? It is no accident whatsoever that the occupations deemed most 'successful' are those that most serve the system. But this *success* business is worth a closer look:

Presidents and prime ministers are puppets of forces dictating their decisions and, in the case of George W. Bush, and many others, it's clear that a moron can be 'successful' by reaching the 'highest office'. He may be called President of the United States, but he is still a moron. His status makes no difference to that, except in our manipulated perception, and to climb the greasy poll of politics you need to have corruption in your blood and the ability to lie by reflex action.
Is that really success?

A lawyer serves the system by administering laws drafted to imprison the population in a mountain of codes, regulations and red tape. Mainstream lawyers charge so much for their system-serving that it denies the great majority of people access to the process or the chance to challenge the impositions of government, courts and police who are able to use taxpayers' money to defend the system from the same taxpayers they are supposed to be serving. They use the people's 'money' to imprison the people. Most of the 'laws' that lawyers administer are a fraud anyway.
Is that really success?

Lawyers that arse-lick the system most enthusiastically and unquestioningly can progress to become an even bigger success called a Judge. These ensure that the system's will invariably prevails and those that can be most trusted to reach the 'correct' decision will always get the high-profile cases that the system most wants to win. They are system-fodder, like politicians, and many are deeply corrupt within a fundamentally corrupt 'legal' cesspit.
Is that really success?

Police officers play the same role, enforcing laws to impose the system's will and defending it from challenge. Even the many genuine ones are forced to conform or they're out. Police officers don't primarily serve the people, they serve the system, with honourable exceptions. It is the system that pays them and, through their uniform or warrant card, gives them the power over others that so many crave.
Is that really success?

The military fight wars and invade countries in line with the system's agenda while selling this insane human slaughter to themselves and the people as 'defending freedom'. Many have seen by their experience in Iraq what pawns they are and how little the politicians who send them into battle care about the consequences for them and their families.
Is that really success?

A doctor is a mobster's moll in the organised crime syndicate known as the pharmaceutical cartel. This dictates the treatment that doctors prescribe (like cancer = chemotherapy) along with the national medical associations that the cartel controls. Doctors are programmed with the official view of the body and health throughout their 'training' and if they accept this Stone Age version of medicine the system rewards them with their qualification papers. As a result, one of the biggest causes of death is *doctors*.

Is that really success?

Leaders of transnational corporations are deemed to be extremely successful people earning gigantic salaries. But what about the mayhem they cause across the world? They seize food-growing land and cause the local people to go hungry; pay them a pittance to work horrendous hours after all alternatives for employment have been destroyed; and bribe corrupt governments and security agencies to target anyone who challenges their corporate dictatorship. What about the murder and genocide that many of these corporations perpetuate and the wars that are fought to defend or advance their interests?

Is that really success?

Stockbrokers can make so much 'money' that some of the most expensive areas to live in London are often referred to as the 'stockbroker belt'. But what are these people, really? They are professional gamblers like those playing the tables in Las Vegas. The only difference is that the stockbroker is playing with the lives of billions across the world who take the consequences of how these guys 'invest' (gamble) their clients' 'money'. A good deal for them can mean poverty and hunger for people they don't even know exist. We have whole television channels dedicated to reporting the roulette tables of Wall Street and the City of London under the guise of the 'financial markets'. They might as well report from a poker game at the MGM Grand. Stockbrokers may be feted for being so rich, but they make their 'money' from the manipulation and misery of others.

Is that really success?

Television newsreaders and their fellow journalists present the world in the form that constantly reinforces the illusion, and report events in ways that suit the system and Problem-Reaction-Solution. Most – though not all – are doing this because they have no idea what is really going on and merely repeat official sources. Other 'stars' of the small screen present the mind-numbing banality that dominates the output and hypnotises the viewers into lifelong slumber.

Is that really success?

No, it's all *bollocks*. There are some within all of these professions who do try to buck the system, but look at what happens to a doctor who wants to treat his patients with methods that challenge the pharmaceutical dictatorship, or the university professor who tries to give his students a wider vision of possibility. Like the genuine police officers, journalists and others, they either conform or they're out of a job. *So the most successful people in these symbols of success are those who serve the system most slavishly.* This is by design, not default.

Whenever 'success' is being calculated, money will be in the mix somewhere, often right out in front. Newspapers and magazines blitz us with reports of how rich people are, as if this was a measure of anything. It's not even a measure of how much money they have because there *is* no money – only recycled debt. If there is no money how can anyone have money or owe money? A guy may be an arsehole, but he's a billionaire arsehole so that gives him status. Why? Often it's the very fact that he's an arsehole that made him a billionaire because of the ruthlessness necessary to acquire all that debt, sorry 'money'. The pursuit of status, power and control through money has made people slaves to its illusions. It has distorted our reality and tethered us to the system through both the desire for success and the desperation to survive. You can work with enormous dedication to help people, or make a profound contribution to human understanding, and earn very little. But you can make a fortune simply by buying and selling a house while doing nothing except living there or leaving it empty until the market goes up.

'I say, Bill and Ethel have made £200,000.'

'Wow, that's successful; what did they do?'

'They lived in their house.'

'And … ?'

'That's it.'

Even this is often more illusion because if you want to buy another house, they are all more expensive, too. All this does is make fortunes for speculators and increase the cost of a basic human right – a home – for everyone else. This is great for the Matrix because it means you have to work for longer to earn the 'money' for a home and serve the system even more unquestioningly. While I was writing this chapter the news in Britain was full of stories about a 'pension crisis' and how millions are going to live in poverty when they retire because they haven't paid enough into a pension all their working lives. People as young as 40 are now worrying about what is going to happen to them 25 years hence. Fear of the future is the biggest fear of all and includes the fear of 'death'. That is what this pension 'crisis' is really all about – generating fear. It is being proposed that people be forced to pay up to 15 per cent and more of their income into a pension scheme and fear is being used to sell the idea. The real motive is to provide an enormous inflow of fictitious funds to the Illuminati insurance companies who invest it in line with the Illuminati agenda. Those who control the banks are the same people who control the insurance companies and the same people who control government taxation. The whole economic system is a magic-show with the same magician in control.

'Money' is only figures moving around computer screens and we can create as much or as little as we choose. It's another illusion within the illusion, another subplot in the movie. We have poverty through lack of money when there *is* no money, and we have people living in mansions through ownership of something that doesn't exist. Yet we spend our lives trying to acquire more and more of the stuff and those with lots of it are given special status. You have got to bloody laugh. The Illuminati have hijacked the means of exchange by introducing the money fraud. As a result, they have hijacked the dreams of the people – which are largely related to the need for money to achieve what they want, or have money as the end in itself. One of the main reasons the Illuminati have targeted the formerly self-sufficient 'Third World' countries is to destroy their self-sufficiency and make them dependent on money. Once achieved, he who controls the money controls the country and its people through dependency on their means of worthless exchange.

What's more, we are urged to pursue the god they call 'economic growth'. We are supposed to cheer when they announce a rise in economic growth because that means the country is 'doing well'. But economic growth is merely the amount of money changing hands for goods and services. That's all it is. When someone is admitted to hospital or when an oil tanker pollutes a coastline they are adding to economic growth because they involve money being spent. A war adds massively to economic growth for the same reason, as we can see with the hundreds of billions spent by the US military alone. On the one hand we say illness, pollution and war are highly undesirable, but on the other the system's balance-sheet records them as economic success! 'Money', the stockmarket casinos, and economic growth are all expressions of the same bollocks.

Much of the clamber for system-style success is motivated by insecurity and a need to be recognised for achievement. Such is the way the system undermines self-confidence that people find it extremely difficult to find security from within. They must have confirmation they are adequate or successful by others telling them so. For this to happen, given the perception of success, they have to achieve according to the system's rules.

Children are prime targets for this programming, particularly the so-called 'tweenies', or 'tweens', aged between eight and twelve. 'Get them young and keep them for life' is the system's motto. A BBC *Panorama* documentary in November 2004 highlighted the 'tweenie' obsession with brand-label clothing produced by the Illuminati transnationals. These companies make fantastic profits often by producing their clothes in sweatshops in the poorest countries and shipping them to the West to sell at top-notch prices. This is called 'free trade', by the way. The marketing and brainwashing is such that children now apparently have a term for kids who don't wear brand clothing. They are called a 'Niki-no-name'. One *nine-year-old* said in the documentary that if she was not allowed brand names she would 'refuse to wear my clothes and … just stay in my pyjamas'. She added that she hated being called a 'little girl' because 'it reminds me of my childhood' and she revealed the tragic extent to which so many young children have submitted to the hive mentality: 'If I see someone wearing something, like for example, a poncho, if I like it I'll count it as one … When I get to five or six [people in a poncho], that's when I think I've got to have it'. A 12-year-old asked how his attitude to brand clothing could be called an obsession when every other kid of his age was like that. This same boy stressed that he did not buy the latest trends because he would be a sheep and look like everyone else. But then he revealed how he only shopped at a certain brand-label clothes store! Mary Macleod of the UK National Family and Parenting Institute made an astute observation:

> 'Children may think that they are making choices when actually they have been captured by a choice. They have been captured by an identity rather than being able to discover their own identity. So there are a range of identities offered to them and they have to slot into one.'

Exactly. And it's the same with adults. There is no greater way to manipulate someone than to make them believe they are making the choice when, in fact, *you* are. It gives them a sense of being in control when they're not and, as I have said many times, people don't rebel about not being free when they think they are. The nine-year-old in the *Panorama* programme told how the Niki-no-name children were bullied and picked on for not wearing brand clothes. Asked what she would do if a friend did not wear brand names, she said: 'I would still be their friend, but I wouldn't hang around with them so much because you are going to get bullied with them'. One parent had the answer to this lunacy – give in to the system: 'If they are getting hassle for something that can be solved so easy by buying the right pair of trainers – buy the right pair of trainers. Why ever have it as an issue?' It took a 12-year-old schooled at home to introduce some sanity to this madness. Imogen Donaldson did not want to wear famous brand labels and she pointed out that we are not what we wear or how much money we have. She said she had only been in schools on rare occasions and she found them 'lifeless, a bit like a prison'. This is what they are and they provide an environment for peer pressure to dominate and indoctrinate. Imogen, free from this environment, was able to see clearly what brand names really represent:

> 'It's as if someone owns you. The original word came from a long pole with a logo on the end that was burned into a cow's side and showed the farmer owned them. So just having the company's name across the top shows that they own you or something.'

The Illuminati network sees the population in exactly those terms – as cattle. It markets pop singers, like Britney Spears, that it believes will best influence the tweenies, and the kids download the image to which they are manipulated to aspire. This includes kitting out the pop icons in the designer brand names, just as they do with sports stars, because they know the programmed tweenies will demand to wear the same. It is an indication of how far the programming has gone when you think that people once used to be paid to go round the streets wearing sandwich boards that advertised a shop or business. Now people pay the highest prices for the privilege of *being* a sandwich board for *Nike*, *Boss* or *Ralph Lauren* and kids are given a hard time if they don't, or can't, do the same. Yet again it is seeking success on the system's terms for the system's benefit. 'My tee-shirt says "*Armani*" on the front, so I've made it! Yours says nothing – you're a failure.'

182

Infinite Love is the Only Truth, Everything Else is Illusion

Mention of pop singers brings us back to the pursuit of status and money as a symbol of success. When you see these *Pop Idol* shows on television, and their burgeoning offshoots, there are thousands of people willing to undergo the most horrendous ridicule for the faintest chance that they will become a 'star'. What agony they go through waiting for some 'celebrity' judge like Simon Cowell to decree their fate and what relief and gratitude follows their progress to the next stage of their exploitation. 'Oh, thank you Simon; I'm so grateful Simon.' I'm not having a go at Cowell as a person, he may or may not be a very nice chap behind his cultivated image, but the way he is seen by wannabe 'stars' encapsulates how the system controls us through a desire to succeed on its terms. Fame is such a drug because the sense of security comes from without, not within, and has to be constantly fed. This is not always the case and there are exceptions to everything I am saying, but it is a common theme. People look to others to tell them how wonderful they are and many of the most famous and lauded actors and singers are the most insecure of personalities. System-dictated success is their emotional crutch.

Once we fall for this one we are handing control of our lives to those we seek to impress. Whatever we think will impress or attract the 'right people', that is what we do. Soon we don't know who 'we' are anymore because the painted personality has taken over. Why do we have to impress anyone? Bollocks to Simon Cowell and the millions of other self-appointed judges throughout society that we concede our power to. You are *already* a star because you are the *Infinite One, All That Is* and *Ever Can Be*. Are we really saying that the Infinite has to impress a hologram called Simon Cowell or anyone else? Are you kidding? The Infinite – YOU – doesn't have to succeed by being a president, lawyer, judge, pop star or anything else. You are *everything*, including Simon Cowell and all the other illusions that people think they have to impress – the boss, kids at school, parents, teachers, sports coaches, the public in general. It's all *bollocks*.

We don't have to impress people because we've already made it and there was never a moment when we hadn't. We are always the One and we have just been manipulated to forget. This amnesia has made us creatures of the DNA Matrix which perceives in terms of division, hierarchy, success and failure, us and them, little me. Simon Cowell is considered a success because of the *Status Through Fame and Money Program*. Why is he thought more successful than a road cleaner or refuse collector? Which one would you miss most if they didn't report for work for a month: the guy taking your trash away on a truck or the guy bringing it to you on a TV screen? The reason the refuse collector is not considered a success is the reverse of what makes Cowell a 'star'. He lacks status because he lacks fame and money. But status is so illusory and irrelevant because it depends on a job title and/or what the system designates as status. One day you can have power and status and the next you retire and it's all gone. It wasn't *you* who had the power and status, but the job title owned by the system. So it is with people in uniform. They don't have the power – the uniform does. We have allowed the illusions of the Matrix to distort our values, perceptions and even our dreams. If you have a need to be seen as successful, the Matrix has you. If you have a need to be liked or respected, the

Matrix has you. If you think someone is more successful than another because of their fame, status and money, the Matrix has you. But it doesn't have to be like that.

Imagine yourself lying on a bed with ten minutes to live. Okay, not the most pleasant of thoughts (unless you follow the same football team as me), but it's an important point I am making and a good way to unplug from the illusions of the Matrix. You know you have a few minutes left in this 'world', so, in that mode, what matters to you now? Does it matter that you didn't get that job you strove for all your life? Does it even matter if you did? Was all that effort, worry and sacrifice worth it for the temporary, illusory, status it brought you in the eyes of those controlled by the system's perverted 'values' of success? Does it matter that you were a president or prime minister, or neither? Does it matter that you were a lawyer or a judge, or neither? Does it matter that you were chief of police, a top businessman, doctor, television presenter or the guy who swept the roads? Does it matter that you were a billionaire or struggled to pay the rent? Does it matter that you had power over people and could tell them what to do? Does it matter that you were seen as a success or failure, a genius or crazy? Success and failure, genius and madness, are only points of observation anyway.

Most people in their last moments can see the futility of it all, the pursuit of money and system-implanted versions of success. The trick is to suss this before such beliefs have dictated your life, but even then it doesn't matter because that's an illusion, too. Vital to this realisation is not to get caught in the subplots, the diversions. All the aspects of society I have described in this chapter are subplots in the movie: politics, religion, celebrity, fame, money, sex, race, nation, success, family, fuck, shit – all of them. Yes, and even the Illuminati conspiracy. It is important to know how we are being manipulated on the five-sense level, but if we leave it there we won't see the true nature of the trap we are caught in. If we get too focused on the subplots we won't see the movie.

The Matrix is a web of flytraps to keep us in the illusion and the way out is to stop identifying with it. That means to change our perception of self from the hologram, with its name and sense of limitation, and know that we are Infinite Consciousness. When we identify with being human we are identifying with the DNA program and that is not who we are. It is this program that frets about people saying 'fuck', having gay relationships or winning *Pop Idol*. It is this that dictates most people's thoughts and emotional responses and in our ignorance we have allowed the computer to control the keyboard. But it cannot do this if we always remember one simple fact:

Infinite Love is the only truth – *everything* else is bollocks.

CHAPTER TEN

Logging Off

To love oneself is the beginning of a lifelong romance
Oscar Wilde

Always forgive your enemies; nothing annoys them so much
Oscar Wilde

Unless we stop this identification with self as a body we call human, we will continue to be slaves to the illusion. What we believe, and how we perceive ourselves, can either hold us in servitude or set us free.

If you identify with your name and your body you will have thoughts and emotions that relate to limitation. Try it and you'll see. It has to be that way because the whole foundation of the DNA program is to project an illusory holographic world based on rules and, by their very nature, rules always mean limitation. It has its 'solid' walls, laws of physics, illness, ageing, cycle of birth and death, and endless lists of reasons why something can't be done. It is the realm where *but* is king. I'd like to do this, *but*, … I'd like to go here, *but*, … I'd like to heal myself, *but* … The Matrix is feeding us the *'but'* mentality through our DNA and when we falsely identify with that program our consciousness becomes enslaved by illusion.

It's fascinating to sit quietly while you listen to your thoughts and feel your emotions in a way that makes you the observer and not the experiencer of them. Normally we operate as if we *are* our thoughts and emotions, and we identify them with who we are. We see them as our 'personality'. According to **hyperdictionary.com**, the definition of 'personality' is: 'The complex of all the attributes – behavioral, temperamental, emotional and mental – that characterize a unique individual'. What that describes is different versions of the DNA software as read by the RNA, or what are known to psychologists as archetypes. There *are* no unique *individuals* because we are all One and, even if you relate the definition only to this reality, there are still no unique people unless consciousness – Infinite Possibility – is involved. 'Behavioral, temperamental, emotional and mental' are all expressions of the program – the archetypes – and only consciousness can provide uniqueness as we perceive it. What makes us 'human', as opposed to Infinite Consciousness, is the program.

We misunderstand what emotions are and therefore identify with them. We relate emotion to love and caring, but it is a false association. 'Love' and 'emotion' are not the same thing, and nor does emotion have anything to do with empathy. Love, in its true sense, is Oneness and within the balance of Oneness there is no emotion in the way we experience it in the illusion. There is only the joy, bliss and love that come with unity. Emotion is a part, not a whole. Empathy comes from Oneness, because only through that can we fully connect with another expression of the One. Emotion is not love or empathy; it is a series of programmed reactions and they are constantly being manipulated.

If you find that quiet spot and listen to your thoughts and emotions, rather than identifying with them, you will realise they are not you. It is important to the experience not to respond or react to what you hear and feel as they glide by. Just observe them, unattached from whatever they are prattling on about, and certainly don't judge them or they will pull you in. In the end it's like listening to the radio. It is said that we are not our thoughts, we are the silence between them, and it is from this level of consciousness that we can detach from the program. When you observe your thoughts and emotions, the chatterbox in your head that never seems to shut up, you can experience the truth of that. The silence is your consciousness; the chatter is your program. Consciousness is silent because it has nothing to say. It doesn't think, it *knows*, and *knowing* doesn't need to constantly waffle on trying to work things out. Nor is it forever worrying about the 'future' or regretting the 'past' – the major source of mental and emotional discourse. In stark contrast to mind and emotion, consciousness is real chilled.

It can be funny to observe how our thoughts and emotions react to daily life. They can be stunningly dumb and dominated by fear. From the observation point of consciousness their reactions become so predictable and their programmed nature so obvious. I mentioned earlier about people in relationships who play emotional pinball with first one reacting and then the other. This can cause terrific conflict, and the cycle can only be broken when the couple stops reacting according to DNA program. Until that happens the rider is being ridden by the horse. When we stop reacting to program all that remains is consciousness and consciousness can tell the RNA 'laser' to read 'physical' reality in a different way. The software is all about reacting; it's what the Matrix wants us to do. When we react we identify with the program and consciousness chases the white rabbit. In doing so, its state of being mirrors the thoughts and emotions it believes to be its own and generates the energy that feeds the Matrix. Once you realise that your programmed reactions are not *you* there will be far more harmony and peace in your life. There are still moments when the program will con you into reacting, but the more you express consciousness the less this will happen and the quicker you will apply the brake when it does.

As you log off from the software and log on to consciousness, you will develop a spontaneity you never had before. This is the worst nightmare for the Matrix because it is a manifestation in this reality of Infinite Possibility. Some of the Illuminati's own documents say that mavericks (spontaneous people) are the biggest threat to their plans. Spontaneity does not concede its freedom to *buts* and the rules and regulations of programmed society. I'd like to do this *but*, ... No *buts*

– just *do* it. But what will people think? Just *doooo* it. Or even better just *beeee* it. How many times have you wanted to do something in the moment and then had your spontaneity mugged by thoughts and emotions listing all the reasons why you shouldn't? By the time you have processed it all, the spontaneity has already been extinguished by a programmed fire hose called 'can't', 'mustn't', 'guilt' and 'what if'? Spontaneity does not operate within such rules or it cannot be what it claims to be.

This also means to allow others to be spontaneous without imposing rules upon them. If you are obsessed with, or intimidated by, rules the Matrix has you. The people who say 'rules is rules', and enforce them without taking circumstances into account are spontaneity-free zones, carousel horses devoid of a rider. They often become government officials, car-park attendants, traffic wardens, security staff, police officers and many others with a rule-book reality that dictates their every thought. They are like speed cameras in uniform, unable to figure out that not every situation should be treated the same. This is the reptilian brain at work again. I had a guy press the doorbell one time who had come to do a routine five-minute inspection of the flat I was renting. His agency had done this every few months for years on behalf of the owners. He only had to walk a very short distance from his office, but when I said Pam was ill in bed and could he come back another day, he insisted that if he couldn't come in I would be charged a £30 fee. He said that this was the day he told us he was coming and there could be no exceptions in his programmed mind. When I observe such people I can see their circuit board being read and the RNA pressing 'enter'. They are computers.

Have you ever seen a computer being spontaneous unless its system is buggered? When you click on '*Google*' that is where the computer takes you. It follows the rulebook. It doesn't say, 'sod that, I'm off to AOL, tough shit'. It acts like a computer program because that is what it is and it's the same with the 'rulebookers' in uniform, the Windows 95s. Spontaneity overrides the program because it is an expression of consciousness – Infinite Love. When a computer goes haywire and refuses to follow instructions it could be symbolically perceived as mentally ill and programmed people can see spontaneous behaviour in the same way. They don't understand it because it doesn't fit with the program that controls them. There is a great line in one of the Matrix movies where the Merovingian character says: 'It is remarkable how similar the pattern of love is to the pattern of insanity'. So it is, at least as perceived. Love in its true sense is All Possibility and that can be seen as crazy to programmed limitation.

All this is not to say that we should go so far as spontaneously jumping from the Eiffel Tower. It is possible to do that and be okay because everything is an illusory reality, but we will only survive such 'miracles' when we are so disconnected from the program that our reality is no longer subject to its basic 'rules' like gravity. This was well illustrated in the first Matrix movie when Morpheus was able to leap between the buildings in the computer program while Neo fell on his face. One was free of the Illusion at a deep level, the other was not. To perform such apparent miracles we have a lot more deprogramming to do, to say the least, but we can make an immediate start by ceasing to be imprisoned by rules that won't give us the illusion of death if we don't conform to them. There are other ways to jump from the tower without doing it 'physically'. You can jump from a job you can't stand and pursue your dream without fear of losing your 'security'. You can do what you feel is right without letting fear of the consequences stop you. You can cease to allow the fear of what other people think decide your experience. All these are examples of consciousness disconnecting from mind and emotions and overriding the program. The 'world' you are afraid of only exists in your head and you can change it any time you want by changing your sense of reality. You are Infinite Possibility and you can manifest anything if you don't let the 'I can't' program control you.

I have been saying in my books that we need to think for ourselves and that is the start of the process that leads to infinite freedom. It is, however, *only* the start. The next stage is to stop thinking at all. But that's crazy, Dave. How can we live without thinking? In fact, we can't truly live if we do. Thinking comes from 'mind' and mind is the program. Mind thinks, consciousness *knows*. I can only go so far with this while using language because it is something people have to experience to fully understand. Everything I have said in this book has been subject to the same limitation of the language available and there is far more to know than I have been able to portray in words, and far more that I have yet to access. It is the same with the chasm of difference between thinking and knowing. I would put it this way: if you have to *think* about something, it's the Matrix. 'Now let me think' ..., 'I'll think about it' ..., 'Hold on, I'm thinking' ..., are all the program at work. When consciousness overrides the software we just *know*. If you seek answers, the Matrix has you.

By seeking answers you must be asking questions and therefore you are not operating as Oneness – the All-Knowing. When you access that level of awareness, there is an answer to everything, so long as you don't ask the question. Or, looking from another angle, there are no answers because there are no questions. There is only *knowing* because we are accessing the *All*-Knowing Infinite One (*Figure 85, overleaf*). When faced with a situation, you don't think about what to do, you *know*. When trying to understand how things are, you don't think and try to work it out, you *know*. When you are connecting in awareness with the All-Knowing, how can you not *know*? To achieve this state of *knowing* does not require us to learn anything or go anywhere. We have nothing to learn and we are *everywhere*.

'I'd like a ticket to everywhere, please.'

'Sorry, sir, you can't go because you've already arrived.'

We don't need to learn, we need to *un*learn what the program has manipulated us to believe. Mind is not the road to enlightenment; it is the *barrier* to it. Knowledge and *knowing* is not the same thing – one is mind, the other consciousness. We don't need to learn, but to awaken from the hypnotic trance and remember who we are. When we do, we cease to *think* and start to *know*. Some call this intuition or 'following the heart' and it comes from a far more aware level of consciousness than is usually at large in this reality. *Knowing* is the decision-making arm of spontaneity.

Illustration by Neil Hague

Figure 85: *When we open ourselves to the Infinite Consciousness that we are, we begin to see through the illusion and the Matrix loses its control of our sense of reality. Those still caught in the illusion see such people as mad, dangerous or extreme*

The program seeks to suppress this by using mind and emotion to pressure us to consider the consequences of intuitive decisions, feel guilty for doing things that *knowing* urges us to do, and question how 'little me' could possibly *know* anyway. This reluctance to accept the magnitude and infinity of who we are is the biggest block to reaching a state of *knowing*. We have intuitive knowing and then immediately begin to doubt it. That is the program kicking in to protect its control. One of the phrases you hear is: 'You have a lot to learn'. But we don't. We only *think* we do. To accept that we have to learn is to accept we are not All-Knowing, and to accept this means to accept we are not Oneness. How can the *All* think small? Only when the Matrix has you.

Vital to ditching 'Little Me' is to replace self-loathing with self-love. The system wants you to feel bad about yourself, to be consumed by guilt and regret, and to see yourself as insignificant, a loser in the game of life. It lays down blueprints for what is a 'success' or 'failure', a 'good parent', 'good husband', 'good wife', 'good this', or 'good that'. And it wags its finger if you don't measure up. If you accept the system's version of reality it holds you in a low vibrational emotional state where the Matrix makes the rules. Religion has done a magnificent job of making people loath themselves. The sinner mentality is in the DNA programming and affects even those who reject the religions that put it there. But we can disconnect from this genetic self-abuse. You are not your mind or emotions, your 'personality'; you are Infinite Love. That doesn't mean Infinite Love for everything *except* 'you'. How can you reconnect with Infinite Love while you consciously or subconsciously despise yourself?? What you have done or not done, said or not said, is irrelevant. You were caught in the program while thinking it was you. Now you can drop the disguise and love what you really are – *Love*. And why can't you love your programmed 'personality', too? After all, that is also Infinite Love; it's just that it doesn't know. Love and forgiveness for self and others, including the programmed manipulators, deletes the software that stimulates the guilt and hatred which holds us in illusory separation.

Once you realise that the world is illusion and the body is a software program manipulated to ensnare consciousness, you can play with reality and have fun with it. I have been asked many times if it is possible to make money or follow this or that career without being caught in the game. Yes it is, so long as you know it's a game and not real – although once you access consciousness this whole 'career' obsession is seen in a different light. I am not telling people they should sit on a mountain top and ponder every day on the nature of Oneness. Illusions control us when we think they're real, and to know it's an illusion is to breach that control. As I showed with the subliminal advertisements in *Tales from the Time Loop*, once you can see the manipulation it ceases to have power. When you look at a subliminal message in a picture it can talk to your subconscious without you being aware of its existence. But when the hidden message is pointed out you see it clearly every time you look. The illusion is like that. Once you are aware of the game, it loses its control. If people want to pursue a career and make lots of non-existent money, go ahead. But they should know that it doesn't matter if they do and it doesn't matter if they don't because both are illusion.

I'll give you an example of what I mean about playing with the game and being trapped by it. Sport is a major global entertainment and that's fine so long as we don't believe it matters. I love watching football, what Americans call soccer, and coaching my young son, Jaymie, who is a brilliant goalkeeper. I have a few teams I like to see win, but if they don't, so what? I know it's illusion, albeit to me an entertaining one. Jaymie would like to become a professional footballer, but if he does or he doesn't he will not have succeeded or failed – both are holographic illusions and he'll be Infinite Oneness either way. If you think in terms of success and failure the Matrix has you. However, football, and other sports, can be experienced very differently when you think the illusion is real. How the team they support is doing becomes everything to some fans and affects their whole life. They go into anger or depression when the team loses and the hatred between many supporters of rival teams is extraordinary to me. They live their lives through their football club and their own sense of success and failure is measured by how well the team is doing. The Matrix has them because they believe it's real and the outcome matters. It is yet another illusion within the illusion; another subplot; a hologram within the super-hologram.

This attitude to sport mirrors the way the *I Am Human Program* views life in general. Attachments chain us to the Matrix: attachment to people, status, race, nation, religion, money and, the biggest of them all, attachment to outcome. Nothing suffocates freedom and peace more than this. If, like sports fans, you attach yourself to 'your team' winning, you are setting yourself up for disappointment because the only way to avoid that is for 'your team' to win. Any other outcome guarantees disappointment and frustration. But if you enjoy the game without attachment to the result, the outcome will not produce emotional upset and trauma because you weren't attached to a specific scenario. You may have preferred a certain outcome, but you were not attached to it emotionally. Once again, it is the same with 'life'.

What keeps us in the illusion more than anything is our identification with polarity. The Matrix depends for its very existence on the duality that divides Oneness, at least in our sense of reality, and creates the poles between which the world of vibration can resonate. This can be seen in DNA with its two strands and in the two halves of the brain. Everywhere you see the polarities of light and dark, negative and positive, left and right, male and female, right and wrong, good and bad, for and against. This entire reality is based on polarity. When we accept this as real, and who we are, we disconnect from the consciousness of the One in awareness of itself. There are no polarities in Oneness and so no vibration. There is only *one* One and it has nothing with which to resonate. If you identify with a polarity – I am a man, woman, British, American, on the Left or Right and all the rest – the Matrix has you.

Infinite Consciousness observing through a female hologram does not make you a woman. It is the program that does that. You can identify with being Infinite Consciousness having an experience without falling for the trap that you are your body or your experience. To the Matrix, women fighting for their rights is just as important as men seeking to deny them because it creates polarities. The Left in politics is as vital as the Right for the same reason, and so on. If we identify with a polarity we create the other. A belief in the 'Light' means that you must believe in the 'Dark' or you would not have to call it 'Light'. It would just *be*, no label necessary. If you believe in the positive you must create the illusion of the negative or you would not have to use the word 'positive'. It would just *be*, no label necessary. A belief in God creates the polarity of the Devil. There is no God and there is no Devil because these are illusions of mind. But if you believe in, and identify with, either of them you create the other. When you fight the darkness you create it by believing in it. Many New Agers have told me over the years that I have to protect myself from dark forces and this usually involves some ritual or other, or asking the 'Light' for help. This is such bollocks. Why do I need to protect myself from an illusion? By believing that I have to defend against attacks from the 'Dark', I am creating the Dark in my illusory reality and giving it power over me. I am telling the RNA to read 'physical' reality in that way.

What you fight you become, as we can see with the way apparently opposing groups replicate the attitudes, behaviour and methods of the other. The resonance between them feeds both 'sides' the same blueprint. They are different poles, but the same *resonance*. This is why apparently 'opposite' extremes have the same reactions, attitudes and methods. The polarities are behind the so-called 'law' of cause and effect, which is nothing more than the 'law' of *reaction*. It is not a 'law', it is a program. When the Matrix and its Illuminati software instigate something like a war, or anything else contentious, they know the reaction will create a polarity – in this case anti-war – and the emotions involved are trawled as an energy source. It is Problem-Reaction-Absorption. Multi-millions of genuine people who want to stop war and injustice have been caught by the Matrix through the illusion of fighting for something. To fight for freedom is to resonate with its pole, fighting to suppress; and fighting in any form is a low-vibrational state. I love the one about fighting for peace. What staggering self-delusion that is. Doing what you *know* to do should not be confused with *fighting* for what you believe to be right. It is a totally different state of awareness that does not identify with being on a 'side' and so does not involve polarity. It just *is*. Reaction is the force behind the desire for revenge and nothing creates polarity more effectively than that. They say don't get mad, get even, but what we really need to do is get conscious.

This brings me to something that I know most people will find extremely difficult to comprehend and again there are not the words to fully communicate what I mean. If you thought 'stop thinking' was weird enough, get this. To truly connect in awareness with the One, we need to stop making choices, stop trying to change anything and have no sense of purpose. *What?* I know, but hear me out. Firstly, this does not mean sitting in a cross-legged position staring at the wall forever more. It is not that experiences don't happen in your life, it is what *makes* them happen and the state of being from which they happen. Once more this is something we have to *know*, not mentally understand, but I'll do my best with the words available. There are a number of lines in the *Matrix* movies that speak about 'purpose'. One guy says:

'Every program that is created must have a purpose. If it does not it is deleted'. And the Agent Smith character, a computer program, observed:

'Without purpose we would not exist. It is purpose that created us, purpose that connects us, purpose that pulls us, that guides us, that drives us. It is purpose that defines us, purpose that binds us.'

He might have added: 'It is purpose that *controls* us'. I am going to state the obvious, but sometimes that is necessary because we miss it: to be Infinite Possibility we need to *be* Infinite Possibility. We cannot be Infinite Possibility by being anything less than that. To identify with a single possibility is not to encompass all into Oneness. When we have a purpose we are not in connection with the One because the One does not have purpose, it just *is*. Another of writer Oscar Wilde's famous quotes was: 'Ambition is the last refuge of the failure'. Ambition is a state of purpose and wanting, not *being*. My dictionary says that purpose is 'an anticipated outcome that is intended or that guides your planned actions'. Exactly, it is association with outcome, not Infinite Possibility. Purpose is a program of the Matrix because, as Agent Smith said, it *defines* us. And it defines us as a *part* not a whole. When what you are can be defined the Matrix has you because Oneness – *Is*ness – is indefinable. When you have a purpose to do something, that is what you become. You are defined by self and people as a politician, lawyer, judge, stockbroker or whatever. To be without purpose does not mean to sit down and do nothing; it is to cease to identify who you are with what you are doing and no longer let what you do define you. What you do just *is* instead of what you *are*.

When I started my journey to expose the conspiracy I had a purpose and it defined me. I was a seeker of truth who wanted to alert people to what was happening. I was doing what I did for a purpose. Not anymore. I have no purpose in what I do and it is a completely different state of being that has to be experienced to be understood. I did not write this book with the purpose of alerting people, changing people or changing anything. I just wrote it. The words just *are*, the book just *is*. Within '*is*' lies purpose and no purpose – the One. When we make choices through mind or emotion we are pursuing purpose. I did not choose to write this book. There was no point when I made the choice to start writing – it just happened, no choice necessary. When we make a choice about anything we are using mind or emotion and creating a polarity with other possible choices. What we call 'guilt' is the resonance between choices made and choices that could have been made. When you don't make choices there are no polarities. To choose is to select and we do this by *thinking*, which is the program. When we are in a state of *knowing* there are no choices to make because we are not faced with alternatives. *Knowing* **knows**, it does not have to select from options.

When we set out to change something we create a polarity with the status quo and empower the control system. I hear that everything is always in a state of change and that without change – movement – nothing could exist. To quote Agent

Smith again: 'Without purpose we would not exist'. That's what the program wants us to believe. The trinity of purpose-choice-change is the Matrix. It is the realm of doingness, not isness. The One does not change in the sense that it is always One, always Infinite Possibility. Therefore, purpose, choice and change can only manifest in a state of illusory disconnection that identifies with form, limitation and time. Purpose implies to move into the future; but there is no future, it's an illusion. To make choices is to identify with personality, not infinity. To seek change is to identify with the movie, the illusion, not the unchanging One. And what we identify with we give power to.

Okay, I can hear the question and I understand it. If we don't pursue purpose, choice and change, does that mean we just sit around and do nothing while the Illuminati impose terror, control and mayhem? Well, yes and no. It is not about *doing*, but *being*. To *do* is to make a choice to do. It is a process of thought and that is the program, the Matrix, creating polarities. To *be* is to *know* – the One. The pursuit of purpose and *doing* gets in the way of that. Oneness is the balance of all, and the Illuminati agenda is not balance, but polarities. To challenge the Illuminati is not balance, but polarity. To *be* is to encompass them *both* and identify with *neither*. When we come from the perspective of Oneness and move with the flow of knowingness, things just happen without us needing to choose, think, fight or pursue. We might appear to *do*, in the sense that I have done something by writing this book. But it is really a manifestation of *beingness* because I did not set out with the mindset of doing anything for the purpose of change. I know it is difficult to get this over with language, but when you drop into this mode of *knowing* and *being* it makes perfect sense in a way that words cannot deliver.

The road to freedom and Oneness is not to create polarities, but to encompass them. When people ask me how I describe myself, I say: I am and I'm not; I'm everything and nothing; I'm everywhere and nowhere; I am all possibility and none. This sounds ridiculous in a world imprisoned by identification with polarity. How can I be all these 'opposites'? Surely I must be one or the other? But if I am a polarity, how can I be the *One*? In science they talk about matter and antimatter, negative and positive polarities in the realm of particles. When a particle and its antiparticle meet they 'annihilate' each other and their entire mass is converted into pure energy. The power produced by this fusion of poles is simply fantastic. The polarities with which we identify are similar in principle to matter and antimatter and we can bring about this 'annihilation' into Oneness only by bringing them together. Instead of identifying with one, we can be *both* and fuse them into balance. You identify with the whole, not the illusory parts. You are *and* you're not; you are everywhere *and* nowhere; everything *and* nothing; negative *and* positive; you can *and* you can't; you will *and* you won't; you are for *and* against; you believe *and* you don't. By being both you 'annihilate' both and what's left is Oneness. As we do this we dismantle the power of the Matrix that depends on polarity.

We are in the midst of a collective transformation, at least at this level of perception, although I don't believe it's the one the New Age and others talk about. I would suggest there are actually two 'transformations' and one is a fake designed to mislead us. The year 2012 would appear very significant to the Illuminati and this is also the point at which the Mayan Calendar says there will be a transformation to a new world. The ancient Mayans, in what is now Central America, developed their own measurement of time and observed repeating cycles that they detailed in the calendar. They said that a Great Cycle began on August 11th, 3114BC and would end on the winter solstice, December 21st, 2012, the point when a 'Great, Great Cycle' of 26,000 years would also come to a conclusion. It relates to the New Age belief about moving from the astrological Age of Pisces to the 'enlightened' Age of Aquarius. This is the moment when new cycles will begin, it is said, and humanity will be infused with love and light. A Mayan Calendar website summarised this basic theme:

'There is no reason not to take a leap of faith into imagining what may be in store. We may trust that it is time for humanity to awaken into a true partnership with each other, with the earth, and the Cosmos. By accepting this partnership we may claim our birthright and become Galactic Citizens who care for and sustain the planet, thus sustaining ourselves. This is clearly the challenge of our times. Yet, arriving just in time and on schedule is the Winter Solstice dawn on the day we may remember that we are truly Children of the World.'

At the risk of upsetting many in the New Age, I say this is the fake transformation. I have no problem with the fact that 2012 is significant in Time Loop terms, nor that the Mayans clearly had a remarkable grasp on the planetary and cosmic cycles they related to time. I just say they were measuring the computer program, the cosmic planetarium, and that the predicted transformation is as illusory as the rest of this holographic reality. It is another part of the DVD, another diversionary subplot. There is no time, and anything that identifies with it is not a transformation to Oneness. We are not 'truly Children of the World', we are truly Infinite Consciousness. Identifying self with the 'world' is identifying with the Matrix. It is a belief system that still relates to form, with being 'human', 'Galactic Citizens', and sustaining a holographic illusion we call 'earth'. Millions are caught by the Matrix in the fake transformation. The Mayan Calendar is one example and so is Ashtar Command.

I attended an event in London in which members of a remaining tribe of Incas told of coming upheavals and change. They lived high in the Andes Mountains of Peru where their people had remained isolated from the rest of society until, as their legends foretold 500 years earlier, a series of signs appeared that told them the transformation of humanity had arrived. The legends said that when they saw the signs they should come down from the mountains and tell the world that the next 'Pachacuti' had begun. Pacha means 'earth' or 'time', and Cuti means 'to turn upside-down'. This is a common theme and, again, I am sure the upheaval and chaos they predict (including major geological events) is designed by the Matrix to happen, as in fact it already is. But I still say the 2012 scenario is a change in the program, not truly a transformation to Oneness in awareness of itself. The latter is

Illustrations by Neil Hague

Figures 86 and 87: *As the energy of Oneness pervades the Matrix, the fear vibration dissolves and the reality of its captive consciousness is transformed*

nothing to do with an Age of Aquarius, which is just another scene on the DVD.

There is something else going on that does not relate to programmed astrological movements or cycles of time. It is a transformation emitting from a level of awareness in which illusions like cosmic cycles are irrelevant. To continue the computer analogy, Oneness is hacking into the system. Synchronicity or coordinated 'coincidence' can have many causes. It can be the Matrix program; it can be consciousness caught in the cause and effect illusion we call the cycle of reincarnation and karma; and it can be reconnecting in awareness – *knowing* – with the One, *All That Is*, and being drawn to similar states of consciousness. The synchronicity of *knowing* frees you from the synchronicity of the program. The trick is *knowing* which is which. It is reconnecting with Oneness that carries the energy of true transformation and anyone can do this by ceasing to identify with the illusion and *being* the One that they are. The Matrix 'transformation' and the Oneness transformation are running together and the way to tell them apart is their effect. Does a change or event bring love or conflict? Balance or imbalance? Justice or injustice? Does it further divide or bring together? Does it imprison or does it set free? The Matrix transformation is about changing the game; the Oneness transformation is about *ending* the game as we have come to know it (*Figures 86 and 87*).

Energy follows sense of reality and when you *know* you are the One, and express that knowing, you become the essence of the One. That's all we need to do to transform from limitation to All Possibility. The balance of Oneness strips away imbalanced thought and emotion and excites the particles of the holographic realm to vibrate ever faster until there is no vibration at all. It will balance the body holograms of those that connect with it, restore them to health and end the ageing process that sees so many play out their physical lives in pain and infirmity. As we are transformed from fear to love, so we send that energy to the Matrix central computer and rewrite its program. From there it is transmitted back to all holograms within the super-hologram and those programs are also rewritten in the language of love. The balance of Oneness will also heal the gaps in the fabric of our collective reality called interspaces. They are a symptom of fragmentation and cannot exist within unity. With that, and the massively increased potential to see beyond the veil of 'visible light', so much that has remained hidden comes into conscious view. As the frequency rises, so our relationship to illusory 'time' changes and those flowing with the transformation experience 'time' as passing ever faster. Oneness has always been there, but now it is being felt again and, for those who are freeing themselves from the program, home is calling.

We have been caught in a dreamworld that we have believed to be real. This includes those other dimensions of the illusion between which the captive consciousness of the Matrix 'reincarnates' from one program to another. The way home is to know we are *already* home and always have been. It is to stop identifying who we are with form, the need to 'evolve', to learn from endless reincarnated experience, and being subordinate to the will of some 'God'. They are all strands in the web of control, subplots in the movie. Instead we can know we are Oneness and see this illusion for what it is, a silly game created by our own fear.

If you live your life knowing you are the One, your entire perspective is transformed (*Figure 88*). What seemed important or fearful becomes the focus for hysterical laughter. When you look at the world from the perspective of being the One, all those things that annoy you or make you frustrated, depressed and in fear are seen to be the irrelevance that they are. It is worth asking when these situations arise: how would the One view this? Would the One care less if someone said 'fuck'? Would the One condemn sexual preference? Would the One get angry because a sports team didn't win? Would the One go to a voting booth or support a political party? Would the One follow a religion or contemplate the potential perils of a Cheese Danish? Would the One have to protect itself from an illusory 'Darkness'? Would the One worry about its astrology or karma or what it was in a previous life? Would the One feel the need to succeed or 'be' someone? Would the One go to war or fight for peace? Would the One worry about anything, regret the 'past' or fear the 'future'? Would the One be frightened of 'death' when it doesn't exist? No to all of them because they are illusions. So why do *we* do these things when *we* are the One? The only difference is between Oneness in awareness of itself and Oneness that has forgotten what it is.

Illustration by Neil Hague

Figure 88: *Transformation from division to Oneness is open to everyone. There are no 'chosen people',*
only Infinite Love

We act small because we *believe* small; and we believe what we are programmed to believe. It doesn't have to be like this. We can let our consciousness sing and *know* we are *All That Is*. We have been living a false identity, an alias that isn't who we are. But we can look in the illusory mirror and re-evaluate what we think we see. We are not our name, body, family, race, nation or religion. We are not our possessions, job, status, fame, success or failure. We are not even our personality, thoughts or emotions.

So what are we?

We are Infinite Love.

How do I know?

Simple.

There is nothing else.

Human DNA is a Biological Internet, Say Russian Scientists

After I had completed this book and it had entered the production stage, I saw an article on the Internet about the findings of Russian scientists with regard to DNA. I was delighted to see that their discoveries supported the main themes of this book and here is a summary of their work available at a number of websites.

The italicised emphasis and comments are mine:

The human DNA is a biological Internet and superior in many aspects to the artificial one. The latest Russian scientific research directly, or indirectly, explains phenomena such as clairvoyance, intuition, spontaneous and remote acts of healing, self healing, affirmation techniques, unusual light-auras around people (namely 'spiritual masters'), mind's influence on weather-patterns and much more. In addition, there is evidence for a whole new type of medicine in which DNA can be influenced and reprogrammed by words and frequencies **without** cutting out and replacing single genes [*as I suggested in chapter five and in previous books*].

Only ten per cent of our DNA is being used for building proteins [*many say 3% to 5%*]. It is this subset of DNA that is of interest to western researchers and is being examined and categorized. The other 90% are considered 'junk DNA'. The Russian researchers, however, convinced that nature was not dumb, joined linguists and geneticists in a venture to explore those 90% of 'junk DNA'. Their results, findings and conclusions are simply revolutionary! According to them, our DNA is not only responsible for the construction of our body, but also serves as *data storage and in communication*. DNA is an organic superconductor that can work at normal body temperature, as opposed to artificial superconductors which require extremely low temperatures to function. In addition, all superconductors are able to store light and information. This further explains how DNA can store information.

The Russian linguists found that the genetic code, especially in the apparently useless 90%, follows the same rules as all our human languages. To this end they compared the rules of syntax (the way in which words are put together to form phrases and sentences), semantics (the study of meaning in language forms) and the basic rules of grammar. They found that the alkalines of our DNA follow a regular grammar and do have set rules just like our languages. So human languages did not appear coincidentally but are a reflection of our inherent DNA [*the program*].

The Russian biophysicist and molecular biologist, Pjotr Garjajev, and his colleagues, also explored the *vibrational behaviour* of the DNA. The bottom line was: 'Living chromosomes function just like solitonic-*holographic computers using the endogenous DNA laser radiation*'. [Solitons are a special type of light wave that doesn't change shape as it travels.] This means that they managed, for example, to modulate certain frequency patterns onto a *laser ray*, and used it to influence the DNA frequency and thus the genetic information itself. [*This process is what we call 'Evolution', as I said earlier*]. Since the basic structure of DNA-alkaline pairs, and of language, are of the same structure, no DNA decoding is necessary. One can simply use words and sentences of the human language! This, too, was experimentally proven! [*This phenomenon is captured in the water crystal images of Masaru Emoto formed by words and frequencies.*]

Living DNA substance will always react to language-modulated laser rays, and even to radio waves, if the proper frequencies are being used. This finally and scientifically explains why affirmations, autogenous training, hypnosis and the like can have such strong effects on humans and their bodies. It is entirely normal and natural for our DNA to react to language. [*It is a computer program that can be rewritten by this data input*]. While western researchers cut single genes from the DNA strands and insert them elsewhere, the Russians enthusiastically worked on devices that can influence the cellular metabolism through suitably modulated radio and light frequencies and thus repair genetic defects.

Garjajev's research group succeeded in proving with this method that chromosomes damaged by x-rays can be repaired. They even captured information patterns of a particular DNA and transmitted it onto another, so reprogramming cells to another genome. They successfully transformed, for example, frog embryos to salamander embryos simply by transmitting the DNA information patterns! [*In others words, they rewrote the program and changed – shapeshifted! – the waveform/hologram.*] This way the entire information was transmitted without any of the side effects or disharmonies encountered when cutting out and reintroducing single genes from the DNA. This represents an unbelievable, world-transforming revolution and sensation! All this by simply applying vibration and language instead of the archaic cutting-out procedure! This experiment points to the immense power of wave genetics, which obviously has a greater influence on the formation of organisms than the biochemical processes of alkaline sequences [*in fact, one is an expression of the other*].

Esoteric and spiritual teachers have known for ages that our body is programmable by language, words and thought. This has now been scientifically proven and explained. Of course, the frequency has to be correct, and this is why not everybody is equally successful or can do it with always the same strength. The individual must work on the inner processes and maturity in order to establish a conscious communication with the DNA [*consciousness can rewrite the program, as I have emphasised throughout the book*]. The Russian researchers work on a method that is not dependent on these factors but will **always** work, provided one uses the correct frequency.

But the *higher developed an individual's consciousness, the less need is there for any type of device!* One can achieve these results by oneself, and science will finally stop laughing at such ideas and will confirm and explain the results. Modern man knows this only on a much more subtle level, as 'intuition' [*knowing!*]. But we, too, can regain full use of it. An example from Nature: When a queen ant is spatially separated from her colony, building still continues fervently and according to plan. If the queen is killed, however, all work in the colony stops. No ant knows what to do. Apparently the queen sends the 'building plans' from far away via the group consciousness of her subjects. She can be as far away as she wants, as long as she is alive. [*The Queen ant is like the Matrix 'brain'.*]

In man, 'hypercommunication' [*communication at levels beyond the five-sense realm*] is most often encountered when one suddenly gains access to information that is outside one's knowledge base. Such 'hypercommunication' is then experienced as *inspiration or intuition* [*knowing*]. The Italian composer, Giuseppe Tartini dreamt one night that a devil sat at his bedside playing the violin. The next morning Tartini was able to note down the piece exactly from memory; he called it the *Devil's Trill Sonata.* For years, a 42-year old male nurse dreamt of a situation in which he was hooked up to a kind of knowledge CD-ROM. Verifiable knowledge from all imaginable fields was then transmitted to him that he was able to recall in the morning. There was such a flood of information that it seemed a whole encyclopaedia was transmitted at night. The majority of facts were outside his personal knowledge base and reached technical details about which he knew absolutely nothing. [*This is like a computer download. A computer does not have to know anything about the information it records.*]

When hypercommunication occurs, one can observe special phenomena in the DNA, as well as in the human being. The Russian scientists irradiated DNA samples with laser light. On screen, a typical wave pattern was formed. When they removed the DNA sample, the wave pattern did not disappear, it remained. Many control experiments showed that the pattern still came from the removed sample, whose energy field apparently remained by itself. This effect is now called phantom DNA effect. The phenomenon encountered most often in hypercommunication is inexplicable electromagnetic fields in the vicinity of the people concerned. Electronic devices like CD players and the like can be irritated and cease to function for hours. When the electromagnetic field slowly dissipates, the devices function normally again. Many healers and psychics know this effect from their work. The better the atmosphere and the energy, the more frustrating it is that the recording device stops functioning and recording exactly at that moment [*I have experienced this many times*]. Repeated switching on and off after the session does not restore function, but next morning all is back to normal. Perhaps this is reassuring to read for many, as it has nothing to do with them being technically inept; it means they are good at hypercommunication.

[*Remember the story of my experience in Brazil during the ayahuasca session when the lights came on without electricity and the music player went off and on.*]

The Russian scientists also found that our DNA can cause disturbing patterns in a vacuum, thus producing magnetized wormholes! Wormholes are microscopic equivalents of the so-called Einstein-Rosen bridges in the vicinity of black holes (left by burned-out stars).

These are tunnel connections between entirely different areas in the universe, through which information can be transmitted outside of space and time. The DNA attracts these bits of information and passes them on to our 'consciousness' [*what I call 'mind' and 'emotion' – the DNA network*]. This process of hypercommunication (telepathy, channelling, [*knowing*]) is most effective in a state of relaxation. Stress, worry or a hyperactive intellect prevent successful hypercommunication or the information will be totally distorted and useless.

[*This is another reason why the system is designed to keep us in a state of stress, worry and constant mental/emotional activity. It is also why left brain 'intellectuals' that dominate 'education' and 'science' cannot access the level of intuitive knowing that would expose their flawed and rigid beliefs.*]

There is another phenomenon linked to DNA and wormholes. Normally, these super-small wormholes are highly unstable and are maintained only for the tiniest fractions of a second. Under certain conditions stable wormholes can organize themselves, which then form distinctive vacuum domains in which, for example, gravity can transform into electricity. Vacuum domains are self-radiant balls of ionized gas that contain considerable amounts of energy. There are regions in Russia where such radiant balls appear very often and it was this that motivated research programs that led to some of the discoveries detailed here.

Many 'spiritual teachers' also produce such visible balls or columns of light in deep meditation or during energy work, and in certain Earth healing projects such light effects also appear on photographs. Simply put, this phenomenon has to do with gravity and anti-gravity forces that are ever more stable forms of wormholes, and displays of hypercommunication with energies from outside our time and space structure [*the Time Loop*]. Earlier generations that experienced such hypercommunication and visible vacuum domains were convinced that an angel had appeared before them and we cannot be sure what forms of consciousness we can get access when using hypercommunication. We have made another giant step towards understanding our reality. Official science also knows of gravity anomalies on Earth that contribute to the formation of vacuum domains. Recently gravity anomalies have been found in Rocca di Papa, south of Rome.

In their book *Vernetzte Intelligenz* (*Networked Intelligence*), Grazyna Fosar and Franz Bludorf explain these connections precisely and clearly. The authors also quote sources who believe that in earlier times humanity was once, just like the animals, very strongly connected to the group consciousness and acted as a group. To develop and experience individuality, we humans had to forget hypercommunication almost completely [*I would say that it was deliberately suppressed*]. Now that we are fairly stable in our individual consciousness, we can create a new form of group consciousness, namely one in which we attain access to all information via our DNA, without being forced or remotely controlled about what to do with that information. We now know that, just as on the Internet, our DNA can feed its proper data into the network; can call up data from the network; and can establish contact with other participants in the network [*exactly as this book describes*]. Remote healing, telepathy or 'remote sensing' [*intuitive knowing*] can thus be explained. Some animals know also from afar when their owners plan to return home. That can be freshly interpreted and explained via the concepts of group consciousness and hypercommunication [*the DNA network*].

Any collective consciousness cannot be sensibly used over any period of time without a distinctive individuality. Otherwise, we would revert to a primitive herd instinct that is easily manipulated [*the Illuminati agenda for the human race today*]. Hypercommunication in the new millennium means something quite different. Researchers think that if humans with full individuality would regain group consciousness, they would have a god-like power to create, alter and shape things on Earth! And humanity is collectively moving toward such a group consciousness of the new kind. Fifty per cent of today's children will be 'problem' children as soon as they go to school. The system lumps everyone together and demands adjustment. But the individuality of today's children is so strong that that they refuse this adjustment and resist giving up their idiosyncrasies in the most diverse ways [*Well, many do but vast numbers do not*]. At the same time, more and more clairvoyant children are born. Something in those children is striving towards the group consciousness of the new kind, and it will no longer be suppressed.

As a rule, weather is rather difficult to influence by a single individual. But it may be influenced by a group consciousness (nothing new to some tribes doing it in their rain dances). Weather is strongly influenced by Earth resonance frequencies, the so-called Schumann frequencies [*a sort of planetary heartbeat*]. But those same frequencies are also produced in our brains, and when many people synchronise their thinking, or individuals ('spiritual masters', for instance), focus their thoughts in a laser-like fashion, then it is, scientifically speaking, not at all surprising if they can thus influence weather. [*The Illuminati are manipulating the weather and geological activity using technology and the vibrational principle is the same.*]

Researchers in group consciousness have formulated the theory of Type I civilisations. A humanity that developed a group consciousness of this new kind would have neither environmental problems, nor scarcity of energy. [*How can you have scarcity within Infinite abundance? Only if you believe in it.*] For, if humanity were to use its mental power as a unified civilisation, it would have control of the energies of its home planet as a natural consequence [*it would rewrite the program*]. And that includes all natural catastrophes! A theoretical Type II civilisation would even be able to control all energies of their home galaxy. Whenever a great many people focus their attention or consciousness on something similar, like Christmas time, a football world championship or the funeral of Lady Diana in England, certain random number generators in computers start to deliver ordered numbers instead of the random ones. An ordered group consciousness creates order in its whole surroundings!

All information is from the book *Vernetzte Intelligenz* by Grazyna Fosar and Franz Bludorf, ISBN 3930243237. Unfortunately, it is only available in German at the moment. You can reach the authors via Kontext, the Forum for Border Science, at **www.fosar-bludorf.com**

[*It's funny how these scientists, geneticists and linguists went to all this effort and expense to discover only part of what came to me by taking a rainforest plant and trusting my 'knowing'. That is not to diminish in the least what they have done because it is great confirmation of the theme, and for this to come through mainstream sources is a significant breakthrough. But it does show that you don't have to train as a scientist to understand these things. Infinite Knowing is there for everyone to tap into because that is what we are. It simply requires us to trust ourselves and not the system.*]

So the Reptilian Connection is Crazy is it?

In January 2005, as this book was in production, I received the following email and pictures from a clinical hypnotherapist in Australia. It is consistent with a stream of experiencers and therapists who have contacted me since the mid-1990s:

Hi David, my name is Barry Newton. I am a practitioner of homoeopathic medicine and clinical hypnotherapy practicing in Australia. From 1994 to 2001, I treated a patient who suffered the monstrous psychiatric condition known as Dissociative Identity Disorder or DID (once known as 'multiple personality') the result of being born into a Satanic Cult and subsequently ritually abused over three decades. This patient provided me with drawings that she had done that to me held no special significance until now 2005, after reading your book, *Children of the Matrix*.

What initially struck me was that your idea of 'shape-shifting' was very much similar to a process known as 'switching' – when patients with Dissociative Identity Disorder switch from one personality to another.

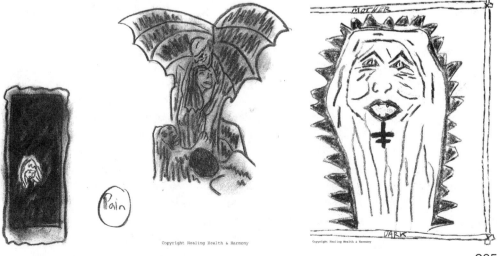

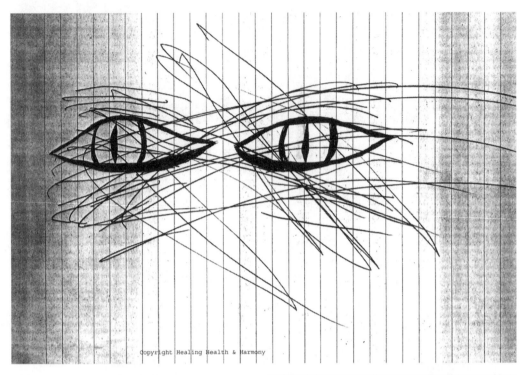

To witness a switch is quite a remarkable and unusual experience. The skin of the host body seemingly becomes fluid, flaccid, and bubbles with upwellings and sinkings and is very difficult to focus upon. The shift is sometimes profound and sometimes discreet. The completion of the shift reveals a facial (even bodily) presence, structure, and demeanour totally different from what was previous. The personality change is no different from speaking to, and being in the presence of, a totally different person.

Reading your work prompted me to recollect such events, as well as connect ideas such as the Annunaki also being called 'The Watchers' by ancient Mesopotamians and others, and this connected my memory with the drawings of eyes that were done by my patient – eyes that she was told were 'always watching'. I went through the case notes to locate the pictures of watching eyes, and to my very great surprise found several more drawings that

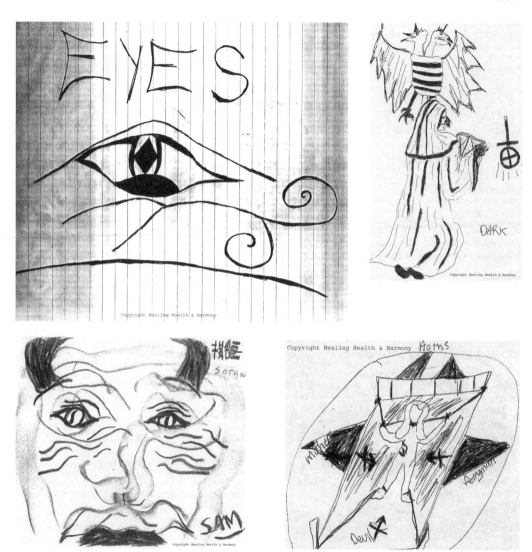

also seem to corroborate your expositions regarding Satanism and reptiles, which I now forward to you.

Note that the eyes of evil are drawn with vertical pupils, and that the two primary perpetrators are depicted as reptilian and snake. Indeed it appears that the presence and use of snakes is integral in all cases of Satanic Ritual Abuse.

Kind regards

Barry

http://www.cdsubliminal.com.au/

INDEX

Page numbers in italics refer to illustrations

INDEX OF ILLUSTRATIONS

Our thanks to the following hologram producers and suppliers for the use of their images

Holography Studio
All-Russian Exhibition Center
C/o Sergey Zharkiy
Tallinskaja Str. 26 – 130
123458 Moscow
Russian Federation
website: *www.holography.ru*

3-D Hologrammen
Grimburgwal 2
1012 GA Amsterdam
Tel/fax +31-20-6247225
website: *www.3-Dhologrammen.com*

Jason Sapan
Holographic Studios,
240 East 26th Street
New York, NY 10010-2436
tel: *212-686-9397*

Royal Holographic Art Gallery
website: *http://www.holograms.bc.ca*

Laser Trend Holographie
Germany
email: *lasertrend@aol.com*

Our thanks to the following chart producers and suppliers for the use of their images

Colon and Eye charts courtesy of:
Bernard Jensen International
1914 W. Mission Road, Ste. F
Escondido, CA 92029
(888) 743-1790 (from USA)
(760) 743-1790
website: *www.bernardjensen.org*

Spine chart courtesy of:
Koren Publications UK
157 Park Road,
Kingston,
Surrey
KT2 6DQ
website: *www.familychiropractic.co.uk*

Unlocking the Imagination

Journeying in the Dreamtime through Art and Meditation.
Workshops with Neil Hague

Everyone is an artist and all have imagination!

Through talking, drawing and painting we will explore primeval imagery, symbols (archetypes), left and right brain activity, colour and the spirit within each of us. Unlocking our mind and opening our hearts enables us to experience multidimensional aspects of ourselves, heal our lives and shape our reality.

Visit **www.neilhague.com** for more information, or telephone Quester on 01637 881613.

Limited edition prints and cards of cover illustrations and other paintings found in this book can be ordered through www.neilhague.com

About the artist

Neil is an artist, author and teacher. Originally trained in publishing, he now writes and lectures on the metaphysics and ancient symbolism found in art. He has had numerous exhibitions of his visionary art and his imagery is inspired by mythology, science, spirituality and a love of nature. Often combining these sources Neil illustrates through his books and imagery a personal and fascinating approach to art and self-awareness brought about through creativity.

Other work by David Icke

ALICE IN WONDERLAND AND THE WORLD TRADE CENTER DISASTER –
WHY THE OFFICIAL STORY OF 9/11 IS A MONUMENTAL LIE   **$29.95   £16.00**
A stunning exposé of the Ministries of Mendacity that have told the world the Big Lie about what
happened on September 11th, who did it, how and why. This 500 page book reveals the real
agenda behind the 9/11 attacks and how they were orchestrated from within the borders of the
United States and not from a cave in Afghanistan.

TALES FROM THE TIME LOOP   **$29.95   £16.00**
In this 500-page, profusely-illustrated book, David Icke explores in detail the multi-levels of the
global conspiracy. He exposes the five-sense level and demolishes the official story of the
invasions of Iraq and Afghanistan; he explains the inter-dimensional manipulation; and he shows
that what we think is the 'physical world' is all an illusion that only exists in our mind. Without
this knowledge, the true nature of the conspiracy cannot be understood.

THE BIGGEST SECRET   **$29.95   £16.00**
More than 500 pages of documented, sourced, detail that exposes the forces that really run the
world and manipulate our lives. He reveals how the same interconnecting bloodlines have been
in control for thousands of years. Includes the background to the ritual murder of Diana, Princess
of Wales, and the devastating background to the origins of Christianity. A highly acclaimed book
that broke new ground in conspiracy research.

CHILDREN OF THE MATRIX   **$29.95   £16.00**
The companion book of *The Biggest Secret* that investigates the reptilian and other dimensional
connections to the global conspiracy and reveals the world of illusion – the "Matrix" – that holds
the human race in daily slavery.

... AND THE TRUTH SHALL SET YOU FREE (21st century edition)   **$29.95   £16.00**
Icke exposes in more than 500 pages the interconnecting web that controls the world today.
This book focuses on the last 200 years and particularly on what is happening around us today.
Another highly acclaimed book, which has been constantly updated. A classic in its field.

I AM ME • I AM FREE   **$21.95   £10.50**
Icke's book of solutions. With humour and powerful insight, he shines a light on the mental and
emotional prisons we build for ourselves … prisons that disconnect us from our true and infinite
potential to control our own destiny. A getaway car for the human psyche.

FROM PRISON TO PARADISE – video and DVD   **$59.95**   **£32.00**

A six hour, profusely illustrated presentation on three videocassettes recorded in front of 1,200 people at the Vogue Theatre, Vancouver, Canada. It will make you laugh, it may even make you cry, but for sure it will blow your mind as endless threads and strands throughout history and the modern world are connected together to reveal the hidden hand, the hidden web, that has controlled the planet for thousands of years.

LIFTING THE VEIL   **$10.00**   **£6.95**

Compiled from interviews with an American journalist. An excellent summary of Icke's work and perfect for those new to these subjects. This title is available from Bridge of Love UK and the Truthseeker Company, San Diego, USA.

SECRETS OF THE MATRIX   **$59.95**   **£32.00**
New – on video and DVD

A six-hour presentation recorded before an audience of nearly 2,000 people at the Brixton Academy in London in which David talks about the history of the conspiracy, its symbolism, goals and methods, and reveals at length the background to 9/11, the 'war on terrorism' and the invasion of Iraq. He also describes the nature of reality, how we create it and how it is manipulated.

TURNING OF THE TIDE – video / DVD   **$19.95**   **£12.00**

A two-hour presentation, funny and informative, and the best way to introduce your family and friends to Icke's unique style and information.

SPEAKING OUT – video   **$24.95**   **£15.00**

A two-hour interview with David Icke.

THE FREEDOM ROAD – video / DVD   **$59.95**

Another triple video by David Icke in which he presents the story of global manipulation. What has happened? What is happening? What will happen? All are revealed in this eye-opening, heart-opening, mind-opening video package. Not available in UK.

Alice in Wonderland and the World Trade Centre Disaster

Why the official story of 9/11 is a monumental lie

Since that horrendous day of September 11th 2001, the people of the world have been told the Big Lie. The official story of what happened on 9/11 is fantasy of untruth, manipulation, contradiction and anomaly. David Icke has spent well over a decade uncovering the force that was really behind those attacks and has travelled to 40 countries in pursuit of the truth. He has exposed their personnel, methods and agenda in a series of books and videos.

Therefore, when the attacks came, it was easy to recognise the Hidden Hand behind the cover story of "Bin Laden did it". Icke takes apart the official version of 9/11 and the 'war on terrorism' and shows that those responsible are much closer to home than a cave in Afghanistan. He explains why 9/11 was planned and to what end. It is vital to maintaining our freedom, and to the memory of those who died and the loved ones left behind, that the light shines on the lies and deceit behind September 11th.

Icke also places these events in their true context as part of an agenda by hidden forces working behind the puppet politicians to create a global fascist state based on total control and surveillance. But it doesn't have to be like this; it does not have to happen. We can change the world from a prison to a paradise and, as Icke explains, the power to do that is within you and within us all.

$29.95   £16.00

The Reptilian Agenda

with Credo Mutwa

David Icke has produced
video and DVD packages totalling more than six hours,
with the Zulu Sanusi (shaman) Credo Mutwa, who David describes
as a genius and the most knowledgable man he has ever met.

The Reptilian Agenda, part one • (3 hours 30 minutes)

Credo Mutwa reveals a stream of astonishing and unique knowledge that, up to now, has only been available at the highest level of initiation in the African shamanistic stream. But, Credo says, the world must know the truth. He tells of how a reptilian extraterrestrial race has controlled the planet for thousands of years. Fantastic confirmation of *The Biggest Secret* and *Children Of The Matrix*.

The Reptilian Agenda, part two • (2 hours 45 minutes)

Credo takes the story on from ancient times and explains how the reptilians have taken over the world and what we can do about it.

These are available from Bridge of Love USA, UK, Australia and Africa.
See back page for contact addresses.

Note: *This is a three-video package in North America.* **$59.95   £32.00**

Tales *from the* Time Loop

David Icke pulls together his fantastic wealth of accumulated knowledge to reveal the multi-levels of the conspiracy. He begins in the 'five-sense' world with a highly detailed exposure of the forces, methods and agenda behind 9/11, the 'war on terrorism', the invasion of Iraq and the planned conquest of North Africa, the Middle East and elsewhere. Icke goes on to explore the other-dimensional connection to the 'human' manipulators and their inter-breeding bloodlines that originate in the ancient world. He then reveals how our sense of reality – what we think is 'real' – is being implanted into our minds while we believe we are thinking for ourselves.

In early 2003, Icke had some amazing experiences in the Amazon rainforest of Brazil that revealed to him as never before that the world we think is 'real' is only an illusion – a lucid and manipulated dream that he calls the Matrix. In **Tales** *from the* **Time Loop**, he shares those experiences and details the scientific support for what he learned about the illusion we call daily life. Icke believes that this book is the most important work he has yet published. It is, he says, the knowledge that will set us free and take us home.

$29.95   £16.00

SECRETS OF THE MATRIX

DVD/VIDEO

Since 1990, David Icke has been on an amazing journey of self and collective discovery to establish the real power behind apparently 'random' world events like 9/11 and the 'war on terrorism'.

Here he reveals that a network of interbreeding bloodlines manipulating through their web of interconnecting secret societies have been pursuing an agenda for thousands of years to impose a global centralised fascist state with total control and surveillance of the population.

The attacks of September 11th – not the work of 'Bin Laden' – and the subsequent 'war on terrorism' are a means through which this is designed to be achieved.

Over six hours with hundreds of illustrations, David Icke reveals the illusion that is life in this 'physical' reality. How is this 'world' a provable illusion – just a lucid dream? How do we create it and how can we change the dream to one that we would like to experience? All is revealed by David Icke before almost 2,000 people at one of London's most famous venues, the Brixton Academy.

3 DVD set – over 6 hours of presentation

$59.95   £32.00

The Arizona Wilder interview

Revelations
of a
Mother Goddess

Arizona Wilder conducted human sacrifice rituals for some of the most famous people on Earth, including the British Royal Family. In this three-hour video with David Icke, she talks at length about her experiences in an interview that is utterly devastating for the Elite that control the world.

This astonishing video is available for **$24.95** in the United States or **£15** (plus **£1.50** p&p) in the UK.

See back page for contact addresses.

Other books available from
Bridge of Love ...

The Medical Mafia

The superb exposé of the medical system by Canadian doctor, Guylaine Lanctot, who also shows how and why 'alternative' methods are far more effective. Highly recommended.

What The Hell Are We Doing Here Anyway?

Guylaine Lanctot brilliantly exposes the mental and emotional prisons that trap the people in a daily illusion and offers the keys to multi-dimensional freedom.

Trance Formation Of America

The staggering story of Cathy O'Brien, the mind controlled slave of the US Government for some 25 years. Read this one sitting down. A stream of the world's most famous political names are revealed as they really are.
Written by Cathy O'Brien and Mark Phillips.

Access Denied – For Reasons of National Security

Cathy and Mark's follow up to Trance Formation of America

What If Everything You Knew About AIDS Was Wrong?

HIV does NOT cause Aids, as Christine Maggiore's outstanding book confirms. Concisely written and devastating to the Aids scam and the Aids industry.

For details of prices and a catalogue of all Bridge of Love books, tapes and videos, please send a self addressed, stamped envelope to one of the contact addresses on the back page or go to **bridgeoflove.com**

www.davidicke.com

One of the world's most visited websites on conspiracy material with millions of visits per week.

5,000 webpages of detailed information on all the subjects covered in this book – and more. The site is updated with current information every day and includes the award-winning *Reptilian Archives*, a library of ancient and modern information, and personal experiences of the Reptilian connection.

Many attempts have been made to close down *davidicke.com* and hack into the system to disrupt this site. But we're still here. See for yourself the information they are trying to block.

Other websites in the David Icke network are **Icke-media.com**, which details David's media appearances and public talks; **DavidIckematrix.com**, which focuses on the nature of reality; and **BridgeofLove.com**, where David's books and tapes can be purchased.

Bring David Icke to your city or conference

If you would like David Icke to speak at your conference or public meeting:

email: *ickemedia@bridgeoflove.com*

tel/fax (England): **01983 566002**

Can you help?

If you have any information you think will help David Icke in his research, please email him at:

ickenews@bridgeoflove.com

Please source the information wherever you can and it will be held in the strictest confidence.

To find out more about Mike Lambert's Shen Clinic
on the Isle of Wight, contact:

www.theshenclinic.com

email: info@theshenclinic.com
telephone: 01983 521811

To order David Icke's books and tapes,
go to:

www.**bridgeoflove.com**

Or Contact:

Bridge of Love Publications
Suite 1
185a High Street
Ryde
Isle of Wight
PO33 2PN
England

Tel/Fax: 01983 566002

UK and Europe
Email: info@bridgeoflove.co.uk

USA and Rest of the World
Email: info@bridgeoflove.com

NOTES

NOTES

NOTES

NOTES

NOTES